THE
RECONSTRUCTION
OF EUROPE

THE RECONSTRUCTION OF EUROPE

TALLEYRAND AND THE CONGRESS OF VIENNA 1814–1815

By GUGLIELMO FERRERO

TRANSLATED BY
THEODORE R. JAECKEL

G. P. PUTNAM'S SONS

NEW YORK

Manufactured in the United States of America

VAN REES PRESS · NEW YORK

PREFACE

I

This book relates how, in 1814 and 1815, Europe escaped
from the predicament in which the creation of the great
Napoleonic Empire had left her ever since the Battle of
Austerlitz and the Treaty of Pressburg (1805). What was
this predicament? The upsetting of the balance of power
on the European continent.

The events in France which had begun in 1789 had,
after 1800, resulted in the creation of a revolutionary
state with a military strength superior to that of the most
powerful states of Europe. By taking advantage of this
force and abusing it, Napoleon had succeeded in destroying a large number of small and medium states, in weakening and mutilating the most powerful states, and in
erecting a vast empire which dominated the whole Continent. At war against England, Napoleon attempted to
unite the entire Continent, over which he ruled, against
the British thalassocracy. But the only way he could do
this was by exerting an increasingly violent and intolerable
pressure on all the large, small, and medium states on the
Continent; draining the submissive territories in his search
for soldiers, provisions, and money; submitting the small
and medium states which he had not absorbed to a more
and more exacting protectorate; and obliging the larger
states, by means of promises, threats, and even wars, to
conclude alliances with him which were solely to the interest of the French Empire. The result was a prolonged
situation which became more and more unbearable to the
whole world.

the phrase, "legitimate governments," as applied to contemporary Europe, and I have gone into the matter at length in the present work. There is only one political form which is possible today for a Western people, and that is a representative government, a government whose powers are all, directly or indirectly, delegated by the people, who are bound to obey them. Even the revolutionary states today recognize this principle; their rulers never cease repeating that they have the right to govern because their peoples are behind them and they are carrying out the latter's wishes. But for a representative government to be, not a travesty imposed by force, but a serious institution possessing a prestige which is indispensable to its sovereignty, two conditions are necessary: that the right of opposition be respected, and that there be free elections. The majority has the right to govern, but the minority has the right to present its case, to criticize the government, and to attempt to become the majority by convincing the people. Elections should be an expression of the free will of the people and not a farce organized by the government so that the people, instead of approving or disapproving of the government as it sees fit, is obliged to vote as the government wishes.

Revolutionary governments today, although they accept in theory the principle of popular sovereignty as the source of legitimate authority, in practice suppress the right of opposition and freedom of suffrage. For reasons explained in this book, states so constituted cannot exist in peace either with other revolutionary states or with legitimate states, just as Napoleon's revolutionary state was unable to preserve peace at the beginning of the nineteenth century. The conclusion to be drawn is easy and obligatory; no one can tell how soon the day will come when Europe will again be so unified that peace and order are possible, as it was between 1814 and 1914. That depends on circumstances and events which cannot be predicted. What is certain—and this is the great discovery of

Talleyrand's doctrine, as explained in this book—is that
Europe will be delivered over to the chaos of wars and
revolutions until the day when the two principles—right
of opposition and freedom of suffrage—are applied by all
the European states; until the day when a state which
suppresses these two principles will meet with the same
reaction as a state which attempts to bring back slavery.

II

This book is the sequel to another whose French title
was *Aventure, Bonaparte en Italie, 1796-97,* and which was
translated into English under the title of *The Gamble.*
Together with *Aventure,* which preceded it, and a book,
Pouvoir, not yet published, which will follow it, the present work will form a historical and philosophical trilogy
which will thoroughly examine the problem of the origin,
development, and nature of the revolutionary state.

Although there are allusions to *The Gamble* in this
book, it is not necessary to have read the former in order
to understand the latter. But I believe it would be useful
to know the fundamental thesis of *The Gamble.* In that
book I undertook to analyze how and why the Revolution,
which at the beginning had been merely a domestic crisis
in France, resulted in a general war which lasted fifteen
years, from 1799 to 1814, except for a breathing space of
one year—from 1802 to 1803. This decisive transformation
was the result of Napoleon's invasion of Italy in 1796.
After a series of complex events, the story of which I described in *The Gamble* and which originated in what may
be called the military dynamism of the Revolution, Napoleon and the Directory finally came to an understanding
with the Court of Vienna, by which the ancient and glorious Republic of Venice was abolished and northern
Italy divided between France and Austria. This agreement,
made in 1797 and sanctioned by the Treaty of Campo
Formio (October, 1797), seemed at first a facile undertaking. What was Venice compared with the enormous

states which were suppressing her—the French Republic and the House of Hapsburg? Merely a small state with four million subjects and only a remnant of its former military might.

And yet it was the forcible disappearance of this tiny state which provoked a general war in Europe that lasted fifteen years. Why? Because the disappearance of Venice upset the balance of power between the various states of Italy, and this in turn caused a general *malaise* and panic in Europe, of which France and Austria themselves were the first victims. This *malaise* and panic resulted in the downfall of the entire European system, as created in the eighteenth century, by letting loose a general war.

In 1940, a similar event took place, but this time on a world scale. Continental France, in relation to the total surface of the earth, is perhaps even smaller than the Republic of Venice, in relation to Europe. And yet the invasion of France and the destruction of her military might was enough to provoke the same unrest, but this time throughout the entire world, that the destruction of Venice had provoked on the Continent of Europe. The annihilation of France's military power upset the balance of power in Europe, just as the destruction of Venice had upset it in Italy; the upsetting of the balance of power in Europe unbalanced the world by causing a world-wide panic, just as the upsetting of the balance in Italy had unbalanced Europe.

The alarm has been particularly prompt and violent in the United States. In less than six months, the defeat of France had three repercussions on the other side of the Atlantic: 1) total rearmament; 2) peacetime conscription, which alone is a tremendous revolution; 3) the policy of all-out aid to Britain. It is difficult to say which of these is the most important, and unquestionably their consequences will be felt in American history.

A tremendous reaction this, but a justifiable one, and one which proves the existence of a strong political sense in American opinion. Indeed, it is not difficult to predict what will happen if a military hegemony, like that which is now dominating Europe, should definitely and permanently arise. Germany and Italy would immediately begin to build an immense navy, so as to be assured of mastery over the seas and to eliminate the weakness of their naval power which during this war has been the cause of their greatest difficulties. This navy would provoke the greatest fears—and the most justifiable—in the United States. The United States would feel herself threatened by Germany, as mistress of the European Continent, and by Japan. Japan in turn would be afraid of the United States and of Russia. Russia would tremble before a possible coalition of Germany and Japan. Germany would fear a coalition of Russia and the United States.

An atmosphere poisoned by intercontinental terrors would envelop the entire globe. All the great powers would continue to overarm, exhausting the last resources of the world. In the universal uncertainty, no sincere effort to re-establish general prosperity would be possible. No one would be able to foresee when this crisis would be resolved. What is certain is that such a situation could only lead to wars and revolutions which would be even more disastrous than those which have devastated the world since 1914.

The upsetting of the balance of power in Europe, accomplished in 1940, unbalanced the whole world. The whole world will be a prey to perpetual fear, to permanent unrest, and to incurable insomnia, as long as the European Continent will not have found a balance and order acceptable to all the states, large or small, which constitute it. That is the situation in which the whole world now finds itself. It is the main difference between the present crisis and that of 1814. Then the crisis had been confined to Europe alone; the rest of the world had watched from a distance. Today the crisis is a world crisis.

Another and no less important difference is that in 1814,

as the book will make clear, Europe had the strength to avert the crisis by itself. It is doubtful that this can be done today. The balance of power has been upset far more than in 1814. But it is exactly for that reason that the question should arise as to whether the day has not come when the United States can become a decisive factor in the situation.

Up until now the United States has played a unique role, suitable to her, in the history of the Western world, and this has taken her in two different directions. In 1776, she created a great state, in which for the first time the hereditary principle—monarchic and aristocratic—was suppressed and replaced by the elective and representative principle. The resistance to the aristocratic and monarchic Europe of the eighteenth century was absolute and complete; for the first time the Western world was about to witness the development of a great state and a great civilization without the benefit of kings, emperors, princes, or nobles, based on the principle that all men are created equal. The democratic state had been founded—a startling novelty in the history of the world. After having gained her independence and created this new type of state, the United States launched out with all her energy into another direction, as original as the first—the development of a civilization which I call quantitative, as opposed to the bygone qualitative civilizations. She took the lead in releasing the great motive forces of nature—heat and electricity—in order to activate machines which became more and more rapid, powerful, and complex; by this ingenious exploitation of natural forces and scientific discoveries she, together with those who followed her, succeeded in fabulously increasing the wealth of mankind.

For a century the United States has accomplished miracles in this field. It has been by her industrial achievements in particular that she has impressed the world, set an example which has had many imitators, and contributed to the creation of a new orientation of the human mind.

It appears that the moment is at hand when the order of influences may be changed and the United States be called upon to exert a decisive political influence. Europe today is faced with the same problem which the United States solved a century and a half ago, that of organizing a state and society which can exist and develop without kings, emperors, princes, or nobles. The obstacles are tremendous because behind Europe stretch ten centuries during which the monarchy and the aristocracy were the two sacred pillars of social order. So long and so great a past cannot be forgotten in thirty years. Every revolutionary government in contemporary Europe has come into power, like that of Napoleon, during the following transition period: between monarchy, which is no longer possible because the conditions which were its *raison d'être* and its strength are no longer in existence, and democracy, which is not yet possible because the conditions required to make it function are not yet in existence. This is a terrible transition period, in which the most civilized peoples of Europe lose their bearings, become unable to find a way out, and allow themselves to be dragged into revolutionary adventures.

If the United States will understand the problem and make an effort to help the great powers in Europe rediscover the path of order and peace, she will render a tremendous service to herself and to the world.

When I visited the United States for the first time in 1909, I was impressed—as I said in the book which I wrote on my return, *Between the Old World and the New*—by the enormous effort the United States was putting forth to "translate quantity into quality"—the expression I used at that time—that is, to draw from the immense wealth which she was producing, something fine, noble, and beautiful. For a century the United States has been seeking this fine and noble use for her wealth, this sublime transformation of quantity into quality, directed toward the past as well as the future, in all the higher activities of the mind: science, art, literature, religion, geographical and archeological exploration, charity, hygiene, sport, etc.

A magnificent purpose, but the task which might tomorrow be given to the United States would be more important than any she has accomplished up till now; and that is to help that part of the Western world which has lost itself in revolution and has become incapable of governing itself according to old political principles or according to new ones, to find its bearings and restore peace and order to the world by rediscovering either one or the other for itself.

Will this be possible? Shall we see Roosevelt become the Alexander I of the new great crisis of Western history? This book gives the real story of the Russian emperor, about whom so many legends have been woven. He had many faults, and he committed many errors, like his friend, Talleyrand; but, in 1814, like Talleyrand, he attained the topmost pinnacle of human grandeur to which the mighty ones of this earth may aspire. Is there, for a simple mortal, grandeur comparable to that which, in the case of these two men, consisted in saving, through courage and intelligence, an entire continent, which was in danger of being lost in an interminable war, and in giving it courage, confidence, order, and the chance to live and work in peace for a century?

To the men who govern the United States today, and behind them to all the American people, will soon be offered the same glory and the same opportunity. They will be offered on an even larger scale, for it will be a question of snatching from fear, from disorder, from the blind fury of wars which must be continued for the simple reason that no one knows how to end them, not only a continent, but the world itself. I am certain that neither the American people nor its leaders will allow this opportunity to escape.

G. Ferrero

Geneva
April, 1941.

CONTENTS

THE
RECONSTRUCTION
OF EUROPE

I

THE GREAT PANIC

---━►≫≪◄━---

For a quarter of a century the world had been tottering. The "great panic" had begun on July 14, 1789, the day of the Bastille. Here is the way an imaginative historian described it:

The fourteenth of July was a decisive day. . . . Suddenly, like the recoil of a spring, the provinces rose. And in the tremendous upheaval, there occurred two very distinct, seemingly contradictory movements. At first there was a sort of general shudder of fear. The long-established royal authority, which for centuries had been shielding the peasants as well as squeezing them, seemed shaken; and, as it was the only form of authority they could understand, it seemed at first to the peasantry that society itself was crumbling and that if they did not defend themselves they would be open to every kind of plundering. In this absence of authority, a frightening rumor arose: "Here are the brigands! They're coming to burn our forests and cut our wheat! On guard and to arms!" From one end of France to the other, peasants armed themselves and started beating the countryside for brigands whom they never found. This time of panic left an indelible impression on the minds of the peasants; in the Midi they still talk about *l'an-*

nado de la paou, the year of the panic. One would say that this memory has obliterated all others.[1]

The book from which this beautiful passage has been taken is a long prose poem glorifying the Revolution as a complete resuscitation of the times, a regeneration of mankind. The poet is rather astonished that the year 1789 was remembered by the peasants of France as *l'annado de la paou;* and he does his best to explain this strange misunderstanding. But the misunderstanding goes deeper than he believes; for it is at the root of the very word—practically unknown before the eighteenth century—with which the latest generations have either intoxicated or terrified themselves without ever quite knowing why—revolution! Revolution is a word with a double meaning, which for a century and a half has concealed one of the most tragic ambiguities in which men can lose themselves. By "revolution" we sometimes mean a reorientation of the human mind, an avenue leading to the future; it is in this sense that we speak of Christianity or the Renaissance as two great revolutions of mankind.

But we also mean by "revolution" the crumbling or the overthrow of an ancient order, the total or partial subversion of established laws. These are two distinct phenomena and, though they may occur simultaneously, do not condition each other. An old regime may disappear with its entire system of laws, and there will be no change in the trend of thought; similarly there may be a reversal of that trend of thought without affecting the political order. But, when an accident of history makes the two coincide, a tremendous confusion results, and the most extraordinary complications set in. The French Revolution was the greatest example of an equivocal revolution from start to finish, because it was dual right from its origin. The old monarchic

[1] J. L. Jaurès. *Histoire socialiste de la révolution française* (Paris: Librairie de l'Humanité, 1927), I, 310. On this important episode, see the excellent analysis by George Lefebvre, *La grande peur de 1789* (Paris: A. Colin, 1932).

order foundered on it while France was attempting to transform the state and society by a new philosophical approach. Two separate revolutions, one creative, the other destructive, took place simultaneously, and the chaos caused by the latter agitated, sidetracked, paralyzed, and finally annihilated the creative forces. That is the secret of the French Revolution, the key to all its contradictions.

When our poet-historian exclaims at the peasants' remembering 1789 as the year of the panic, he is thinking of the Declaration of the Rights of Man. The Declaration is the magnificent avenue to the future: the Revolution in the sense of a reorientation of thought and the promise of a new reign, not of fear, but of liberty, equality, and fraternity. But one month before the sublime Declaration, after the fall of the Bastille, the monarchy, petrified and weakened by two centuries of absolutism, had within a few days collapsed from sheer decrepitude throughout France. The convocation of the States-General and the events following had merely given a final shove to a withered tree whose roots had been rotting for a long time. Immediately the people rose and authority became paralyzed; a correlation between them was at once established: the masses rose because they felt authority paralyzed; authority ceased to exist because it felt that the masses had freed themselves. Barracks and monasteries all through France were emptied; soldiers and monks deserted; the army scattered; the courts and the police became idle; neither taxes nor rents were paid; everywhere castles and monasteries were sacked and pillaged.

But at the same time the "great panic" began, a panic not only of the peasants but of everyone, of the nobility as well as of the clergy and the people. Great and humble, rich and poor, wise and ignorant—all dreaded the fact that what had held them together—the law—had been overthrown. While, on the one hand, the peasants took up arms the moment they heard the news of the Bastille, in order to repulse imaginary brigands, on the other hand the nobility began to flee the country before a danger, not yet present, which their very flight would create. The King's own brothers set the example. The same fear, the great panic, occurred in all classes.

The Declaration of the Rights of Man and all the great reforms of the Assembly were to calm this panic for only a short time. After the Bastille, Louis XVI was a frightened king, and he had cause to be afraid, for he still had all the responsibilities of power without the power. He emphasized that in his messages to the National Assembly. With neither army, judges, police, nor laws, and with the Treasury empty, how could he function as the chief executive, in accordance with the wishes of Parliament, and as the faithful servant of the people's sovereignty? His arms had been cut off, and he was expected to continue wielding his scepter! But the National and Legislative Assemblies were no less frightened by their own impotence. They represented the new legislative power, the proof of the new orientation; yet they were powerless for the same reason as the executive power: the state no longer had any army, judiciary, police, or money. Law and order must exist to insure that a representative system of elections, discussions, and polls may function. Without laws and their enforcement, parties and political cliques resort to violence rather than discussion; and no assembly will have either the authority or the power to assume the majesty of the legislative body.

Both equally powerless, the former authority, which was collapsing, and the new, which wanted to replace it, distrusted each other more and more; and the more they distrusted each other the more they weakened and frightened each other. After countless evasions and hesitations, the King ended up by fleeing, by being caught at Varennes, and by soliciting the help of his brothers, the kings and emperors of Europe. Acts of fear, which the Revolution interpreted as long-planned attacks.

A still more dangerous paradox: the Revolution's fear

was to become an aggressive fear because it had to be concealed. Until April 20, 1792, there had been no more than misunderstandings between the Revolution and the Court of Vienna; none of these misunderstandings had been worth a war. But on that day the King appeared before the Legislative Assembly and said, "in a voice trembling with emotion," that war should be declared on the King of Bohemia and Hungary, stating that all France preferred "war to further outrages against the dignity of the French people and threats against the national safety." Once again fear in its headlong flight became aggression. The outrages and the threats complained of by the King were no more than hallucinations of the Girondists. Frightened by the powerlessness of the Assembly and by the general anarchy, and feeling the ground crumbling beneath their feet, for several months they had been preaching a sort of holy war, in the hope of winning back the people and the government by leading them against Austria. Frightened in his turn by the Girondist agitation, Louis XVI had yielded. And so the first Austrian war, and so, too, the storming of the Tuileries on August 10. The monarchy, deprived of its powers, was nevertheless feared to such an extent by the Revolution that the latter abolished it and proclaimed the Republic, at the very moment when France was invaded.

Without an army, without an administration, without police, without law, without a Treasury, the Revolution was forced to make war on three frontiers. Its fear was convulsed into terror; and the terror produced the twins of the guillotine and war without rules. But the Revolution succeeded in overcoming its fear for a while, long enough to overthrow the terroristic dictatorship and to try to give France a decent representative government with the Constitution of the Year III. On the day that the five Directors met for the first time in the Luxembourg Palace, they were sincere in wanting to give France the liberty which the Revolution had promised her. But the prerequisite to a free people is a government without fear. And the government, which needed a great deal of courage, did not even have, on that day, a table to sit at during its deliberations. This is what one of the five Directors has written about the first meeting of the new government:

We found every room in the Luxembourg bare; there was not one piece of furniture of any description. After a useless search, we took refuge in a small chamber. The porter, Dupont, had a small rickety table brought in, one of whose legs had been eaten away by old age, and four chairs, all that he had. He also lent us some logs, for the weather was very cold.[2]

Is it strange that the Directory, in spite of its noble intentions in the beginning, was not long in also succumbing to fright? France was discontented, uneasy, restless; on the right the Catholics and the royalists were taking advantage of the new freedom to get excited and arouse public opinion; on the left the equalitarians, the purists, the first precursors of socialism, were crying out against the scandalous fortunes of the Revolution and the *nouveaux riches,* more detestable than the aristocracy; in the press, in the clubs, in the legislative bodies, elected with a certain amount of freedom, the opposition was gaining ground. Freedom was turning against its mother, the Revolution. What would happen when the royalist and Catholic opposition would gain a majority in the Councils and would have the right to govern? Two years after its advent, the Directory was able to stay in power only by a series of *coups d'états,* which, provoked by fear of the right- or left-wing oppositions, only multiplied the hallucinations called up by fear. It lived constantly in terror of real and imaginary conspiracies, the latter more frightening than the former. This whirlwind of fear dispelled the liberal policy of the Revolution; in the general panic the new democracy went out the window.

[2] *Mémoires de La Révellière-Lépeaux,* published by his son (Paris, 1895), I, 316-317.

But at any rate there was no longer the Terror and its permanent guillotine, even if the new regime was one of arbitrary authority. The really serious danger became war without rules. The nineteenth century was convinced that the Revolution had invented total war by abolishing the rules with which the eighteenth century had bound it. But those rules had not been the arbitrary invention of a capricious formalism; they had been a bridle and rein used by the powers to control war and prevent themselves from being destroyed by it. Why did the Revolution hypnotize itself into the belief that it had discovered a wonderful secret in the suppression of rules, when instead it had only provoked an intensification of misused strength? Because it needed to gain courage by terrorizing its enemies. But it succeeded in terrorizing them only at the cost of getting caught in the vicious circle of fear leading to abuse of force and abuse of force intensifying fear. The Directory started it all with the Italian adventure. Carried away by its initial successes, it became more and more involved. But war without rules, though guaranteeing unhoped-for successes to the French army, provoked a rapid dissolution of the Old Regime in Italy, a general anarchy that threatened to engulf the invaders. Unable to leave this Italian anarchy to its own devices and not wishing Austria to profit by it to seize the whole of Italy, the Revolution accepted at Campo Formio the partition of Italy between France and Austria, between the Revolution and the Old Regime. An impossible partnership, which caused the great panic of France to be followed by the great panic of Europe. Until the peace of Campo Formio the only effect of the Revolution on the rest of Europe had been the increased watchfulness of the police, charged with the surveillance of the malcontents and hotheads. Since 1789, these agitators had been increasing both in numbers and in activity. But after 1797 all the great courts were beginning to feel great anxiety and to be affected by the spirit of adventure. France had brought the Revolution to Italy; why, she might spread her subversive doctrine over all Europe! The Court of Vienna, by taking up arms against the Revolution, had obtained no less a prize than Venice, had even extended her Empire to the banks of the Po. Could one not, by entering the lists against the revolutionary monster, obtain as rich a haul? In its turn the Directory, which prided itself on having concluded a glorious and lasting peace at Campo Formio, became more uneasy than ever about the contact established in the Po Valley by the peace treaty between the Old Regime and the Revolution; it distrusted the Court of Vienna as much as the latter distrusted it. One year after Campo Formio the war was renewed on a larger scale, with Russia helping Austria.

At last domestic instability and the military campaigns led the Revolution to attempt the most preposterous of its adventures, the 18 Brumaire. This *coup d'état* was not the work of Bonaparte but was carried out by part of the Directory; and the idea was not to polish off the Revolution by establishing a dictatorship under a victorious general, but to save the Revolution by opposing, on the left to the attacks of the extreme radicals, on the right to those of the royalists and Catholics, a kind of inverted democracy—a regime in which the popular sovereignty would be directed by the government which it had created. A monstrous distortion and a product of fear, the Constitution of the Year VIII enslaved the people at the very moment it proclaimed them sovereign. An even greater temerity was to set this Herculean task—enslaving the sovereign yet keeping him sovereign—on the shoulders of a young soldier of thirty, who had so far distinguished himself by losing half the fleet and the best army of the Republic in Egypt, and by the adventure of Italy, which, having crushed the Italian system and laid the peninsula open to anarchy, split Europe wide open.

And at first the adventure seemed successful. With the treaty of Lunéville, Austria finally acceded to the French plans for the Rhineland; the treaty of Amiens forced the acquiescence of England. Peace was re-established; the Revolution had triumphed, and Europe recognized its natural boundaries. The zenith of French history? No, merely a brief illusion. The upheavals began anew; one transformed the decennial consulate into a life consulate; another re-established the monarchy in revolutionary form —Empire. At the same time the war broke out again, the peace of Amiens having lasted only one year. A craving for power? The illusion of grandeur? Headlong ambition? No: fear, and only fear! Napoleon was a product of the Revolution; the fundamental secret of his whole policy, like that of the Revolution, was fear. Entrusted at the age of thirty by the men of Brumaire with putting into practice in France the paradoxical formula of the people being sovereign yet shackled, Bonaparte was terrified by his power and the task before him. He was afraid of every-thing: real and imaginary plots being organized, or about to be organized, to assassinate or depose him; discontent; criticism; resistance provoked by his acts; the responsibilities which he had to assume. He could not have been anything else but terrified, for the problem he had to solve was insoluble.

The series of *coups d'états* which culminated in the Empire was thus inspired less by the ambition of the absolute government than by fear of the illegitimate power, exorbitant yet powerless, given to it by the men of Brumaire in order to accomplish an impossible task. Meanwhile, Italy was giving Napoleon no peace. At Lunéville the partition of Campo Formio had become definite. But Austria represented the Old Regime, and France, the Revolution; in the Cisalpine Republic the upper classes appealed for Austrian help against revolutionary oppression; in the provinces under Austrian rule, the radicals hoped France would destroy the Old Regime. On both sides, there were fear and suspicion leading to the renewal of war. Fearing a new war with Austria in the Po Valley, Bonaparte annexed Piedmont in 1803 to secure his communications with the Cisalpine Republic. But the annexation of Piedmont ended the peace of Amiens.

A war began which lasted eleven years; an unprecedented war, governed by periods of partial and insecure peace, by alliances and counteralliances; a war which was to become an intensification of the abuse of force, provoked and aggravated by fear. It was not ambition which led Napoleon to mutilate, dismember, absorb, fetter, and violate so many states: it was fear, the anxiety to reduce the losers to absolute impotence; but the result was always the opposite: the more Napoleon maltreated his victims, the more he feared them. He took fright at the least sign of life in his prostrate enemy; he wanted to snuff it out altogether and transform Europe into a cemetery of countries and peoples. After Austerlitz and the Treaty of Pressburg, he was frightened by the mutilations which he had inflicted on Austria and by the revenge which Austria might attempt. To forestall that revenge he abolished the Holy Roman Empire, proclaimed himself protector of the Confederation of the Rhine, and provoked the war of 1806. With the Prussian army destroyed at Jena and Prussia dismembered, he should have been able to relax, for he had conquered the two great Germanic powers. Vain hope! After Jena and Tilsit it was terror of the whole of Germany revolting which haunted him and pushed him into irreparable abuses of force. He disarmed Prussia and planned to disarm Austria; though an ally of Russia, he wished to resuscitate Poland, but only partially, without head or arms. He created the Duchy of Warsaw, the fragment of a nation which could only have existed by expanding and could only have expanded if Russia had suffered the fate of Austria and Prussia. The contradiction between the Russian alliance and the Polish policy was obvious; Napoleon alone failed to see it, because he was blinded, not by pride but by terror of his victories. Added to this terror was the anxiety characteristic of an illegitimate ruler. The more he tried to identify himself with the ancient dynasties, the more he distrusted them. No, these authentic kings and emperors were never to accept him in all sincerity as one of them; they greeted him with a dagger up their sleeve. Spain was the victim of the most wretched of these families: a fool for a king, the queen's lover for a minister, the heir to the throne a semi-insane prince fighting with his father, his mother, and his mother's lover. But these wretches were authentic Bourbons, and they inspired the usurper of the Bourbon throne in France with such fear that he invaded Spain in order to eliminate them. At the same time he multiplied the princely and royal marriages of his brothers, sisters, brothers-in-law, and sons-in-law—in Italy, in Spain, and in Germany. But with all this he succeeded only in augmenting his own anxiety and the general insecurity of Europe. The more numerous became the spurious dynasties, the more formidable the authentic ones seemed to Napoleon.

He abused his strength to frighten Europe because he was afraid. Symbol of revolutionary power, his fear was aggressive and increased with his strength. But the royal houses of Europe failed to understand that they were facing a fear as great as their own; they saw before them in practice, seemingly real, the childish myth of the desire for power, invented by subsequent generations to satisfy their ignorance. And, hating it, they armed themselves, made alliances, planned coalitions; but they were always eager to come to terms with the enemy. Making one concession after another, the Hapsburgs finally legitimized the false emperor by marriage—a tremendous scandal in all the courts, an incurable autolesion which the monarchy inflicted on itself through fear. Prussia, Austria, the small dynasties of Europe ended up by accepting the direction and the superiority of this revolutionary might, which seemed to them invincible because it had violated all the rules; until the day when, in 1812, Russia dispelled so monstrous a conglomeration of fears. In spite of the fear which paralyzed the courts of Berlin and Vienna, the coalition was at last reversed; Russia succeeded in overcoming the final waverings of Austria and Prussia and drawing them into an attack on the French Empire. The Coalition invaded Germany in 1813, forced Napoleon to cross back over the Rhine, invaded France, and marched on Paris.

But the nearer it came to the final victory, the more it was obsessed by fear: fear of the adversary and of itself, fear of defeat and of victory. Master of the art of surprising his enemies, Napoleon gave an astonishing display of superb tactics and strategy in the French campaign; he formed swift and unexpected combinations which succeeded in partially checking the Coalition, one day at one point, the next at another. From then on, however, the Coalition called into play such forces that the setbacks it received could no longer change the outcome of the war. No matter; fear mounted with each fresh defeat; endless discussions were engaged in by the councils of war. To their fear of Napoleon was added the fear of France. Supposing the people of France should rise against the invaders, like the Russians or the Spanish? Every Cossack patrol which fell into an ambush of peasants made ferocious by terror of invasion, seemed to indicate a general insurrection. To the terror of war and its contradictory vicissitudes was joined the terror of victory and of peace, nevertheless so desirable. The spurious monarchies of the Emperor were collapsing all over Europe; Italy, Spain, France, parts of Germany and Poland were already, or were to be in several weeks, without governments; the regime of mediation in Switzerland was tottering. And no one knew what to put in this tremendous void.

The Revolution was an immense paroxysm of fear which ended by terrifying Europe. Blinded by fear, Europe, in 1814, no longer knew where it was, where it was going, or what lay ahead. In what cataclysm was the great panic, begun on July 14, 1789, going to end?

II

A CASE WITHOUT PRECEDENT

While Paris was in the throes of the great panic, during the terrible winter of 1813-1814, there was one man who, far from succumbing to it, was giving serious thought to the matter. Whence came this deep universal fear? Night and day he asked himself that question. An original thinker, he had spent all his life at odds with himself and the whole world. His destiny and the part he played were unique; he had no precedent. That is why he is so difficult to understand. Yet, without an understanding of their protagonist, the events of 1814 and 1815, and consequently the whole history of the nineteenth century, would be incomprehensible. Let us therefore try to pierce the veil.

All society is an organized system held together in part voluntarily, in part by a combination of moral pressure and coercion—a kind of prison guarded by warders and policemen. Everything depends on the number of warders and policemen, on where they are placed, and on the orders given them. It was by means of this rule of force that the Old Regime recruited part of the clergy in the Catholic countries. In each generation a certain number of men and women from the upper classes were compelled by irresistible pressure on the part of family and society to enter either the secular or the regular clergy. One of the last and the most famous of these prisoners of the Church was Charles-Maurice de Talleyrand-Périgord, born in Paris in 1754, descendant of an ancient and illustrious noble family of warriors. As he had a lame foot which kept him out of the army, his family determined that he should enter the Church. His aversion for such a career was ignored; in spite of all his tearful despair, the pitiful story of which has been set down by his friends, he was forced to follow in the path of countless others of his generation and to become a priest at the age of twenty-five. This misfortune was common enough in his day; and the victim seemed to merit envy rather than pity, for with his name and intelligence he would doubtless become Archbishop of Paris and a Cardinal within a few years.

He became nothing. Nine years after taking orders on December 18, 1779, Talleyrand was still abbé of Périgord, a disgrace for someone with his talents and also for his family. But he had only himself to blame for a ruined career. He had led such a scandalous life that his mother, an ardent Catholic, had refused to see him any more. For a century historians have described this conduct as the preliminary indication of a depraved nature, an initial error of judgment on their part, which falsifies from the very start both the individual's character and his career. If he had been a cynic and a monster, he would have concealed his vices rather than displayed them; and he would have had a high career in the Church without depriving himself of any forbidden pleasures. This was a common procedure in France during the last half of the eighteenth century. But might not the young abbé's disgraceful career have indicated something else—a revolt for instance? He might have confronted his century and said: "You have forced me to become a priest. Very well. But don't expect me to fool the public in the role of the good priest. Compelled to be a priest, I will be a bad priest, and everyone will know it." If, like many others, he had become a priest against his wishes, at least, unlike the others, he rebelled. He rebelled against his mother, his family, the Church, and the epoch, which was the accessory to his violence. He rebelled whenever he could, disgracing the cloth, but giving up all the advantages which resignation to his fate would have assured him, the most dangerous kind of rebellion for him, since it set his whole class against him and condemned him to poverty and obscurity.

This revolt of one lone victim against society as a whole might have been foolish, but it cannot be attributed to the shamelessness of unchecked depravity. There was a kind of hopeless courage in it. An old aristocracy now and again gives birth to proud, courageous individuals who can neither bow nor adjust themselves to acts of violence that are committed against them, and who, heroic or foolish, or both, take up arms in the face of immense risks. Was the young abbé of Périgord one of those men who are incapable of submission to force? We are not yet far enough removed from the period to answer that question. It is certain, however, that his father must have considered the aberrations of the young abbé to be at least partly excusable, for on his deathbed he asked Louis XVI to give his son a bishopric. Still unrelenting, his mother begged the King not to disgrace the Church with such a bishop. Louis XVI yielded to the dying man and appointed the abbé of Périgord, bishop of Autun on November 2, 1788. He was consecrated on January 16, 1789; after a month's incumbency, he left never to return. He had been elected a member of the States-General, and departed for Versailles, for the Revolution, for a new history. In short, he had been appointed bishop by the Old Regime, then *in extremis* and at the brink of the Revolution, in a last attempt to achieve aristocratic solidarity; and he had held his office for only a month. The Revolution was beginning, the Revolution, which, although it was eventually to give a measure of freedom to France and to Europe, at the same time was to give them even heavier chains than any they had borne before. But it was also to accomplish the secularization of France and the invaded countries, wherever it went destroying the social and political power of the Catholic Church. Good or bad, that destruction was its main accomplishment, its immediate and definite achievement. Where was the new bishop going to take his stand?

He completed his revolt, begun by a deliberate campaign of depravity, and he completed it by striking a decisive blow against the temporal power of the Church, a blow that upset the entire structure of the Old Regime. On October 10, 1789, he initiated a bill in the Legislative Assembly which provided for the secularization of all Church property. Stripped of its immense wealth by this law, the Church reverted to a purely spiritual power in a laicized society. By this action, the bishop of Autun made a clean break with the Church. In fact, after having been a constitutional bishop for some time, he definitely made up his mind. In January, 1791, he threw off his cassock and returned to the laity, sending his resignation to the King and ignoring the Pope. Apostasy! thundered the Church. Escape! must be the historian's reply. The rebellious prisoner had taken advantage of an earthquake to flee over the ruins of his prison.

Unfortunately he had fled from the Old Regime to the Revolution, only to be caught in the Terror which began. Although he had hated the Old Regime, he was horrified by the Terror. This time he did not revolt: he merely disappeared. Having secured a passport, he left for London on September 7, 1792, and there attempted to help the Revolution—meanwhile keeping a safe distance—in a manner both strange and unexpected, by presenting to it a grandiose plan of foreign policy, drawn up in the form of a *Memoir on the Present Relations of France with the*

Other States of Europe. The plan began by establishing the fact that the foreign policy of a state and the principles governing its domestic policy are closely related. Since that which distinguishes a free people is the will "to resolve their polity along the principles of reason, justice, and general utility," it follows that "a liberal Constitution by its nature tends constantly to order all things in it and outside of it for the particular benefit of mankind," and that an arbitrary government naturally tends constantly to order all things within and outside of it for the particular benefit of those who govern.

The Revolution must therefore repudiate the entire policy of the Old Regime, declaring unhesitantly to the world that: "True pre-eminence, the only one both useful and rational, the only one worthy of free and enlightened men, consists in being master in one's own house, and never in possessing the ridiculous ambition for mastery over others"; that "all territorial aggrandizement, all those usurpations by means of force and cunning which an old and illustrious tradition had concealed under the names of *rank,* of *consistency of policy,* of superiority in the order of powers, are naught but cruel games of political folly, untrue estimates of power, whose real effect is to increase the expenses and difficulties of the administration and to diminish the happiness and safety of the people in favor of the fugitive interest or the vanity of those who govern."

Therefore, all thoughts of aggrandizement by the Old Regime must be abandoned. France must remain within her natural boundaries and make no alliances with any great power. In principle, an alliance is rational and just only when it is limited to a reciprocal defense pact. Since it is incredible that a great power should wish to attack France, which has no desire to expand and is interested only in improving to the greatest possible extent her own territory, the latter should only contract alliances with little states, especially with those which she will have aided in becoming free "less for her own interest than ... to speed up the ultimate development of the great emancipation of peoples. . . . After having freed the Savoyards, the Belgians, and the Liégeois; after having raised the banner of freedom on the shores of the Atlantic and the Mediterranean, France will formulate solemn treaties of brotherhood between herself and all these peoples, in which the interests of common defense will be established and determined forever, and in which new sources of commerce and industry will be freely opened to the needs and activities of the human race."

The *Memoir* ends on a really extraordinary note. France and England must agree to free all their colonies and get Spain to do the same. Colonies will never develop their resources until they have gained their independence.

Such was the plan for a foreign policy proposed to the Revolution in November, 1792, by the youthful Talleyrand. It is a strange document. He condemns the wars waged for over a century by the great European dynasties for territorial gains and for the balance of power. Instead he offers a simpler constitution and firmer foundation for their states. He goes further, condemning all wars, the very idea of war, as a contradictory, absurd, and largely fictitious means of increasing one's power and wealth, which each state could more easily do by a greater improvement of its own territory. But if, on the one hand, the *Memoir* disowns the wars of the Old Regime, it foreshadows a potential revolt against the Revolution. Talleyrand advises it to lay down its arms forever, just when it is about to launch the longest, most widespread, and bloodiest war of expansion of the eighteenth century. Nothing could have been more inappropriate!

What kind of a man was this unfrocked bishop, this outcast noble who preferred to serve the Revolution at a distance and by advising it to do the opposite of what it was doing? His attitude was so peculiar that it immediately became suspect. The *Memoir* came out on November 25. On December 5, the Convention dispensed with the unwanted services of the former bishop by issuing a formal accusation against him, based on certain papers found in a safe. Talleyrand always claimed the accusation was untrue; whatever the case, he became a refugee. Already rejected by his mother and her family, disowned by the nobility, and execrated by the Church, he was finally driven away by the Revolution. He took refuge in England, but only for a short time. England, too, would have none of him and expelled him on January 28, 1794. From there he went to the United States. Had he then, at forty, become an enemy of the human race, spurned by the whole world, without one place of refuge? But in the general excommunication to which he was subjected, he retained a few faithful friends of both sexes. These he was always to have: a sort of compensation for the hatred which never ceased to pursue him. On September 4, 1795, his friends obtained a decree from the Convention which annulled the accusation of 1792 and permitted him to return. He returned, at a time when the Directory was at the height of its power, minus fortune, position, and family, suspect to the new leaders because of his former connections with the aristocracy and the Church. What could he do? Anything can happen during a period of revolution. A woman, Mme. de Staël, in one day made him Minister of Foreign Affairs. He was forty-three.

For five years the Revolution had been waging a war in search of its natural boundaries. At Leoben it had agreed to the partition of northern Italy with Austria. It was engaged in the pursuit of profitable alliances in every direction, and with as much *élan* as any eighteenth-century court. In accepting the Ministry, the erstwhile bishop of Autun was bound to follow a foreign policy which was the negation of the plan elaborated in his *Memoir*. What was the explanation for this retraction? Historians have had no trouble in finding one. The vicious and depraved abbé, the apostate bishop, was going to transform himself into one of the most skillful turncoats in history. Thenceforward he would serve under every regime and get ample reward for his services, only to betray them when they began to waver. Cupidity and ambition were the only standards he acted by. Supposing this were true, what is the explanation for the following passage from a report which he sent to the Directory a few months after the Treaty of Campo Formio?

When a republic has been able to establish itself in Europe against the wishes of the monarchies, some of which have come to grief through their hostility, and it then launches forth upon a reign of terror, can one not say that the Treaty of Campo Formio and every other treaty we have signed are nothing but military capitulations by the enemy of little permanent worth? The rivalry, momentarily subdued by the amazement and consternation of the loser, is not of a nature to be definitely ended by force of arms, which is transitory, whereas hatred lives on. Because of the great incongruity between the contracting parties, our enemies look upon the treaties they sign with us as no more than truces similar to those which the Moslems resign themselves to concluding with enemies of their faith, without ever making any agreements for a lasting peace. . . . Not only do they continue to plot secretly against us but also remain in coalition against us. We are alone in Europe with five republics that we have created and that are a new cause for anxiety to these powers.[1]

This passage is political philosophy of the highest order, the rarest of all types of human wisdom, for in general philosophers do not know how to act, while politicians do not know how to think. Talleyrand, anticipating events, revealed in that statement one of the greatest secrets of history: why the wars of the Revolution were never to result in a lasting peace. They were never successfully concluded because the two adversaries represented irreconcilable principles, continued to suspect each other, did not even think in the same way, as in the case of Christian and

---

[1] Cited by Albert Sorel, *L'Europe et la révolution française* (Paris: Plon-Nourrit & Cie., 1887-1903), V, 282.

Mohammedan. And also because the Revolution, dazzled by the physical side of force and by the apparent successes of war without rules, had lost all notion of the metaphysics of force and of its limits.[2] It believed that by winning battles it could obtain everything. "Force of arms is transitory, whereas hatred lives on." This sentence should be engraved over the entrance to every ministry of foreign affairs. But it is also obvious from the foregoing that no minister of foreign affairs had ever uttered so merciless a condemnation of the narrow-minded empirical policy he was forced by his government to follow, as did Talleyrand in this passage. It does not seem logical for a turn-coat, exclusively interested in his position and its rewards, to announce to the Directory, which prided itself on having concluded a glorious and lasting peace at Campo Formio, that it had obtained nothing but a false and precarious truce? I will say more. A turncoat minister, as intelligent as Talleyrand, would never have even dreamed of making such a report to the Directory. Ambition and cupidity place their entire faith in the present, providing it favors them. In order to pierce the veil of the present and look into the distant future, the clear, unbiased vision of a prophet is needed, a steady determination to see the light, to know, and to be neither the dupe nor the victim of circumstance. In 1798, when he wrote his report, Talleyrand was already in full revolt, if not against the Revolution at least against its foreign policy.

Nevertheless, he continued to serve it for ten years. In 1807 he was still the minister of the "political folly" whose cruel and fallacious games he had disclosed and denounced in his *Memoir*. The contradiction is obvious. If he judged the foreign policy of the Revolution to be both absurd and fatal, then why did he continue to be Minister of Foreign Affairs under the Directory, the Consulate, and the Empire? If he could not bring himself to resign be-

[2] Concerning the physics and metaphysics of force, see *The Gamble* (London: G. Bell and Sons, 1939), pp. 95 *et seq*.

cause of the position and the salary, why, at the risk of losing them, did he condemn both himself and his masters? And then came 1798-1799, those two frightful years, during which an avalanche of disaster, set in motion by the Treaty of Campo Formio, buried Italy, France, and all Europe! Everywhere there were wars, *coups d'état,* chaos, misery, and a rain of blood; everywhere the rumble and panic of laws toppling under the fanatical blows of unrestricted force. Talleyrand ended up by taking part in the greatest and most inevitable lunacy of the age: the 18 Brumaire, that monstrous distortion of democracy. It is likely that Talleyrand, terrified by the frightful chaos in Europe, was under the same delusion as his colleagues—the possibility of setting up a government which would be a contradiction of the very principle it was based upon. Be that as it may, out of this paralogism in action came a sort of counter-revolution which reconciled the Church, re-established absolutism, restored the aristocracy, increased to twice its former size by the creation of a new nobility, and abolished equality and liberty. And there was Talleyrand, pillar of a counterrevolutionary government which speedily transformed the citizen Minister into an Excellency, a high chamberlain, and finally into no less than a prince. Was the eminent rebel going to be reconciled with the Church and the Old Regime by taking a magnificent place in the new nobility of the Counterrevolution? But just then a marriage made him once more an outcast.

Since 1798, Talleyrand had been living with a French-woman who possessed the distinctions of having been born in India and divorced by an Englishman. Mme. Grand seems to have been very pretty. In 1802 the First Consul requested his Minister of Foreign Affairs to set his domestic affairs in order, giving him the alternatives of marriage or rupture. But Talleyrand had been a consecrated bishop. The First Consul exerted all his influence in Rome. The registrars, the theologians, and the canons were mobilized. A waste of time. If he had remained what he had been

nine months before the Revolution—abbé of Périgord—
Talleyrand, as a mere priest, might have been able to join
the ranks of the renegades. But he was a bishop, and in
eighteen centuries the Church had not once given its
consent to the marriage of a bishop. A bishop, once consecrated must remain pure; the Pope was uncompromising.
What was to be done? In 1802, Talleyrand was forty-eight
and his mistress forty; neither of them was at an age when
two lovers are ready to defy the world and fate to be
united. Talleyrand was not unaware of the danger to which
he would be exposed if he chose to ignore the laws and
his own position in the Counterrevolution, by making
Mme. Grand his wife in the sight of man, when God
denied her recognition. A civil wedding would constitute
a new revolt against the Church and a new rupture with
the old nobility, who were nearly all on the point of rallying to the new regime. At the moment when the Church
and the aristocracy were getting ready to forget the fact
that the man so high in the ranks of the new government
had been the former bishop of Autun, they were about
to be faced with a fresh horror—a married bishop. A cynical
and covetous opportunist, as history has been pleased to
paint Talleyrand for us, would not have hesitated for an
instant to sacrifice Mme. Grand to his career. Talleyrand
married her in the sight of man, since God refused his
consent.

To sum up, after having rebelled against the Old
Regime and the Revolution, in 1802 he clashed with the
Counterrevolution over a middle-aged woman, meanwhile
continuing to work for it. It was probably he who had the
greatest share in the most decisive step taken by the Counterrevolution of the 18 Brumaire: the founding of the
Empire. If he had had any illusions at the start, his keen
intelligence could not have long deceived him about the
real nature of the Constitution of the Year VIII. This
masterpiece conceived by Siéyès, a final effort on the part
of the Revolution to free itself from the contradictions

that were strangling it, was nothing but a hoax. Far from bolstering authority, this absurd Constitution required bolstering itself, by a combination of force and trickery. It was impossible to govern France in the name of the people while suppressing the free and honest expression of the sovereign will, whether real or presumed. Since the Republic had been choked to death by its contradictions, nothing was left but to restore the monarchy under a new dynasty, for, in 1802, Talleyrand could have neither desired nor been able to facilitate the return of the Bourbons. When one is desperate and one's safety in danger, the impossible can seem possible even to the most perspicacious of men.

The Empire showed itself grateful to Talleyrand. It overwhelmed him with honors and riches, made him a high chamberlain in 1804, and Prince of Benevento in 1806. But on October 17, 1805, the eve of the capitulation of Ulm, Talleyrand wrote a letter to the Emperor in which he suggested a peace proposal which he described as "the most durable that human reason could hope for." Following victory, the Emperor was to expel Austria from Italy, withdraw his own troops, resurrect the Republic of Venice, separate the two crowns of Italy and France, allow Austria to seek compensation in the East, and propose peace conditions which would clear the ground for a Franco-Austrian alliance.

This letter had no more favorable a reception than the *Memoir* of 1792. The Treaty of Pressburg expelled Austria from the peninsula, transferred her territories to the Kingdom of Italy, and subjected the whole of Italy to the sovereignty or the suzerainty of France—the reverse of what Talleyrand had proposed. The Emperor and his Minister were already in disagreement. The Minister balked at the foreign policy of the Empire for the same reasons that he had balked at the foreign policy of the Directory. Napoleon merely carried on where the Directory had left off. And, as before, Talleyrand's scruples did not result in open

rupture; once more he submitted, playing the docile pup-
pet of imperial policy through all the fatal developments
of the Pressburg Treaty. He even drew up the decree for
the continental blockade, one of the most dangerous abuses
of force ever produced by fear. This time one can hardly
help coming to the conclusion that Talleyrand was thinking only of his position and that he cared little for his
ideas, since he was able to change them so easily at the
behest of his chiefs.

Nevertheless, in the long report which preceded the decree of blockade and which had been drafted by him, the
following lines occurred:

Sire, three centuries of civilization have bequeathed to
Europe a law of nations for which, in the words of a famous
writer, human nature will never be grateful enough. This
law is founded on the principle that nations should in time
of peace do each other the most good, and in time of war
the least possible harm.

In accord with the maxim that war is not a relationship
between men, but between states, in which individuals are
only accidentally enemies, not as human beings, not even as
members or subjects of the state, but solely as its defenders,
the law of nations does not permit military law and the law
of conquest, which derives therefrom, to have jurisdiction over
peaceful, unarmed citizens, over dwellings and property devoted to the commodities of trade, over the shops which contain them, over the conveyances which transport them, over
the unarmed vessels which carry them on the rivers or over
the seas—in a word, over the private individual and his
property.

This law, the child of civilization, has furthered the growth
of its parent. To it Europe owes the preservation and the
increase of her prosperity, even at the height of the frequent
wars which have divided her.

It would be difficult to find a clearer picture of the
reasons for and results of the great effort made by the
eighteenth century toward limiting the destructive furies
of war. But at the same time it would be impossible to

imagine a more pitiless condemnation of the continental blockade. Why did Talleyrand remind his master so forcibly of the principles implicit in the law of nations which denied him the use of such barbarous methods? If one accepts the traditional view of Talleyrand, that question becomes unanswerable. Throughout his life, this enigmatic man remained a living contradiction, and no one has been able to guess the reason. And, as he rose in his career, the contradiction became even greater. There he was, in 1807, a married bishop, a fictitious chamberlain, a farcical prince, a conscious instrument of political folly, to all appearances firmly attached to his position.

When, all of a sudden, in August, 1807, after the Treaty of Tilsit, with Napoleon at the height of his power and everyone in Europe believing that his Empire would out-last the Roman Empire—this strange grasper, doggedly holding on to his position, chooses that moment to hand in his resignation! Have you ever seen an ambitious man, subject to every vice, whose only thought is to acquire money, throw away the power which gives him enormous rewards at the very moment that this power seems to be resting on unshakable foundations?

This resignation was really the outburst of his hitherto latent revolt against the Empire and its foreign policy. Coming after so long a period of dissension, the resignation should this time have brought about a final break. Not at all. Talleyrand continued to serve Napoleon as Vice-Grand Elector at a salary of 330,000 francs, which, added to his various perquisites, gave him a fixed income of half a million francs. The former Minister did not intend to feel the pinch of poverty in his retirement! Blessed with such an opportunity, he should have done everything in his power to hang on to it. Yet, only a year later, this amazing man was to accomplish the so-called "Erfurt betrayal" against his Emperor!

Obsessed by fear of a German revenge, in the spring of 1808, Napoleon deposed the Spanish Bourbons so as to prevent a possible stab in the back, should he be forced to fight Prussia and Austria. But this action provoked a nasty war on the other side of the Pyrenees, whereupon Napoleon's fear returned. He now dreaded that Prussia and Austria would take advantage of his war in Spain to attack him in the rear. Terrified by this dual fear, he conceived the plan of disarming both Prussia and Austria. Prussia, too feeble to resist after Tilsit, became the first victim. He ordered her to disarm, and in Paris on September 18, 1808, he signed the Convention which placed the Prussian army in French hands. Austria, still a great power, in spite of Pressburg, was a more difficult proposition. Napoleon could not disarm her without the support of Russia. To obtain this, he invited Alexander I to meet him at Erfurt, under pretext of discussing Eastern affairs. He arrived there in October, 1808, with Talleyrand to help him in the difficult negotiations. Instead, Talleyrand went to see Alexander and encouraged him to resist Napoleon's demands with all his strength. If Alexander resisted, it was because he had Talleyrand behind him.[3]

It appears that Napoleon never did know exactly what took place between his Minister and the Czar of Russia. But he might have found out; in that case Talleyrand was risking his head. While admitting that Napoleon might never have gone that far, it would have been natural for him to have dismissed from office, stripped, and banished his Minister. Talleyrand was at least risking his position. Why? To gain the friendship of the Russian Czar, or of the Austrian Emperor? What good would that have done him, if he had lost Napoleon's favor, which supported

---

[3] To my knowledge, Albert Vandall is the only historian (*Napoléon et Alexandre Ier;* Paris: Plon-Nourrit & Cie., 1893-1896, I, 390-417) who perceived that the real purpose of the meeting at Erfurt was the disarming of Austria, desired by Napoleon. M. A. Sorel (Vol. VII, p. 317) alludes to the disarming of Austria demanded by Napoleon but without attributing any particular importance to it, as if it were a minor point. The writer fails to grasp the primary importance of the point, on which depended the fate of Europe. Lanfrey, *Histoire de Napoléon Ier* (Paris: Charpentier, 1867-1875), whose book comes closest to the truth, completely ignores the disarming of Austria as one of the problems discussed at Erfurt.

him? For revenge? The events which were later to justify his hatred did not begin until the following year. One fails to see what Talleyrand would have wanted vengeance for, in 1808, at the risk of losing all.

No, the "betrayal" at Erfurt was inexplicable. The Talleyrand that tradition has handed down to us would have "betrayed" Napoleon when the odds were all in his own favor; he would never have "betrayed" him, as the real Talleyrand did, when the odds were all against him and when there was no profit motive. What kind of man was he, then? His life seemed fated, by some mysterious predestination, to be a permanent revolt against all the powers of the world, including those he served, which were, until 1814, revolutionary powers, that is, very dangerous ones, as all powers are which suffer from a persecution complex. But of all these revolts only one, the first, against the Church, resulted in a complete break. The others never resulted either in a complete break or a substantial modification of the policy which provoked them. Only the revolt at Erfurt seemed to have brought results. What was the meaning of these continuous revolts, which were useless to mankind and dangerous only to him? One must not look on the surface for the key to these enigmas, but in the depths of history, in the struggle between two eternal forces over the direction of world affairs: the spirit of adventure (or of enterprise, as Talleyrand called it), and the constructive mind. In the preceding volume we have studied the spirit of adventure; now we must analyze the constructive mind.

III

THE CONSTRUCTIVE MIND

If all human beings were to react similarly to a given set of circumstances, so that their actions could be foreseen, human society would resemble nothing so much as a bee-hive or an anthill. Every problem would be solved before it came up. Intelligence and will power would have no functions to perform. The life of the individual and the history of the group, would, like that of the bees and ants, be reduced to a predetermined and invariable co-ordination of instinctive and unchanging actions.

But, in a universe which is governed by the law of causality, the human mind is alone distinguished by its freedom, a word used somewhat equivocally by certain philosophical schools. Every piece of iron exposed to heat always reacts in the same way. It expands, turns red, then white, softens, and finally liquefies. The forecast is unmistakable, and all human labor is based on the security afforded by countless similar forecasts. The reactions of the human mind to physical or mental forces acting upon it, are on the contrary variable and far more unpredictable. One man will react quite differently from another to the same circumstances; the same man will not necessarily react tomorrow as he reacts today. Collective reactions seem even more capricious and difficult to foresee than individual reactions. Every human mind is the condensation of a mysterious force which explodes under the shock of life with intensity and in different and unforeseen directions, at will or as it can. That is why no science of the mind and of history analagous to the science of matter and nature has been formulated; one is even forced to consider whether the word "science" can be applied in the same sense to the physical and intellectual life of men, to the chemistry and history of societies.

This sovereign independence through which the mind acts and manifests itself, is the essence of human nature. But it is also responsible for the agony and the hardship in man's existence. Obviously, in order to live together, men must be able to foresee, at least to a certain extent, and under not too exceptional circumstances, what their actions or reactions will be. Take, for instance, the family unit. Would it be endurable if the husband and wife, parents and children, never knew, among the daily vicissitudes of life, whether they could count on mutual respect, obedience, and love, or whether they should live in fear of revolt, indifference, and hate—an equally possible alternative? The same may be said for all human societies, even the greatest ones, like the state. If the central nucleus of the human mind enjoys unlimited freedom and is capable of ignoring fixed laws, social life becomes permissible only if each one of us can more or less foresee the conduct of the majority of our fellow creatures under every known circumstance.

Society, then, is founded upon a contradiction between human liberty and the social necessity for reactions that can be foreseen. How did men get around this contradiction? By discovering and imposing laws which maintain a certain order, namely by guaranteeing some possibility of foreseeing what will happen in the course of human relationships. For disorder is only the result of the unpredictable made permanent in human relationships. Order means the possibility of predicting the reactions of the people we live with, at least under ordinary circumstances. The constructive mind is the union of those intellectual and moral qualities which are necessary in order to discover and impose these laws. But the task presents extreme difficulties because man is a contradictory creature, continually striving to attain goals which are beyond his grasp and which he is unable to abandon. He is timid and seeks to be brave; he is wicked but would like to be good; an evanescent mote, he aspires to the eternal and the infinite; though an egoist, he has need of society; though senseless, he obstinately wishes to be rational. And he is also eternally in revolt against the order he creates with such strenuous effort and without which he could not live. In fact the first creation of a constructive mind is a juridical order, law in the strict sense of the word, the civil and penal codes—the entire organization of justice, which, through force, imposes respect for a certain number of elementary rules, without which not one of us would ever be sure, upon leaving his house, of not being murdered or robbed.

Although the juridical order is the simplest creation of the constructive mind, in order to make good laws and apply them seriously, a number of rare virtues are required: a strong and clear sense of justice tempered by a deep humanity, acute powers of reasoning, encyclopedic intelligence, a sure and profound knowledge of human nature, and a great deal of energy. And yet, even if the constructive mind makes use of all these virtues in the simplest of its tasks, it never succeeds in imbuing man with a fully developed respect for justice. The independence of the human mind is never completely subjugated; it is a permanent menace to the juridical order, ready at any moment to burst into crime. But juridical order, in spite of its weakness, rests on firm foundations: specific laws and the means to enforce them.

When, however, it invades the higher plane of ethics, where coercion is no longer possible, the constructive mind has a far more difficult task. Moral principles are present in each individual conscience, but in a nebulous condition and submerged in a welter of passions. Men can easily abuse their freedom by confounding these principles and inverting them at will. What is good for one man may be bad for another; that which a man considers good today, he may consider bad tomorrow. How is one to bring order out of this anarchy? The constructive mind attempts a solution by formulating rules of ethics and by seeking to impress them firmly on individual consciences and, through persuasion and example, to establish them as categorical commands to be universally observed. Religion is the most powerful instrument at the disposal of the constructive mind to establish and maintain moral order. But advice and examples are no more than aids. All forms of coercion being out of the question, the human conscience must, after all, at the moment of choice, follow its own dictates. Moral order is achieved through the self-regulation of each individual conscience, an extremely difficult operation, because, in spite of advice and example, violations of the rules are easily justifiable. The constructive mind wearies of giving advice and examples which, from lack of sanction, are too often sterile. Too often, it is satisfied with appearances: the absence of notoriety rather than respect for the law. It succumbs to the gangrene of hypocrisy.

But juridical order and ethical order are only two superimposed sections of universal order. To be complete, the system of order needs, as a house needs a roof, a certain political order of dual nature, external and internal. The problem of internal political order consists in seeing that the power made use of by the administration to impose the law does not become an instrument in its hands for the transgression of law and morality. As sovereign, the executive power has no obligation to respect the laws which it or an ethical code imposes on its subjects. It can kill, steal, break faith, betray, and lie at will. So that it may be checked and not become hated and feared by those whom it should protect, it must agree to submit voluntarily to certain restrictions, the greater part of which can only be imposed by public opinion. This contract must be so complete that not even the temptation remains either to overstep these restrictions or to consider the possibility of overstepping them without danger and with profit. In certain countries the aggregate of these restrictions or checks is called constitutional law.

The same difficulty, on a larger scale, occurs in the relationships between states. As soon as peoples no longer want or are able to live in the barbaric isolation of a permanent state of siege, they begin to feel the need for international order, that is, the possibility of being able to predict when and under what conditions each of them might be attacked. But this becomes possible only when the states agree voluntarily to observe certain rules pertinent to their intercourse. The aggregate of rules which the European states had discovered in the seventeenth century and continued to observe until 1914, constituted the law of nations, or international law.

Political order, then, like moral order, can be maintained only by a process of self-discipline. But political self-discipline is the most necessary and the most difficult of all the tasks faced by the constructive mind. The most necessary, because without it men are condemned to an everlasting and frightful inhumanity. The most difficult, because it becomes possible only when the state is governed by an elite which has succeeded in distinguishing between the physics and the metaphysics of force; in catching sight, over and beyond its immediate and visible effects, of its fundamental and invisible reactions; and in discovering the simplest and hardest of truths, which the human intellect is both capable and incapable of grasping: that the usefulness of force to man is measured by his ability to control it, that for it to be intensified is suicidal, and that the abuse of force terrifies the one who commits it more than the victim.

In this discovery, and through it, the constructive mind attains its highest perfection and power, thanks to the most difficult of all its efforts—an effort which calls for an extremely rare combination of intelligence and courage. Intelligence alone is not sufficient; courage is also needed. For if man, in his fickleness and ignorance, tends to believe only in the physics of force, in its immediate and visible consequences, this tendency becomes irresistible when he is afraid. Governments based on fear are no longer capable of the least self-discipline because they are no longer able to foresee the more far-reaching consequences of the use of force. They confuse their well-being with immediate success, as if the latter were the only reality, present and future, even when it has been secured by the most dangerous abuses of force. Only a government with ample intelligence and no fear will be able to see through the illusion of force, to recognize the limitations and the snares, and to understand that beyond those limitations force will injure its possessor more than its victim, that self-discipline although it may appear to limit internally and externally the sovereign power of a state, in reality maintains and guarantees it. Such a government will observe the rules because, by being able to foresee the far-reaching consequences of its actions, it will be strong enough to forswear any immediate advantages obtained through violating those rules.

Now that we understand the nature of the constructive mind, let us reread the *Memoir* of 1792. It was an indictment against war, made just when a twenty-three-year war was beginning in Europe. Its conception was too vast, too theoretical, and too ineffective to become the policy of a future minister. But neither was it a utopian dream, on the order of that proposed by the abbé Saint-Pierre. What was it? The utterance of a profound horror of force, and consequently of war, the sincerity of which is unquestionable, chiefly because the plan is impractical. Most men submit to force and sometimes, through weakness, even admire it. Some admire it in all sincerity, and even go so far as to worship it, through inhumanity. At the opposite end of the scale, a small, select group composed of entirely humane individuals, either saints or sages, has a deep horror of it. In 1792, Talleyrand was still only a sage who distrusted force and hoped that the Revolution would put an end to the wars of expansion and balance of power which characterized the eighteenth century. Those wars had been caused by the increasing disparity between the distribution of territory among the powers and the forces which guaranteed it: the ambitions of the courts, wealth, the *Kultur* and military strength of the states, the needs and aspirations of the peoples. Europe had been fighting for a century to establish a new balance of power, but the task had proved tremendously difficult. Wars had multiplied, and they had become so lengthy, so bloody, and so costly, that a reaction by the elite of Europe occurred, which produced the famous law of nations.

What was this law of nations which had set so many lay and clerical pens to scribbling in the seventeenth and eighteenth centuries and which Talleyrand had so paradoxically eulogized in the decree announcing the continental blockade? It was a complex movement, somewhat confusing and incoherent, which sought to check the multiplication and violence of wars and to establish a permanent peace by subjecting force to a system of rules capable of correcting its abuses and originating in human nature. Two badly co-ordinated impulses—intellect and feeling—determined seventeenth-century Europe to check the abuse of force, the danger of which was becoming apparent in the development of armies and war. The philosophers and jurists—Grotius, Wolf, Puffendorf, Vattel—had primarily set up principles of law against the unleashing of force. Churchmen like Bossuet and Fénelon had endeavored to set up justice and charity, drawing from Christianity everything that could help man to resist the onslaughts of passions released by the use of violence. Finally, the writers—Montesquieu, Voltaire, Rousseau, Volney, the encyclopedists—had combined reason and feeling, law and humanitarianism, to create for statesmen models of wisdom and humanity that were sometimes rather visionary. It was Montesquieu who had written these famous lines, which sum up the entire effort of his century:

> The law of nations is genuinely based on this principle, that the divers nations should do each other the most good during peacetime and the least harm during wartime without harming their true interests.

This movement, which had been most active in France, had exerted a strong influence on the statesmen, warriors, and monarchs—including Louis XIV and Frederick the Great—of the seventeenth and eighteenth centuries. It had contributed enormously to the creation of warfare with rules and of the whole system of self-discipline which had prevented the wars of the eighteenth century from becoming irresistible outbursts of violence, destructive of social order. But in spite of this magnificent effort, wars had plunged Europe into an atmosphere so saturated with violence, treachery, intrigue, and suspicion that Talleyrand could write of them as "cruel games of political folly." Talleyrand had studied the religious and lay writers who had been trying for a century to set up against the ever more menacing abuse of force, principles of law, justice, charity, wisdom, humanity, philosophy, and the Gospel. Having an enlightened mind, he had been greatly impressed. To understand Talleyrand and his place in history, one must never forget that he was essentially a product of the eighteenth century and a disciple of the movement which had been its greatest achievement. In his *Memoir,* for example, we rediscover the spirit which inspired Fénelon's criticism of war in the *Examen sur les*

Devoirs de la Royauté, the same distrust of force, the same
horror of war, the same conviction that a civilized state
must, in its relations with other states, minimize as far as
possible the use of violence. If this be kept in mind, it is
easy to explain why Talleyrand, in 1792, still hoped that
the Revolution, by turning history into more humane
channels, would be able to re-establish peacefully the balance between force and law in Europe.

Six years later when, as Minister, he wrote his report
on the Treaty of Campo Formio, he was no longer the
humanitarianist, hating war for itself in complete freedom
of conscience. Instead, he had become a statesman and
diplomat who was witnessing the wars of the eighteenth
century multiplying and escaping from that self-discipline
which up till then had held in check their destructive
power, by their escape causing the total destruction of the
law of nations, created by previous generations. He was the
servant of a government which, preyed upon by fear, saw
only the physical side of force, and its apparent invinci-
bility. The spirit of adventure had unleashed all its fury
upon mankind, spreading terror wherever it went, a terror
all the more awful because, like Frankenstein's monster, it
had turned upon its creator. If Talleyrand had been like
the others, he would have succumbed to the general
panic and would also have hailed the victories in Italy and
Switzerland of Napoleon, Brune, and Championnet, as
the salvation and the glory of France. But he was not like
the others; he had read, studied, and assimilated Grotius
and Vattel, Fénelon and Montesquieu; he was blessed with
a strong philosophical intellect which desired and knew
how to comprehend and to subjugate the changeable and
fragmentary reality of the universe by the only efficacious
method, that of restoring it to fixed principles. Through
no fault of his, that intellect had been trained in one of
the most famous dialectical schools of the age, that of
Saint-Sulpice. And, finally, he did not become a prey to
the general panic.

Thus, in a generation which believed only in the physics of force, he rediscovered its inner significance. Alone in his era, he began to understand the paradoxical drama of the Revolution, with its sterile victories and wars that would never end because they had transgressed the limits beyond which force ceases to be effectual and destroys itself. And in that realization he revolted once more. To his own epoch, dominated by the spirit of adventure and the fears it engenders, he began, as early as 1798, to oppose the constructive mind which had awakened in him and which was a combination of courage and perspicacity. This was to gain strength in proportion as his resistance grew to the illusory fears of the age and of the government he served. Why, several days before the Battle of Austerlitz, did he propose his peace plan to the Emperor? Understanding that the future of the world hung in the balance, he became the courageous spokesman for the constructive mind at a time when he was engaged in a hazardous adventure. Though it is doubtful whether the Republic of Venice could have been revived in 1805 with a modern constitution, Talleyrand was right in stating that there would be neither peace nor a balance of power in Europe until Italy had recovered, in one form or another, the independence which it possessed in the eighteenth century; and that, by weakening Austria in order to help herself to Italy, France was splitting up the whole European system and was signing its own death warrant into the bargain. The whole history of Europe from the Treaty of Pressburg to the second world war has been a bloody confirmation of that prophetic letter. Fearing that Austria would revolt against the Pressburg treaty, Napoleon was to destroy the Holy Roman Empire, attempt to reduce southern Germany to the status of a French protectorate, invade and dismember Prussia. From then on it was to become a duel to the death between France and the German states, the cause of perpetual anguish on the part of the Western world, waiting for the ultimate outcome, never certain, of this war of extermination. A prophet in the midst of blind leaders, Talleyrand saw in 1805 that Austerlitz might turn into one of the greatest disasters of French history if the victor did not know how to make peace. He told him so, even before the battle, at the risk of alienating the man upon whom his career depended.

Why, at the outset of the continental blockade, did he invoke with such vehemence the principles contained in the law of nations, which charged peoples to do each other the least possible harm in time of war? Because he did not believe in the blockade, which was really a frenzy of fear; and he did believe in the eighteenth-century law of nations, the masterpiece of the constructive mind. Why did he hand in his resignation in 1807, at the height of the Empire? Because he knew that the Empire, which seemed solidly built, was really full of invisible cracks which would burst and topple the whole structure at the first violent blow from the outside. They were the same weaknesses which he had found in the jerry-built construction of the Directory, but far more dangerous: every peace was nothing but a truce; the victor's position was becoming more precarious after each victory; his fear was growing with the success and the expansion of the Empire; the end of each war was followed by preparations for a greater one, equally futile.

Why, after the resignation, did he betray Napoleon at Erfurt? Because the disarming of a great power like Austria, and the subjugation of its military strength to France and Russia, constituted a monstrous abuse of force, instigated by fear, which would have precipitated all Europe into frightful chaos. Europe at that time, as also during the nineteenth century, consisted of a system of states in equilibrium. So that this system could be held together, a certain balance was needed among all the elements of power: territory, wealth, population, and army. To destroy this balance at one point by the forceful disarmament of a great power was to upset the whole system and allow chaos to set in. The Treaty of Tilsit made Prussia a small power; yet she reacted to the disarmament which Napoleon imposed on her by giving birth to Prussian militarism, which in turn engendered German militarism, the terror of Europe since 1870. Two monsters, one the issue of the other. What even more horrible monster would Austria have let loose on Europe if she had had to submit to the same violence? The disarmament of Austria was the greatest folly of a fear which no longer believed in anything but violence, and which threatened the total annihilation of Europe. Constructive genius, great philosopher of force, Talleyrand alone understood the terrible danger and risked his position, perhaps also his life, to save France, Austria, Europe, and Napoleon himself. The danger was too great for him to hesitate.

A prophet revolting against his blind masters. Such was the contradictory life led by this enigmatic man during the whole Revolution. But this astonishing contradiction is still not the explanation of the enigma, for it is the enigma. One cannot understand Talleyrand until one can explain the reason for the contradiction he lived under between 1797 and 1814. Many eminent men bowed to the inevitable and served the Revolution, in spite of their disgust for its violence and its mistakes. Others, incapable of concealing their disgust, preferred either to emigrate or to hold aloof. Talleyrand took a third course: he served the great panic of his age, but only up to the point at which it began to commit irreparable follies. At that point he suddenly revolted and set up the invisible truths of the metaphysics of force against the deceptive illusions of its physics; but he made no definite rupture with his blind masters, and continued to serve them. It is obvious that such an attitude made his extraordinary clear-sightedness useless to the world and dangerous to him, because it forced him to live a perpetual lie, in permanent opposition to revolutionary powers, that were suspicious, violent, and cruel. How is one to explain the fact that a man who had no inclination to be a martyr, who on the contrary was ambitious for power, glory, and wealth, took such an attitude, ridiculous both from the point of view of public interests and that of his personal interests?

The answer is that after having revolted against the Old Regime he could not also break with the Revolution. The man who had disestablished Church property, the bishop who had married, would not have known where to go or what to do, if he had broken with the Revolution. Even if he had retired into complete seclusion, for which he was not suited anyway, he could not have escaped the hatred that he had engendered. During his whole life, Talleyrand was a prisoner of his first revolt against the Church and the Old Regime. What was this revolt? If we concede what was assumed at the start, that he was one of those true *grands seigneurs,* courageous and proud, who are unable to submit to force and who must revolt; if we add that this *grand seigneur* was a constructive genius who had rediscovered the secret of force—then we shall understand the singular drama of his life. This had been a permanent revolt against the Revolution's spirit of adventure and its fears, which he was forced to serve and which he was unable to serve all the way. He had to serve them because he naturally required an important position and an executive function. He could not serve them all the way because the courage of the *grand seigneur* always ended up by revolting, when abuses of force, for which he would have had to take the responsibility, became too absurd and dangerous. As in his youth he had refused to act the hypocrite by playing the part of a good priest, even at the risk of falling out with the whole world, so, in the prime of life, did he balk at expressing a hypocritical admiration for the Treaties of Campo Formio and Pressburg, the continental blockade, the Treaty of Tilsit, the disarming of Austria, and all the other errors committed by the Revolution. He protested as often and as strongly as he could without breaking completely with the Revolution.

There lies the real truth in all the contradictions of his extraordinary life. Alone in his age, alone even in history, for he had no predecessor to serve as model, this smiling yet tragic figure was constantly struggling with himself and with others. Struggling with himself, because he was the servant of blind men and saw the precipice they were nearing, yet was unable to stop them; with others, because the Church despised him, the aristocracy disowned him, the Revolution and the Counterrevolution distrusted him, Napoleon pampered and tormented him at the same time. What an antithesis between these two men! One, an outcast noble; the other, a great parvenu. The one stood for the constructive mind; the other was the spirit of adventure incarnate. The one was a great philosopher of force; the other, a ruthless manipulator of force. To the one, force was useful only when it could be controlled; to the other, only when it could be unleashed. The one based thought and action as far as possible on principles; the other scorned principles and used them for the sake of deception. The one was a true realist; the other—Napoleon—was an eternal visionary.

Friendly enemies to the last! They could have lived and acted together all their lives, without understanding one word of what they said to each other. Toward the end of the Empire their friendship, continually poisoned by suspicion and aversion, became strained to the breaking point. Napoleon abused, humiliated, and harassed Talleyrand; he distrusted, feared, and hated him, partly because he detected in his Minister a more formidable enemy than the armies of the Coalition, partly because he was jealous of a superior intellect. Nothing is so annoying to great parvenus than a subordinate who excels them. However, he did not dismiss him, but kept him always within reach, partly to make use of him and partly to have him where he could do the least harm. All the fears that haunted the Emperor seemed to be personified in this courtier, supreme terror of the man who was terrorizing all Europe. Talleyrand endured everything—insults, humiliations, suspicion, vexations—without a quiver, with the impassivity of the *grand seigneur* who despises where he cannot rebel.

From 1810 to 1814, Talleyrand's life must have been a hell. Forced to be a courtier after having been a bishop; living in a spurious Court, chained to a task that was futile yet engrossing; spied upon from all sides by unseen powers; pulled this way and that by relentless animosities which waited only for a favorable opportunity to fall on him and destroy him; completely at the mercy of a man in the clutches of a persecution complex, who hated him and seemed to be playing a cat-and-mouse game with him. This resembled the endless agony of a man condemned to death, whose execution is constantly deferred. No history has yet given an account of this drama, because every historian has passed over the perpetual danger in which Talleyrand lived between 1806 and 1814. They compare his position with that of a Minister or high functionary of the Third Republic, living in Paris in complete personal safety, free to say anything he wanted. Instead, he was forced to suspect everyone, to be on constant guard in his conversations, even with friends, and take care with the most insignificant letter that he wrote, never knowing what would happen to him from one day to the next: whether he would be entrusted with an important duty to perform for the Empire or whether he would be locked up in Vincennes.[1]

What patience, what self-control, what dissimulation, what courage must have been necessary to endure this interminable anguish! But, while identifying himself more and more with the agony of a Europe devastated by fear and violence, in the depths of his solitude he

[1] The Château de Vincennes, in which political prisoners were incarcerated.

sought obstinately for his own well-being in the common salvation. During the winter of 1813-1814, during that grim winter when the mortally wounded Empire made mankind tremble with its death pangs, he immersed himself in long and profound reflections by which he uncovered the roots of the great panic. These reflections once saved mankind; they could save it again if mankind would only understand them. Let us reread the pages on which he has expressed them; or, rather, let us read them, for mankind has not yet read them.

IV

THE PRINCIPLE OF LEGITIMACY

The *Mémoires* of Talleyrand, published in 1891, are unusual, in that the author objectively, calmly, and almost familiarly reduces everything, large and small, to the same scale.[1] This has given rise to difficulties in understanding and making use of an otherwise simple and lucid book. For example, all of a sudden, in the middle of Volume II, the reader finds himself, without any warning, in the middle of a philosophical dissertation on the foundations of government, which goes on for seven pages. There is no introduction to this weighty discourse; the tone of the book never changes; it seems as though the author were merely jotting down a few elementary ideas as they occur to him while at work. Led astray by this nonchalant manner, readers have been skimming the surface of these pages for half a century, as if they were "bare

[1] Today everyone agrees that the *Mémoires,* published by the duc de Broglie (Paris, 1891), are authentic. For my part, I incline to the belief that they underwent mutilations and perhaps also revision. As for the passages discussed in this chapter, there can be no question of their authenticity. Talleyrand alone was capable of thinking and writing these ideas.

of novelty and interest," the phrase used by a recent biographer of Talleyrand. But these seven pages contain the key to the whole history of Western civilization from the French Revolution to the present, and very probably the key to the history of subsequent generations. I am going to quote the whole of this important passage, transposing a little and adding here and there commentaries of my own. Both transposition and commentaries will be useful for getting the most out of what the author seems to have written without ever suspecting that he was bringing a powerful light to bear on several centuries of history.

I have already mentioned that during the last days of the Empire I had often asked myself this question: What form of government should France adopt after the fall of Napoleon?

To have restored the dynasty of the man who had led France to destruction would have been to sink to the lowest and most abject misery. Moreover, Austria, who alone would have had no objections to the regency of Marie Louise, had only a weak voice in the councils of the Allies. She had been the last of the great powers who had undertaken to avenge Europe's wrongs, and certainly Europe did not make any strenuous efforts to put the throne of France at the disposal of the Court of Vienna.

Russia might make an ingenious bid for Bernadotte, in order to rid herself of a troublesome neighbor in Sweden; but Bernadotte was only a new form of the Revolution. Eugène de Beauharnais might perhaps have been carried by the army, but the army had been beaten.

The duc d'Orléans was supported by only a few individuals. In the eyes of some, his father had committed the crime of having dishonored the name of equality; for others, the duc d'Orléans would have been no more than a usurper of better family than Bonaparte.

And, meanwhile, it was becoming increasingly urgent to form a government which could be hurriedly substituted for the one that was falling to pieces. A single day's delay might bring about the realization of those ideas of partition and subjection which secretly threatened our unfortunate country. There was no question of entering into any intrigues; they would all have been futile. What was needed was to find exactly what France wanted and what Europe must have wanted.

A ship without rudder or sails, the Empire was about to founder. How was it possible to prevent it from dragging France and Europe into the depths? Talleyrand answers this in a passage which must be thoroughly digested to be understood. This passage is unprecedented in Western history, for it is the first to state the problem of the legitimacy of power.

Strangely enough, when the common danger was drawing to an end, it was not against the doctrine of usurpation that men were fighting, but against the man who had had the best luck in using it, as though he alone were responsible for the danger.

The fact that tyranny had triumphed in France had not made the impression on Europe that it should have produced. People were more impressed by the results than by the causes, as though the former were independent of the latter. France, in particular, had fallen into no less serious error. Seeing the country strong and peaceful under Napoleon, enjoying a kind of prosperity, people were easily persuaded that it mattered little to a country what the laws were that upheld the ruling government. With a little reflection, they would have seen that this strength was uncertain, that this peace had no solid foundation, and that this prosperity, partly the result of other countries having been laid waste, had no lasting quality.

What kind of strength was this, which succumbed to its first reversal! Spain, invaded and occupied by courageous and numerous armies; Spain, without troops or money, sickened and weakened by the long, disastrous reign of a worthless favorite under an incapable king—Spain, finally, deprived of its government by treachery, struggled for six years against a gigantic power and at the end emerged victorious. France, on the contrary, having under Napoleon apparently attained the optimum of power and strength, fell after three months of invasion.

It is true that she was tranquil under Napoleon, but she owed that tranquillity to a hand of iron which held in check and threatened to crush everything that might disturb it, and which could not safely release its grasp for a single moment. Moreover, it is impossible to believe that the tranquillity would have outlived a man who was hardly able to maintain it by devoting all his energy to the task. Master of France by the rule of might, he set a precedent for his generals, who, at his death, would have done their best to acquire the title by the same rule. The example he gave showed that ability or luck were all that was necessary to seize the power. Which among his subordinates would not have tried his luck and taken great risks for such a brilliant future? France might have had as many emperors as there were armies, and, thus split up into rival factions, would have perished in the throes of civil war.

Her prosperity, superficial though it was, might have grown deeper roots but would have been confined to the brief term of one man's life, each day of which might be the end thereof.

There is nothing more baneful than usurpation to nations whom rebellion or conquest have placed under the yoke of usurpers. The same is true of their neighbors. The former are faced with a permanent prospect of disturbances, shocks, and domestic upheavals. The latter are constantly threatened with aggression and destruction. Usurpation means death and annihilation for everyone.

Europe's most pressing need and greatest concern was, therefore, to do away with the doctrine of usurpation and revive the principle of legitimacy, the only remedy for all the evils which had beset her, and the only one which would prevent their recurrence.

In this passage Talleyrand takes for granted that he and the reader agree in their definitions of usurpation and legitimacy. The only way to understand this conclusive passage is to define those terms, and we can be sure of having defined them properly if the passage, at first reading somewhat diffuse and obscure, becomes clear and precise with our definitions. Why do some men command

and others obey? That problem is essential to the whole
social order. The answer is simply: Force. "If you don't
do what I say, I'll knock your block off." One must confess the argument has a certain persuasion. But only in
the extent to which force can act. Now force—the collective means by which man is able to terrorize his fellows—is merely a continually fluctuating state of affairs
of uncertain value. He who is most powerful today may
no longer be so tomorrow; he who thinks himself the
strongest may be deceiving himself and really be the weak-
est. Bringing it down to a mere matter of force, government would be no more than a perpetual struggle between those who, considering themselves the strongest,
would desire to be in control. Under these circumstances,
how can a government assume its proper function as an
instrument of reason and a source of laws which limit and
direct the unbridled independence of the human mind?
Contest unleashes passions; and passions are intrinsically
a revolt against reason and the laws which it decrees. In
order that a government may accomplish its organic function as the instrument of reason and creator of laws, its
subjects must conform jointly and spontaneously, obeying its commands voluntarily, at least to a certain extent;
and they will not give their spontaneous submission unless they recognize that the government has the right to
command, apart from the force necessary to impose its
orders. Man began to emerge from barbarism when he
upset the relationship between force and justice; when
he asserted that government does not have the right to
command because it is strong, but that it must have the
strength to command because it has the right to do so.
Strength is not the parent, but the servant of the right to
command.

But how may the right to command be justified?
Theoretically, the answer is easy: "The men who have
the right to command must be more intelligent, wiser,
and more just than those who are bound to obey them."

The only title to power that reason and feeling can claim is the superiority of the one who commands over the one who obeys. But how may this superiority be recognized? No illusion is impossible, when it seems to justify passions or interests. Everything is contestable by passion and interest, especially merit. If there have been so many civil wars, it is because it is only too easy to perceive in oneself the qualities of lord and leader, and too difficult to make others acknowledge them. How is the problem to be resolved? There is only one way: to submit the jurisdiction and the transmission of power to laws which are accepted as just and reasonable by those who obey them, and are respected as obligatory by those who command. On the day when everyone in a community, both high and low, decides that the men who are to have the privilege and the responsibility of exercising power shall be chosen according to a specific law, the right to command will be acknowledged as long as that law is observed.

But how are these laws to be set up? Where should they originate? Principally in the presumption that they will assure the power to men who are worthy of it, or at least that they will exclude men who are not. The presumption may be founded more or less on reality; but, if it is founded on illusion, then at least it must be a sincere illusion, for only this presumption, after all, can justify the law. In the Western world, the laws for the jurisdiction and transmission of power have been drawn from two principles—heredity and election. Until the end of the eighteenth century these were combined, but in the nineteenth century the elective principle gradually took the place of heredity. Yet both principles are equally justifiable on the ground of ability: heredity of office because, granting a careful education and stalwart traditions, it may provide the state with a well-equipped personnel; election, because every elective system presupposes the widespread conviction that the electors, whoever they may be—cardinals in conclave, the prince-electors of the Holy Roman Empire, or the universal suffrage of our time—have a certain ability, innate or transcendent, to choose their leaders.

The principles whence spring the jurisdiction and the transmission of power—heredity and election in the Western world—are the principles of legitimacy which establish the right to command and the obligation to obey. We may now formulate the definitions of usurpation and legitimacy implied by Talleyrand. A government is legitimate when its power is assigned and exercised in accordance with a principle of legitimacy which is accepted by a majority of those who obey, and respected by those who command. It is usurpatory when the power is justified by a principle of legitimacy which is not accepted by those who obey (or at least by a majority), or is not respected by those who command. Therefore, one must not interpret legitimacy of power as the exclusive privilege of certain forms of government, by which they alone would become legitimate—the absolute monarchy of other times, for instance. That is the false interpretation which the legitimists have given to the doctrine. Talleyrand is very explicit on this point:

This principle, it may be seen, is not, as unthinking men imagine and fomentors of revolutions would make one believe, solely a means of conserving the power of kings and sanctity of their persons. It is above all a necessary element of the peace and happiness of peoples, the most solid, or rather the only, guarantee of their strength and continuance. The legitimacy of kings, or rather of governments, is the safeguard of nations; for that reason it is sacred.

I speak of the legitimacy of governments in general, whatever their form, and not only of that of kings, because it must be applied to everything. A legitimate government, be it monarchical or republican, hereditary or elective, aristocratic or democratic, is always the one whose existence, form, and mode of action have been strengthened and sanctioned over a long period of years, I might even say over a period of centuries. The legitimacy of sovereign power stems from the ancient state of possession, as also, in the case of individuals, does the legitimacy of the law of property.

Therefore, there may be as many legitimate or illegitimate governments as there are principles of legitimacy. Monarchies as well as republics, aristocracies as well as democracies, may be legitimate or illegitimate, according as the principle of law, which justifies power in each of these forms of government, is accepted or refused by those who must obey, respected or violated by those who have the right to command. It follows from this that all governments are born in a state of illegitimacy and only become legitimate with the passing of time. We have seen that principles of legitimacy always spring from the presumption of efficacy; but this presumption is at all times only partial and relative. To govern men with intelligence and justice is the most difficult task of all; if it be compared with a model of absolute perfection, the best of governments will be found full of faults. Take, for instance, the two principles of legitimacy accepted by the Western world—heredity and election. It is easy to see that no conceivable form of hereditary law, no system of election which the human mind can invent, will be able to give more than a partial guarantee that only the worthiest men will possess power, and then only under certain conditions which are not likely to be permanent. Therefore, no principle of legitimacy is acceptable at its inception because of indisputable efficacy; at its first appearance every principle gives rise to objection, aversion, and resistance. It always takes a long time and a great deal of persuasion to make it acceptable in spite of its faults. Is the legitimacy of a government only a question of time, therefore? Is it sufficient for a government to last one or two generations in order to become legitimate, regardless of its origin and its formula? Talleyrand's words would seem to indicate this. He compares legitimacy with the prescription of civil law. But here his train of thought becomes too summary and obscure. We must disentangle the contents of his formula by specifying.

Time is necessary for the creation of a legitimacy, but it

is not sufficient. Although every government needs a period
of time before it can be accepted as legitimate, it cannot
succeed in being accepted merely because there is a time
element in its favor. This is a distinction which escaped
Talleyrand and is of prime importance. Entirely apart
from the question of time, to be acceptable a principle of
legitimacy must have certain attributes: simplicity, clarity,
and especially consistency, both theoretical and practical.
Thus, a government based on the principle of heredity will
never be acceptable if the rule of succession is not firmly established. Why in the Roman Empire did the monarchy
never succeed in becoming the legitimate government of
the state? Because it never succeeded in establishing a fixed
rule of succession which would have kept internal peace
and preserved the unity of the Empire. The Empire never
had more than a precarious unity, which was continually
being made over and broken up by rival sovereigns fighting
for power. The peoples were unable to take hold of the
monarchic principle in this constant stream of wars over
the succession, which were its very negation. The Directory, at its accession, and the Third Republic, until the
end of the nineteenth century, were not legitimate governments because under each of them large sections of France
did not accept popular sovereignty as a principle which
was capable of establishing the right to rule. The Third
Republic, however, became a legitimate government with
the advent of the twentieth century. The Directory never
did. Why the one and not the other? Because the Third
Republic was wise enough to respect and apply faithfully
the principle of popular sovereignty; whereas the Directory
suppressed it, with the *coup d'état* of Fructidor, and, after
the *coup d'état* of the 18 Brumaire, completely distorted
it, giving the executive power the means to make the public exercise its sovereignty as the power directed. The
people's representatives may legitimize the power only
when it is done freely. A sovereign in chains is a contradiction in which the principle of legitimacy is destroyed by

its application. A principle which is destroyed by its application becomes a hoax, and time cannot transform a hoax into a principle of legitimacy capable of guaranteeing peace and order. The inverted democracy of the Constitution of the Year VIII could not have become a legitimate government, even if it had lasted for centuries, because in practice it denied the principle of popular sovereignty, which it declared to be the foundation of the state. The same can be said of the modern totalitarian states. They are inverted democracies, founded more or less on the model provided by the 18 Brumaire. They may last for centuries, but they can never become legitimate.

To sum up, a principle of legitimacy is always partial, limited, disputable, and reversible, yet must always be sincere. When it is transformed into a hoax, it can never legalize the government, which becomes simply an instrument of coercion. That is what the passage quoted from the *Mémoires* would have revealed, if mankind had known how to read and understand it. Through these reflections, during the dreadful winter of 1813-1814, Talleyrand was able to uncover the roots of the great panic that was terrorizing the Continent. Europe was afraid because, ever since 1789, the number of illegitimate governments, the "usurpations," had been steadily increasing. The evil had begun in France with the fall of the monarchy in 1792. The Convention government which had followed it had not been legitimate because the new principle of popular sovereignty was understood and accepted by only a small minority; and, in the frightful anarchy produced by the collapse of the monarchy, the new principle had been applied awkwardly and imperfectly. But an illegitimate government which knows and feels that its right to rule is not recognized by the majority and that the latter is in a state of latent or open revolt against which it has no defense but force, is a government continually in fear of its own power. The Convention would have been afraid even if it had possessed the means of defending itself; but without money, without arms, without an administration, with adventurers for officials, it had been forced to fight internal revolution and foreign wars, unleashed partly through fault of the Revolution, partly through that of the monarchies. The great panic had begun and it had spread to the regimes which succeeded the Convention.

Crazed with fear to the point of violence, these regimes had completely ignored the limits beyond which force becomes suicidal. The guillotine, terrorization, tyranny by the police, the totalitarianism of the Consulate and the Empire—these were their methods of preserving internal order. And in their foreign policy they relied on war without rules, ephemeral victories, confiscations, unilateral annexations, oppressive treaties, despotic protectorates, wholesale manufacture of counterfeit republics, and, under the Empire, artificial monarchies. Because all these governments were illegitimate "usurpations," they had fallen into the vicious circle of fear which provokes abuse of force, which in turn aggravates the fear; and they had dragged Europe into this circle with them. The obvious conclusion which Talleyrand reached was that the great panic had to disappear, and that for this to be accomplished legitimate governments had to take the place of usurpations, especially in France. Napoleon had been able to maintain his illegitimate monarchy just as long as he had been bolstered by the illusion of victory. Once beaten, he would never have had either the courage to sign a treaty which named him the loser or the strength to impose it on France. Only a legitimate government would have had the strength and the courage; and the only legitimate government still possible for France was the old monarchy. A part of France still believed in the divine right of kings, whereas no one had any more faith in the democratic principle after it had been so falsified by the Revolution. Talleyrand said as much with his usual clarity and concision.

Sick of the horrors of invasion, France wished to be free and respected; in other words she was ready to welcome back the Bourbons and the principle of legitimacy. Europe, still fearful in victory, demanded guarantees that France would disarm and stay within her old boundaries, so that peace did not have to bear constant watching. This also indicated a desire for the Bourbons.

And so, once the needs of France and Europe were recognized, everything rendered the restoration of the Bourbons easy, for a sincere reconciliation became possible.

Only the House of Bourbon could veil the stain of defeat on their flag from a people who are proud of their glorious military past.

Only the House of Bourbon could immediately get rid of the foreign armies on French soil without endangering Europe.

Only the House of Bourbon could without shame restore France to the happy proportions indicated by policy and by geography. With the return of the Bourbons, France ceased to be a monster and became a great power once more. Relieved of the weight of her conquests, France's only hope of regaining her high position in the social order lay with the Bourbons. Only they could ward off the revenge which twenty years of excesses had piled up against France.

Was it then sufficient to recall the brother of Louis XVI and re-erect the throne of French kings in the form it had preserved for centuries? Talleyrand did not think so. For him the principles of legitimacy had their existence in the sincere approval of human beings and were therefore never crystallized by tradition or by documentary titles into the fiction of unalterable perfection. Like all living things, they never stopped changing. Heredity was still valid as a qualification for government in France, because it was recognized by a considerable portion of the people. But it had lost a great deal of ground during the Revolution, and it had to be strengthened by something else. Restoring the monarchy was not an excuse for resurrecting the corpse of the pre-Revolutionary sovereignty. Talleyrand's thoughts

29464

on this subject are to be found in his report to Louis XVIII from Vienna the following year.[2]

But, however legitimate a government may be, the nature of its authority must vary with the objects to which the lattter is applied, with the time, and with the place. Thus, in the more civilized states today the belief prevails that the central power may rule only in conjunction with certain assemblies chosen from the society over which it rules.

.   .   .   .

In another age, when religious sentiments were deeply engraved on the hearts of people and exerted tremendous influence over their minds, it was easy for them to believe that the sovereign power came from above.... But in an age where hardly a trace of religiosity remains, where the tie with religion, if not broken, is at least loosened, there is no longer any desire to ascribe a divine origin to legitimacy.

Today there is a widespread belief, which it would be impossible to shake, that governments exist only for the benefit of the people. From this it follows logically that a legitimate power is one which can best guarantee their peace and happiness. Therefore, the only legitimate power is one which has lasted a great many years. And furthermore, strengthened by tradition and by the affection which men naturally possess for their rulers—owing them an allegiance which becomes a law in the eyes of every individual, corresponding to the laws regulating private property—this power is less likely than any other to deliver up its people to the grim horrors of revolution. In other words, it is one which people are serving their best interest by obeying. But, if one reaches the sad conclusion that the abuses of this power make it take advantage of its position, one is forced to regard legitimacy as an illusion.

What will give the people confidence in the legitimate power, so that they will show it the respect upon which its security is based? It must indispensably be so constituted that people will have no cause to fear it in any way. It is as much to the interest of the sovereign as to that of the subject that the power be so constituted. For absolutism would be as much of a burden to the one who exercised it as to the object of it.

[2] This report was published in Vol. III of the *Mémoires de Talleyrand,* pp. 195 *et seq*. The following passages are taken from pages 214, 217-220.

Before the Revolution, the central authority in France had been restricted by ancient institutions. It had been modified by action of the august bodies of the magistracy, the clergy, and the nobility, which were elements necessary to its existence, and which it made use of in order to govern. Today, these institutions are destroyed; the old methods of governing have disappeared. Others must be found that meet with public approval; in fact they must even be chosen by the public.

Formerly, the authority of the Church was able to lend its support to that of the sovereign power. It can no longer do this, now that indifference to religion has spread to every class and become universal. Therefore, the sovereign power's only support is in public opinion, and to obtain that support it must conform to the wishes of the public.

That support will be given if the people have satisfied themselves that the government which is all powerful in making their happiness can do nothing to harm it. They must be certain that there is nothing arbitrary about the methods used by the government. It is not enough for them to believe in its good intentions, for they might fear that these intentions would change or that the methods were wrong. It is not enough that confidence be based on the sterling virtues and talents of the sovereign, for they are as perishable as he. It must be based on the strength of permanent institutions. Even more is necessary. No matter how well these institutions guaranteed the happiness of the people, they would not have the latter's confidence if they did not establish the form of government which the era regarded as the only one capable of securing that happiness.

Guarantees are wanted both for the sovereign and for the people. The following are demanded:

Individual freedom must be secured by law against any impairment.

Freedom of press must be fully guaranteed, and the laws must confine themselves to the punishment of offenses against it.

The judiciary must be independent, and therefore its members must be irremovable.

The right to judge must be the exclusive right of the tribunals and never of the administration or any other body.

The ministers must be jointly and severally responsible for the exercise of the authority of which they are the trustees.

No person without responsibility must be included in the councils of the sovereign.

And finally, the law must be the expression of a will formed by the union of three separate wills.

What was it that Talleyrand said to the King in the language of the court?

"You are the lawful King of France; but you alone cannot bear the weight of authority. The era has become too rationalistic to believe in your infallibility, while the institutions which formerly restricted royal authority and prevented many abuses and mistakes, are no more. In order that your authority may remain legitimate, not because of your title but in the conscience of the people, you must surround yourself with representative institutions and recognize the right of opposition with all its concomitant liberties. The revolution should have granted the right of opposition to France; it fell because it did not succeed in doing that. Now your turn has come; the Bourbons will rule France if they can succeed where the Revolution failed."

Talleyrand did not believe monarchy to be the only legitimate form of government. But early in 1814 he had come to the conclusion that only the dynasty which had been overthrown in 1792, providing it recognized the right of opposition and surrounded itself with representative institutions, could give France a government whose right to govern would not be too seriously contested and which therefore would have the courage to tell France the truth. Everything that had happened since 1789 had been a tremendous adventure ending in the great panic; the time had come to face reality and begin the reconstruction of Europe. The fears of the spirit of adventure were to give way to the clear-sightedness and courage of the constructive mind.

V

DEATH PANGS OF THE EMPIRE

The fall of the Empire was the chef-d'œuvre of the constructive mind, but it was accomplished clandestinely. Talleyrand had discovered both the reason and the remedy for the great panic, but what could he do to liberate mankind? According to tradition, Talleyrand spent the winter of 1813-1814 in feeling out the ground on all sides and seeking whatever solution would be most advantageous to himself. The historians have forgotten that Talleyrand was more than ever the prisoner of Napoleon during that terrible winter. In November, 1813, Napoleon had offered him no less a prize than the Foreign Ministry. Upon his refusal, the Emperor had at first considered locking him up in Vincennes. On second thought he had appointed him a member of the Regency Council, which substituted for Napoleon during the latter's absence from Paris. This Council was a safer and less obvious prison than Vincennes; Talleyrand would be rendered harmless. And this time he did not dare to refuse.

On February 25 he wrote to the duchesse de Courlande: "The news from Paris never reaches me, for I see and wish to see no one." [1] In her *Mémoires* of that period, one of his friends, Aimée de Coigny, duchesse de Fleury, states that all Paris was visiting him in secret. These two statements are contradictory only on the surface. With his reputation for shrewdness, Talleyrand, in that dreadful hour, became the last hope, even of his adversaries and enemies. He alone, they thought, could find a way out of the mess. All these desperate people caught hold of him and begged to see him. Talleyrand, though protesting, even to his most intimate friends, that he wished to see no one, received them secretly, talked to everyone, yet never revealed his innermost thoughts. Thus it was that the lovely Aimée de Coigny, an ardent royalist, received quite a shock when she made a furtive call on Talleyrand during that winter to convince him that the Bourbons must be restored. He told her that if Napoleon should abdicate or die, there could be no question of what to do. A regency under Marie Louise would be set up until her son had reached an age at which he could accede to the throne. Unable to convince him, the ardent royalist tried again and again, but never with success. She wrote in her *Mémoires:*

For several days running we saw each other during the morning. I spoke on the subject without his interrupting me or giving me an answer, and I used to leave very much frightened by his plans. In particular I feared the watching and waiting that was a part of his character and which enabled him to use everything to his own advantage and take credit for having foreseen it and acted secretly, when all he had done was to await it in silence. As it was important that the event I wanted should be brought about and as this could not be done in the natural course of events, I found the indifference of M. de Talleyrand insupportable. Although I realized that this attitude served his own ends, I felt that it was fatal to what I devoutly wished for. I exhausted myself in arguments and even in witticisms, for I knew how important it was not to bore

[1] *Revue d'histoire diplomatique*, I, 246.

him; and I rather skillfully played on the deadly monotony of Bonaparte's court, where subtlety and taste were lacking.

The lovely Aimée never suspected that the man she could not convince was already just as convinced as she was of the necessity for restoring the Bourbons, and from far more serious and deeper reasons than her love for the King. But it was impossible for him to tell her. His life would have been in danger if the slightest indiscretion had given the imperial family, its advisers, or Napoleon any reason to suspect that he was working for the ruin of the Empire. His real thoughts on the subject are to be found in the *Mémoires*, rather than in his relations with the men and women come to consult the oracle. Furthermore, he did not have the solution of the catastrophe caused by the Revolution in his pocket, as certain historians seem to believe. The solution did not depend upon him but upon the course of events, upon the war, the Coalition, and its policy. But the policy of the Coalition, at the beginning of 1814, seemed to be running counter to all his plans. On January 11, Austria had managed to entice Murat into an alliance. Article IV of the treaty read as follows:

His Majesty, the Emperor of Austria, King of Hungary and Bohemia, guarantees to His Majesty, the King of Naples, and to his heirs and successors, the free and peaceful possession of, as well as the complete sovereignty over, all the states which His Majesty at present holds in Italy. His Imperial and Royal Apostolic Majesty will endeavor to bring about the agreement of his Allies to this guarantee.

Still more serious was the first secret Article:

In order to remove all pretext for strife between Their Majesties, the King of Naples and the King of Sicily, His Majesty, the Emperor of Austria, King of Hungary and Bohemia, pledges himself to use every means of securing in favor of His Majesty, King Joachim Napoleon, and his descendants, a formal renunciation from His Majesty, the King of Sicily, of all his claims on the Kingdom of Naples, to be observed by him and his successors in perpetuity.

This renunciation shall be recognized and a guarantee thereof given by His Majesty, the Emperor of Austria, to His Majesty, the King of Naples, and His Imperial Majesty will approach the other allied powers with regard to obtaining similar recognition and guarantee.

In compensation, His Majesty, the King of Naples, renounces, for himself and his heirs, all claims on the Kingdom of Sicily, and declares himself ready to guarantee its possession to the dynasty now ruling.

Since, however, the allied powers are unable to secure the guarantee of the Kingdom of Naples to King Joachim except as against a reciprocal agreement contracted among them to provide a suitable indemnity for the King of Sicily, His Majesty, the King of Naples, pledges himself forthwith to concede the principle of this indemnity, and, whereas the efforts of His Neapolitan Majesty should be directed to the furtherance of the aims of the great European Alliance, he therefore undertakes especially to extend these aims to include the indemnity for the King of Sicily." [2]

In order to defeat Napoleon, Austria did not hesitate to recognize, to guarantee, and to lend her assistance to one of the "usurpations" which the Emperor had imposed on Italy. In the midst of all this diplomatic juggling, what was to become of Talleyrand's doctrine, according to which peace would never be established in Europe until it had been swept of the Napoleonic "usurpations"? An even greater cause for concern were the negotiations being carried on between the Allies and Napoleon. Although these had been instigated at Frankfurt on November 8, they did not officially begin until three months later, at Châtillon, on February 5. This delay was enough to show how difficult the negotiations were to be, and difficult negotiations could become dangerous. Here, in the words of a spectator, is Talleyrand's summing-up of the situation cre-

[2] D'Angeberg, *Le Congrès de Vienne at les traités de 1815* (Paris: Amyot, 1863), I, 84-87.

ated by the negotiators at the end of February or the beginning of March. It is taken from a conversation with a friend to whom he could talk freely, the duc de Dalberg.

You see, [the rest of] Europe is ignorant of our position, ignorant of what it can and should do for the good of all. It opens negotiations with a man whom it should destroy, and it opens them at the one time it could do so. He will twist the others around his finger; peace will be signed, and then what will become of us? He knows what we want, and he will never forgive us. . . . At any cost, we must make the allied sovereigns see the real state of affairs, how far they can go, and the danger of letting themselves be inveigled into negotiations. But how? Where can I find a man who can be trusted and whom I may send to see them in order to enlighten them, reassure them, and give them courage by raising their hopes? [3]

Dalberg found him such a messenger. M. de Vitrolles agreed to go before the Allies to show them that peace could only be obtained by breaking off negotiations with Napoleon and officially recognizing Louis XVIII. Talleyrand sent a note to Nesselrode [4] in invisible ink, which ran as follows: "The man who will deliver this to you is completely trustworthy. Listen to him and recognize me. The time has come for frankness. You are walking on crutches, where you could make use of your legs to greater advantage." [5]

The historians have made great fun of the precautions taken by Talleyrand on that occasion; nevertheless, it must not be forgotten that he was risking his neck. M. de Vitrolles succeeded in penetrating the lines. On March 12 he held his first conversation with Metternich at the headquarters of the Coalition in Troyes. He was cruelly disillusioned. Metternich, polite but frigid, told him that

[3] Baron de Vitrolles, *Mémoires et relations politiques* (Paris: E. D. Forgues, 1884, I, 61.
[4] Alexander's plenipotentiary at the Congress of Vienna.
[5] Dupuis, *Le ministère de Talleyrand en 1814* (Paris: Plon-Nourrit & Cie., 1919), I, 116.

the question of France's future government could only be
decided by France, and that the Allies were ready to make
peace with whatever government France would recognize.
In the meantime, Napoleon still represented the government of France; they were carrying on negotiations with
him which they hoped would meet with success. As to the
restoration of the Bourbons, Prince Metternich was very
skeptical. Where were all the royalists and malcontents of
whom the *émigrés* had said France was full? The Allies
had been in France for two months, and they had not
seen a trace of either the one or the other. As though the
rebellion simmering throughout France could have broken
out while the Allies were negotiating with Napoleon and
declaring him to be the present and future sovereign of
the country! On the seventeenth, the comte de Vitrolles
had an audience with the Czar. The latter, though less
frigid than Metternich, did not hide the fact that he disliked the Bourbons and believed them no longer capable
of ruling. He had been thinking of giving France Bernadotte or Eugène de Beauharnais, or even a discreet form
of republic! As though such tremendously different alternatives had ever been possible in the history of any people!
Finally, on the nineteenth, he saw Castlereagh at Bar-sur-
Seine. The polished aristocrat concisely and sententiously
told the envoy that he himself and the Regent of England
were in favor of restoring the Bourbons, but that, since
popular opinion in England was against it, there was nothing he could do. As though the destiny of France could be
dependent on the fluctuations of a misguided and irresponsible foreign opinion! [6]

In short, the trip was a complete failure. Talleyrand's
fears were justified. The Allies had not the slightest
inkling of the real reason for the war they were fighting;
and what was worse, they were unable to see it. What was

[6] Vitrolles, *op. cit.* I, 91-143. The summaries of the conversations that
M. de Vitrolles had during March with Metternich, Alexander I, and
Castlereagh, are of the greatest importance to the history of this period.

taking place in Europe had never before occurred in history. The Allies were victorious. They had defeated Napoleon in Russia, in Germany, and in Spain. They had forced him to retreat across the Rhine, to restore Spain to her King, and to free the Pope. They had invaded France and were marching on Paris. But, as their victories increased, they became more and more fearful. Each victory overthrew one of the despotisms Napoleon had created. By the beginning of 1814, the Duchy of Warsaw, the Confederation of the Rhine, the Kingdom of Westphalia had disappeared. In Switzerland the mediation government was breathing its last. In Italy the Revolution was collapsing under the blows of Austria and of Murat. Murat had occupied Rome and Tuscany for the Coalition and was marching on northern Italy, where Eugène de Beauharnais, the viceroy, was offering what resistance he could to the Austrians. But, as each despotism was overthrown, it left a country without government, and the Allies had to substitute the "central department" and the "governor generals" which they had created in October, 1813. These regimes were provisional regimes under military supervision and were regulated with gross severity. As the armies advanced toward France and Paris from north, south, and east, the void which they left behind became larger and larger. They created an immense desert of countries without governments, where, in spite of the military occupation and partly on account of it, seethed the revolutionary ferment which had been created by the Napoleonic regime and then suppressed by it; and where the apocalyptic horrors of famine, pestilence, and war took hold of imaginations with the speed and violence of a deadly epidemic. What if the provisional military governments throughout this immense waste haunted by ghosts should collapse, dragging with them the armies of occupation? Speed was needed to finish the war, even if that meant an alliance with Murat and an attempt to corrupt Beauharnais. Forward was the cry! They were trying to gain a decisive victory over Napoleon in the shortest possible time. In order to accomplish this they were ready to follow him to the gates of Paris, into the very heart of France, even to the shores of the Mediterranean and the Atlantic. But they were advancing through France in a confusion of fantastic fears and hopes, sometimes believing that the people would rise to help them against the tyrant, and again fearing that they would be faced with an uprising directed against them and that the story of the French army in Russia would be repeated. But France seemed totally indifferent to everything, to the invasion and the liberation, to the victory of the Empire and its defeat. It submitted passively to the invasion, a reaction which at times made the Allies more uneasy than they would have been at a determined resistance, which at least would have been tangible and calculable. The King of Prussia was the most frightened; and in his moments of despair he would bewail this "unfortunate invasion."

With his superior intellect and in his position as a by-stander, Talleyrand could see everything clearly. The allied monarchs and their ministers did not have his far-sightedness, and furthermore they were in the thick of the battle, and were unable to see the forest for the trees. They did not understand what was happening because they were too frightened by the perils which surrounded them, and they became more and more frightened because they failed to understand what was happening. Under the circumstances, it was not surprising that for a while they clung to the hope of coming to an agreement with Napoleon. But from the time that the Allies began to consider making peace with their incomprehensible adversary, they were faced with a new and still more frightening impasse: the more they fought him the more impossible became the chance for peace. The established monarchies of Europe were fighting against an illegitimate state, which, instead of having the support of a recognized and accepted principle of law, was held up by a reputation for extraordinary power. Each defeat which it suffered diminished its reputation and thereby weakened it: but the more that reputation was impaired by successive defeats, the less likely it was that the head of this unusual state would sign a treaty which admitted his defeat. Once he had made such an admission, the state would have disappeared together with the reputation upon which it was based; and the peace which he had signed would not have had the slightest value.

At Frankfurt in November, the Allies, not knowing whether they would be able to cross the Rhine, had let it be understood, without making any definite promises, that they would be prepared to allow France to keep her natural boundaries. But if he had been able to hold the Rhine, Napoleon would not have been satisfied with those boundaries. He would have asked for greater concessions in order to strengthen as much as possible the reputation of his extraordinary power. However, Napoleon had lost the river. Once the Allies had crossed the Rhine and reconquered the German territory on the left bank, they were no longer in a position to offer France her natural boundaries; Austria and Prussia would have incurred rebellions at home. Napoleon, on the other hand, after having lost the Rhine, had to demand at least the natural boundaries as the price of peace. If he had not, it would have been a confession of defeat, and his strength would have evaporated. The contradiction was insoluble. It had its roots in the illegitimacy of Napoleon's government, in this novel phenomenon which the Allies were unable to understand. Fearful novelty: the allied armies were marching through a waste land toward a peace which got farther away as they advanced! Unable to understand this mirage, for which they had no precedent, the allied sovereigns and their ministers lost heart, slowed up their armies, and hesitated. Talleyrand alone understood; peace could only be made with a legitimate government. That was the crux of the matter. But, since no one else realized it, what could he accomplish by himself, almost a prisoner in his palace on the rue Saint-Florentin?

And then, all of a sudden, a rumor spread through Paris. On March 12, Bordeaux, taking advantage of the entry of the English, had hoisted the royal standard on the highest tower in the city. For Talleyrand, this was the first favorable indication for his plan for the welfare of Europe. But only on condition that the Allies had the courage to break off the negotiations at Châtillon. He wrote to his niece: "It appears that Louis XVIII has been proclaimed in Bordeaux just as the English entered the city. When the mail coach left, the city was in the throes of counter-revolutionary activity. If the peace negotiations fail, then Bordeaux will have a tremendous significance. If peace be made, Bordeaux will lose its significance."

"If peace be made" means "If peace be made with Napoleon." But would it be made? No one knew; everything depended on the answer. Be that as it may, Talleyrand seems to have decided, after the revolt of Bordeaux, on a rapprochement with Louis XVIII. Aimée de Coigny began to haunt Talleyrand in order to convert him to royalism. During one of her frequent visits, one day toward the end of March, Talleyrand got up, went to the door of the parlor, made sure it was locked, and came back to his seat, saying with a shrug: "Madame de Coigny, I have the greatest sympathy for the King, but... The King knows nothing about me. I must confess that I have no desire to expose myself to a pardon instead of gratitude or to have to vindicate my actions...."

The duchesse de Fleury was probably the first person to whom Talleyrand revealed his true colors. He must have been throwing out a line for someone who would act as a mediator between him and the Old Regime. In fact, the marquis de Boisgelin volunteered his services in the attempt to reconcile Louis XVIII and the former bishop of Autun. And then at last came the great news: on March 19, the negotiations at Châtillon had fallen through. The stumbling block had proved to be the Rhine, claimed both by Napoleon and the Allies. The danger so greatly feared by Talleyrand had been averted. But the situation remained critical. On March 20, Talleyrand wrote his niece:

The Congress may be expected at any minute, but what will it be? Today people were talking about a conspiracy against the Emperor which included some generals, but it was all very uncertain. If the Emperor were killed, his death would assure the succession to his son, which is now jeopardized by what has happened in Bordeaux and by the general trend of thought in France. As long as he is alive, nothing can be certain; and no human being can foresee what will happen. With the Emperor dead, a regency would satisfy everyone because a Council would be chosen to meet the approval of everyone and because steps would be taken to see that the Emperor's brothers had nothing to say about state affairs. Marconcy is bringing you this letter; destroy it as soon as you have read it.[7]

Talleyrand is not revealing his plans in this letter; he is giving news. At that time he gave so little thought to the regency of Marie Louise that he considered an assassination of Napoleon the only thing that would make it possible—too uncertain an event on which to count. With Napoleon alive and the peace negotiations broken off, anything in the nature of a forecast had become impossible. That is the substance of Talleyrand's letter of March 20, and there was nothing more he could say. Of the three possible solutions, he had told Dalberg that a peace with Napoleon would be as dangerous for the world as for him. The restoration of the Bourbons seemed to him to be the best solution for France and for the world, but he did not know whether it would be good or bad for him. He had said as much to Aimée de Coigny. The third solution—a regency under Marie Louise—he considered inadequate and dangerous. He gave his views on this subject with his usual precision and ludicity in his *Mémoires*. The only thing he had

[7] *Revue d'histoire diplomatique*, I, 247.

been able to do toward preventing the first solution had been to send the Allies the enigmatic message borne by M. de Vitrolles. Up until March 20 he had been unable to do anything for the second solution, except to formulate in his mind a series of plans which he could not guarantee would be practical. He considered the third solution beneath his notice.

And then, beginning with March 20, matters suddenly came to a head. Defeated at Arcis-sur-Aube on that day and the next, Napoleon, instead of retreating toward Paris, decided to march east, to Lorraine, in the hope of drawing the Allies after him to avoid having their communications cut. Alexander, however, was not to be drawn; the Russian and Prussian armies made for the capital. For a moment, the allied and French armies were back to back. Panic broke out in Paris at the news of the enemy's approach. On the twenty-seventh Talleyrand again wrote to his niece:

The news this morning is much worse. Social disintegration is spreading rapidly. There is no discipline, and nobody dares give an order.[8]

On the twenty-eighth King Joseph convoked the Regency Council and proposed that the capital be abandoned. Finding the majority against such a move, he produced a letter from Napoleon dated March 16 which officially ordered the Empress and the King of Rome to leave Paris in the event of a threat to the capital. The Council bowed to the command and began preparations for a hasty departure. On the afternoon of the twenty-ninth the Empress left. The same evening Alexander arrived at the château de Bondy, and on the morning of the thirtieth, the Russian and German troops launched their attack on Paris, which was defended by the dukes of Ragusa and Treviso. In the afternoon King Joseph departed, having authorized the marshals to enter into negotiations with the enemy for the surrender of the city and to withdraw to-

8 *Ibid.*, I, 247.

ward the Loire. The Regency Council followed Joseph, and a few hours later, about four o'clock in the afternoon, the Duke of Ragusa sent a flag of truce to the enemy. That evening two Russian emissaries, Count Nesselrode and Count Orloff, one Austrian emissary, Count Paar, and the two French marshals met in a tavern near the Saint Denis lines to discuss the terms of capitulation. As no agreement had been reached after a long and fruitless discussion, Nesselrode returned to inform the Czar. Taking advantage of the interruption, the Duke of Ragusa invited Orloff to dinner at his house on the rue de Paradis. The house was full of people seeking the latest news. Everyone was eating and talking while they waited for Nesselrode to appear. Suddenly, there was a commotion. Talleyrand had appeared! They had all thought that he had left with the Council. But he explained that he had been stopped at the barricades along the Champs-Élysées and that he had come back to find out what roads were free. He chatted with the Marshal, stopped for a while with various other people, and finally, just before leaving, he came up to Orloff and said: "Sir, have the kindness to convey to His Majesty, the Emperor of Russia, the humble and sincere respects of the Prince of Benevento."

Having learned that Napoleon was abandoning Paris to the enemy and that the allied armies would be in Paris by the morrow at the latest, Talleyrand had realized that the time was ripe for the execution of his long-cherished plan. After six months of waiting and watching, he swung into action. It was a fateful moment. He was risking his life and the salvation of mankind on a throw of the dice. His own fate depended on whether he could save mankind.[9] If he failed, he would be destroyed.

[9] Even the best historians (Sorel, Thiry, Dupuys) have ascribed little or no importance to the interview of March 31 between Talleyrand and Alexander I. They have treated it as though it had no more importance than a meeting between the French Premier and the British Prime Minister would have had in 1939. But that interview was an event which any sane man would have judged impossible, so numerous and dangerous were the obstacles confronting it. Talleyrand was a man high in the

councils of the French Empire; Alexander was the head of the Russian Empire. The two Empires had been at war for more than two years. Any attempt by Talleyrand to communicate with the Czar was a treasonable act which might lead to extremely serious consequences for him. The precautions he took with the message carried by Vitrolles to the allied headquarters are ample proof of this. Furthermore, an interview of that sort usually had to be arranged beforehand through intermediaries, could not be secret, and had to take place at exactly the right moment, which was often very brief. It is easy to see how difficult it must have been, during the last days of the dying Empire, to find trustworthy intermediaries in Paris and to pick the right time, which lasted only twenty-four hours. If Talleyrand had not given his enigmatic message to Orloff on March 30, if Orloff had forgotten it en route, if Alexander had not understood or had ignored it, the interview on the thirty-first would never have taken place. Alexander would not have signed the manifesto of April 1, and it is impossible to tell when and if peace would have been concluded. No one, from Alexander on down, had any idea what to do next, and terrible catastrophes are caused by such a situation. If Talleyrand and Alexander were able to meet in Paris that day, it was due to the vision, the resolution, and the courage of Talleyrand, to his unselfish devotion to the cause of world peace and order. What prevented him from biding his time, like the marshals, and waiting for the end of the war to declare for the winner, risking nothing thereby? I know that for those people who still get angry over the fate of Napoleon and his Empire, in the belief that they were a blessing, Talleyrand's act was sheer treason. In the eyes of those who realize how terribly endangered the whole future of mankind was by Europe's great panic of 1814 and the resulting threat of endless war, Talleyrand, at the risk of his life, accomplished one of the most heroic deeds in history, a deed which saved France, Europe, and the whole of mankind. These two points of view are irreconcilable, and all discussion on their merits are therefore futile. But, in summing up, the situation on March 30 can be stated thus: Talleyrand and Alexander had to meet for peace to become possible. But such a meeting could only be lawful after peace had been made. Talleyrand severed the Gordian knot of a contradiction on which the fate of Europe depended.

VI

AN ACT OF COURAGE

———————————————————·≫≫≪≪·———————————————————

Talleyrand believed that only a legitimate power—that of Louis XVIII—could make a durable peace, providing the Allies were intelligent enough not to make excessive demands. So long as the Allies dealt with Napoleon, he had kept this belief to himself. After the rupture, his theory could be crystallized into a political maneuver, if there were a government which had the will and the means to achieve it. But until March 28, such a government was nonexistent. On that day, at the meeting of the Council when Joseph had read the order to abandon Paris, Talleyrand learned that Napoleon was not going to defend the capital. Thus, in a day or two, what everyone had believed for twenty years to be impossible would take place: the King of Prussia and Alexander would enter Paris at the head of their troops. An idea, a wish that had long been nourished in Talleyrand's mind, blossomed forth into a definite plan. What if he should stay in Paris and manage to gain an interview with Alexander, his old friend of Erfurt, as soon as he had entered the capital? What if he should persuade him to declare publicly that the Allies would not make peace with Napoleon and that they would respect the honor and integrity of France? Talleyrand might then get the Senate, heartened by this declaration, to decree the deposition of Napoleon, the recall of Louis XVIII, and the grant of a liberal constitution to France. By one stroke of a magic wand, he would have created a government that could make peace.

This simple and daring plan carried with it several difficulties and a certain amount of chance. The greatest obstacle for Talleyrand was how to stay in Paris when Napoleon had ordered the Council—and with it, him in particular—to leave the capital. As long as the French army remained in Paris, Napoleon was still a menace to his enemies. To show open insubordination by refusing to leave would have brought swift punishment. Talleyrand had hurdled this obstacle by a clever stratagem. He had asked M. de Rémusat, a friend and admirer, who commanded the National Guard in the lines along the Champs-Élysées, to prevent him from leaving when he went to join the Empress. This difficulty removed, a second arose. In view of the presence in Paris of the French army, how could he let Alexander know that he wanted an interview without being caught in the act of communicating with the enemy? They had been friends since Erfurt; but officially they had been enemies since 1812. The night of the thirtieth he had gone to the Marshal's house, where he expected to find either Orloff or Nesselrode, or both. He had gone with the intention of seeing one or the other and asking them to convey his respects to the Emperor of Russia. The real message behind the rather banal sentiments expressed in courtier style which he confided to Orloff, read as follows: "Shall we have another conversation about the welfare of Europe, as at Erfurt? If you agree, I am ready." But at this point elements of chance crept in. Would the message be delivered? Would it be understood? Would it meet with favor? In what mood were the Emperor, his advisers, and his Allies?

Up till then the Allies had stated many times, at Frankfurt and after the rupture at Châtillon, that they were ready to make peace on reasonable terms. But up till then they had been weak. Now they were strong. Were they, like Napoleon after Austerlitz and Jena, to succumb to the victor's fear and do their best to annihilate their adversary? The real struggle was about to begin, the decisive struggle between the victors and themselves. No one had more cause to fear that struggle than Talleyrand, who had seen from close-up Napoleon, preyed on by terror of his victories, devastating Europe for ten years. In any event, the decision he was going to ask the Czar to make was fraught with tremendous consequences. Only the King of Prussia was at hand to advise him. The Emperor of Austria and Metternich were at Dijon; there was no representative of the English government at the headquarters of the Russo-Prussian armies. Might not Alexander hesitate before taking on such a heavy responsibility without having consulted his Allies?

That was possibly the greatest hazard. There was not a moment to lose; it was that day or never. The Allies were at the gates of Paris, but the war was far from over. Napoleon, if he were not already there, would soon be at Fontainebleau, from which he could march on Paris and attack the Allies from the flank. If his fangs were not drawn, Napoleon could keep up the war for a long time by forcing the Allies to occupy the whole of France, at the risk of causing her complete destruction, which would be the prelude to the destruction of all Europe. The decisive moment had to be caught on the wing. Under the combined stimulus of the allied forces entering Paris and a solemn declaration that France would retain her position of a great power before the Revolution, the Senate would have unresistingly decreed the deposition of Napoleon and the recall of Louis XVIII. On this point, Talleyrand had no doubts whatsoever. He had reasoned the matter out thoroughly, probing into every aspect, and he had been reassured. And once the Senate had been won over, the rest would follow quickly. It would be easy to make the' soldiers lay down their arms. A lasting peace would be concluded without too much difficulty, after which the restoration of the Bourbons, with the addition of parliamentary institutions, could be imposed on those who were indifferent or hostile. If, on the other hand, several days were lost, a new war would begin, one that would be even more terrifying than before. The Senate would no longer dare to act; opinion would continue to shift this way and that; the Allies would be obliged to overrun France in search of a peace that had become impossible. Such an event would be nothing but a desperate adventure, a frightful nightmare, that, in a Europe half of which lacked any government, might result in universal chaos.

The die had been cast. It was now a question of putting an end, in twenty-four hours, to a war which had lasted for twenty-two years and which people were convinced would never end. Never had a more grandiose plan been conceived by a statesman in a time of universal despair. And never had one been carried out with such dispatch, such courage, and such unselfishness. We know now that his plan succeeded; but Talleyrand had no way of knowing how it would turn out. And what about his own fate, if he had failed? Posterity has not yet forgiven him for having "betrayed" Napoleon, although by this so-called "betrayal" he succeeded in saving all Europe, including France. What frightful disaster would his own tormented and contradictory life have ended in if he had failed? But he was no more concerned with his own future in the event of failure than in the event of success. The friendly mediation between Louis XVIII and Talleyrand, undertaken by Boisgelin, could not have borne fruit by March 30. When he was setting things in motion for the restoration, Talleyrand had no idea as to whether Louis XVIII considered him a friend or an enemy. But, as with all heroes in their hour of destiny, his predestination carried him along over all obstacles, including ambition, egoism, personal interests, and the instinct of preservation. He was predestined to be the most constructive force of his age, in a state of permanent revolt against the spirit of adventure and its insane fears. In a world which no longer believed in anything but violence, he was predestined to rediscover the most fundamental and the most difficult truths which the human mind is at once capable and incapable of comprehending: that force is useful to man only when he knows how to control it, and that it destroys itself when intensified. He was predestined to be the only man of his generation to understand that the Revolution would never make peace because its wars had everywhere overstepped the limits beyond which force becomes suicidal. And finally he alone was predestined to discover the fundamental causes of the great panic that was sweeping the world and to find the cure for it. This unique and complex predestination had been thwarted and humiliated for forty years by a malignant fate. During the frightful chaos of the Revolution it had been revealed only by intermittent gleams, which had been incomprehensible and, for the moment, futile. Now, after forty years of this repression, it burst forth with a terrific explosion of energy. In twenty-four hours a definitive peace was made, a peace for which the Revolution had spent twenty years of fruitless search; and in twenty-four hours the deadly circle of fear creating abuse of force, which in turn augments the fear, was broken. In the presence of this suddenly arisen opportunity everything else ceased to count; there was nothing that could prevent destiny from taking its course.

But would Alexander understand the message? Would he send an answer? And, above all, would he accept Talleyrand's proposal? Everything depended on him. Talleyrand could not have had much sleep the night of March 30. On the morning of the thirty-first he was with his coiffeur when a message came that Nesselrode was waiting. Leaping to his feet, he ran into the anteroom and embraced the Czar's envoy so vigorously that the latter was covered with powder from head to foot. Nesselrode has described the incident. It is not very difficult to explain this outburst of joy from a man usually so self-controlled. The fact that Nesselrode came at such an early hour indicated that his message had been understood. Indeed, Nesselrode had come with a message from the Czar that he would be in Paris that morning with the King of Prussia, at the head of the allied armies, and that he wanted to see him in the afternoon.

The Emperor Alexander [related Nesselrode] asked me to tell M. de Talleyrand that he had been warned that the Élysée Palace, where he wished to stay, was mined and that he must not go there. M. de Talleyrand told me he did not believe this rumor but that if the Emperor found it more convenient to take up his headquarters elsewhere, he would be glad to put his own house at the Emperor's disposal. I accepted this offer, and that is how the Emperor came to live in the rue Saint-Florentin.[1]

Talleyrand now had only to wait for this decisive meeting. That morning there occurred an astonishing and unprecedented spectacle. Paris, the revolutionary monster feared by the whole world, the volcano expected to erupt à la Moscow, received the Emperor of Russia, the King of Prussia, and the two representatives of the Austrian Emperor, at the head of their troops, with a thunderous ovation. Alexander was hailed as a liberator and showered with flowers and cheers.[2]

That afternoon, still under the influence of this unexpected welcome, the allied chiefs convened in the rue Saint-Florentin. Present were Alexander, Frederick Wil-

---

[1] All this is related with his customary brevity in Talleyrand's *Mémoires*, II, 163.

[2] Castlereagh, *Correspondence, Despatches, and Other Papers* (London: J. Murray, 1848-1853), IX, 418-420. In this letter from Sir Charles Stewart to Castlereagh, there is a moving account of the reception given the allied sovereigns by Paris.

liam III of Prussia, the two Austrian representatives, the princes of Schwarzenberg and Liechtenstein, Nesselrode, General Pozzo di Borgo, Dalberg, and Talleyrand. There was no English representative at the meeting. And then began the discussion that was to determine the fate of Europe, a discussion in which Talleyrand and Alexander, the two friends of Erfurt, took the leading roles. History's judgment on this encounter has been that it was the meeting of two thieves. Such an explanation is far too simple. We already know Talleyrand. It is time we knew something about Alexander, this young ruler, aged thirty-seven, who was going to decide the fate of France and of Europe. And to know him, we must read a document which, like the letter from Thugut to marquis Gherardini on December 27, 1796,[3] and the letter from the Directory to Bonaparte on April 7, 1797,[4] is one of the keys to an understanding of Western history that lie buried in archives. This document contains the "Confidential Instructions to M. de Novosiltzow on His Visit to England," signed on September 11, 1804, by Alexander and countersigned by his Foreign Minister, Prince Adam Czartoryski.[5] Novosiltzow was going to England to negotiate the alliance which became known as the Third Coalition. The young Emperor, then twenty-seven, put into this document his thoughts and plans on war and peace for his envoy to submit to the British government. After stating that the French had convinced the world "that their cause is that of the freedom and prosperity of peoples," he declared:

It would be shameful for mankind to consider such a noble cause to be the property of a government which under no circumstances is worthy to defend it. . . . The welfare of mankind, the true interests of legitimate authority, and the success of the enterprise to be launched by the two powers [England

---

[3] See *The Gamble,* pp. 137-140.
[4] See *ibid.,* pp. 180-185.
[5] These instructions appear in the *Mémoires du prince Adam Czartoryski* (Paris, 1887), II, 27-45.

and Russia] require that they deprive the French of this formidable weapon and appropriate it for use against them.

Thus, it was a question of liberating France and all the countries under French rule from the despotism which was crushing them; but not in order to give them back the Old Regime.

Liberty based on true principles. That is the theory on which I believe the two powers should act; their conduct, their language, and their proclamations should consistently be in accordance therewith. By winning victories on the battle-field and manifesting our principles of justice, liberty, and good will, we shall have commanded respect and succeeded in stimulating a universal and well-merited confidence.... Then we shall declare to her [France] that we have no grudge against her, but only against her government, a government as tyrannical for France as for Europe.

Liberal constitutions inspired by "wisdom and good will" were not the only condition for the happiness of peoples, but they were the only means of "establishing the future peace of Europe on firm and durable principles." In fact, the Emperor adds:

I am certain that this noble aim could not be regarded as having been attained until, on the one hand, the various nations have acquired an affection for their governments, which they will if the latter be made capable of functioning only for the good of their peoples, and, on the other hand, the relations between the states have been established by more precise laws, the respect for which would be to the interest of the governments. Deep thought on the subject, together with centuries of experiment, are enough to prove that these two results would be impossible of achievement unless the internal social order is based on sensible principles of liberty which seem to consolidate governments and preserve them from that unbridled ambition or megalomania which often possesses their leaders, and unless the law of nations which governs the relations of the European federation is re-established on its true principles.

These secret instructions set up with admirable logic, as early as 1804, three conditions for the peace and order of Europe: a liberal regime for France; the progressive humanization of government in all Europe by the free consent of the people; and rules of international law which could only be respected by wise and just regimes. (It was too early for Alexander to say "legitimate.") There is a relationship between the foreign and domestic affairs of a state; there will be peace only between states which are ruled by governments not subject to "unbridled ambition or megalomania." It is impossible to doubt the sincerity of these thoughts, appearing as they did in an extremely confidential document during negotiations vital to Russia and Europe in general. Even if they had been written by his advisers—Czartoryski for instance—the young Emperor deserves credit for having listened to such sage advice. If he had not agreed with it, he would certainly have rejected it.

There is no doubt but that in 1804 the youthful Emperor was an ardent disciple of these ideas, the same ones which inspired Talleyrand and were the crowning glory of eighteenth-century thought. What was the explanation for their championship at the beginning of the nineteenth century by the head of a distant empire, half-civilized and scarcely part of Europe? The answer is not easy, an obscure mixture of personal factors and historical circumstances. A cruel fate had put Alexander on the throne of Russia at the age of twenty-two, at the cost of a parricide which he had neither desired nor ordered, but whose consequences he had tacitly accepted. His accession came at a turning point in the history of the West, after the second and third partitions of Poland had made Russia a neighbor of Austria and of Prussia at a time when the old European order of the eighteenth century was beginning to topple under the swift expansion of the French Empire. Russia was faced with the great problem of what foreign policy to follow. Should she let France expand freely or take up arms against her? Should she seek an alliance with Napoleon, and obtain a share of the spoils? But in Russia neither the court nor the bureaucracy understood the significance of the problem caused by the fall of the French monarchy. Despite the westernization carried out by Peter the Great, Russia still differed radically in her customs and institutions from the West and had been separated from Europe by Poland. Consequently, up to that time she had taken only an occasional role in European affairs—the Seven Years' War, for instance. Even after the extinction of Poland, she would have preferred to continue nibbling at the Ottoman Empire and to expand in Asia. Moreover, Catherine the Great, taking advantage of the confusion in Europe caused by the Revolution, had seized eastern Poland and extended the Russian frontier to the Dniester mainly in order to give Russia a more convenient base of operations for the conquest of the Danubian countries. The Polish partition did not alter Russia's chief concern with the East. Yet meanwhile the French Empire was growing vaster year by year, frightening both Europe and itself in the process.

The young Emperor could not govern Russia as if the French Empire did not exist merely because his people did not want to be bothered by its expansion. Corresponding to this paradoxical situation which the young Czar found on ascending the throne, Alexander himself was one of the most unique personalities in history. The son of a madman and the grandson of a nymphomaniac, he was an unbalanced genius and a restless unadaptable rebel. Talleyrand was a man who had revolted, but Alexander was a born rebel. Talleyrand had been in a state of permanent revolt against every regime he had served until 1814, but his revolt had not come from the restlessness of an unhealthy temperament; it had been caused by external circumstances: at first by the ecclesiastical chains and then by the contradictions and paralogisms of the Revolution. Alexander, on the other hand, was a man who could adapt himself to no discipline of any sort, particularly those which were the most important for the Czar of Russia. Power always enslaves those who exercise it. The Czar of Russia was invested with tremendous power, but as the serf is attached to the soil, he was bound to a number of traditions, principles, interests, and opinions, which he had to observe. He was obliged to keep in touch with the thoughts and wishes of the nobility and the civil and military bureaucracies, the parlors of Moscow and the bureaus of St. Petersburg. Alexander had been at odds from the very beginning with the nobility and the bureaucracy, whose opinion counted for a great deal. And he had been in revolt against the traditions, principles, and interests which he should have defended, particularly the principle of autocracy. It was chiefly because liberal ideas were the antithesis of his own autocracy, that he became for years their sincere and ardent advocate throughout Europe. His whole life was dominated by an unswerving spirit of contradiction.

In short he was a revolutionary, an instinctive rebel against the rules which he should have observed and made others observe. A revolutionary Czar was quite a paradox in itself. But this living paradox was able to govern his Empire and accomplish great deeds only because this contradiction was complicated by many others. He managed to rule over a vast Empire while in constant conflict with everyone—people, family, ministers, and Allies—and above all with himself. It would be difficult to conceive of a man in the clutches of a more frightful mental unbalance. He was at times a genius and a hero. But this genius and hero was also an eighteenth-century monarch who was frightened of a crown stained with the blood of parricide, preoccupied with his personal prestige and constantly threatened safety, and buried to his neck in the diplomatic and military intrigue going on between the courts and chancelleries, in which he joined with a bitter fury. The two individuals—brilliant hero and political gambler—were never completely separated. The former would always draw on the latter for help, while the latter was continually being tortured by the distant remorse of the fallen and powerless hero. When the hero was uppermost, Alexander was no longer a cunning statesman but a champion of humanity who threw himself into the fray with the odds against him. When the political gambler took the place of the hero, Alexander became a paltry, lying, intriguing, twisted monarch, sometimes even wicked, who no longer understood the ideas of his other self and sometimes completely reversed them.

And so, at the age of twenty-seven, in 1804, he had conceived the plan set forth in the secret instructions for the reconstruction of Europe, and had offered it to England with the strength of the Russian Empire to carry it out. This plan is one of the grandest conceptions of history, a true work of genius, because with utter clarity he fixed the essential conditions under which the nineteenth century, and many centuries after that, might have a European system that would give balance and peace to the continent. Furthermore, Alexander was not only theorizing; he was prepared to take the chances of a terrible war, which was not wanted by his people, in order to put his plan into execution. But the task had been too much for his inexperience. He had been disgusted and later frightened by Austerlitz, Friedland, the inertia of Prussia, the weakness of Austria, and the constant vacillations of England. Whereupon he completely reversed his policy. Instead of reconstructing Europe on the ruins of the French Empire, he sealed its destruction by promising Russia compensations in an alliance with Napoleon. By one of those violent fluctuations which were the great weakness of his character, Alexander flung himself into the alliance with the same enthusiasm he had shown in making war on France. But official and social Russia was no better pleased with the alliance—an alliance with Revolution—than she had been with the war. She laid the blame for both to the great inexperience of the youthful sovereign and continued to demand the third solution, neutrality, which was impossible. In the end, the Treaty of Tilsit came to naught, and a war to the death broke out. There was no concrete reason, no conflict of interests, but a sort of spontaneous internal combustion similar to those which cause a large haystack suddenly to burst into flames for no apparent reason. Then occurred the war of 1812, the invasion of Russia, the occupation and burning of Moscow. For the only time in his life, the Czar and his people were reconciled by the urgent task of defense.

Thus, at the age of thirty-seven, Alexander had accumulated enough responsibilities to have crushed several monarchs: an unwanted but advantageous parricide; the Third Coalition against France and the alliance with Napoleon, both of which he had forced on Russia; the war and invasion of 1812; the invasion of France and the march on Paris, also forced on Russia by Alexander against her will. In 1812, Napoleon's army having been driven out of the country, a strong party in Russia had demanded that Alexander withdraw from the war and let France, Germany, and England settle it among themselves. It was he who had stood out for pursuing Napoleon all the way to Paris, and then taking part in Europe's reconstruction.

And now he had entered Paris at the head of his army. Moscow had been avenged. The task was now to make peace, a general, permanent peace which would give mankind a chance to breathe. During the last few weeks, when he had been confiding to everyone that he was going to bring peace and liberty to mankind, he had not exactly been inspired in his clemency by motives *à la* Titus. He had asked too much from his Empire and people; he knew that only a really permanent peace would spare him the fate of his father. But with whom was he to make peace after the rupture of the negotiations at Châtillon and the capture of Paris had made peace with Napoleon impossible? Would he and his army, together with his Allies, lose themselves in a more terrifying waste than the steppes

on which Napoleon's army had perished—the fact that
there was no one with whom he could make peace?

It was because of this that he understood the enigmatic
message of his old friend of Erfurt, and did not hesitate
an instant before sending Nesselrode to him. Now they
were meeting again, this time at the bedside of a part of
dying humanity. What would be the outcome of their
meeting? One was the loser and the other the victor of a
tremendous war. One was only the rebellious minister of
a sovereign about to be deposed, a private individual with
no authority to back him up. The other was Czar of all the
Russias, and, at least for the time being, master of Europe.
But the ordinary citizen spoke thus to the most powerful
sovereign in the world:

Neither you, Sire, nor the allied powers, nor I, to whom you
credit a certain influence, can give a king to France. France
is conquered, and she has been conquered by your arms, yet
even now you have not that power. Any king who is *imposed*
on her will be the result either of intrigue or of force; neither
one nor the other would do. In order to establish something
lasting which will be accepted without protest, one must have
a principle on which to act. We are strong if we have a principle, and we will meet with no resistance. At any rate, resistance will die down after a while. As for a principle, there is
only one—Louis XVIII is a principle. He is the lawful king
of France.[6]

After twenty-five years of turmoil and panic, the great
problem of world peace and order had been stated, as it
had to be stated so that it might be resolved. The Revolution had devastated France and Europe and in the end
had destroyed itself because, blinded by panic, it had come
to believe only in violence, and that through violence it
could accomplish everything, even create governments and
impose peace. If the Allies were to avoid their own self-
destruction, they had to be wise enough in victory to
understand that the right to command can no more be

6 *Mémoires,* II, 165.

created than a lasting peace can be forced on a people. Both must be agreed to by those concerned. But the Czar and his Allies must not be frightened by this situation, far from it! Their safety and that of the world were dependent on their remaining calm. The victors should declare publicly and solemnly that they would never make peace either with Napoleon or any of his family, and that they would not take advantage of their victory. After that, the restoration of the Bourbons would come about naturally. Talleyrand vouched for the Senate, which would do everything necessary to save France and Europe. Louis XVIII was the only man who could make a permanent and honorable peace, for his was the only authority whose legitimacy was generally if not universally recognized. All difficulties could be solved if the Allies were wise enough not to take advantage of their position and abuse their power.

That afternoon of March 31, 1814, while he was talking in this fashion to Alexander, marked the zenith of Talleyrand's strange career. At that time he was sixty. Forty years of misfortunes, of humiliations, of sorrows, of activity and meditation, of dangers and ridiculous adventures, of terrible confusion and skillful planning, of good luck and bad luck—all had pointed toward this amazing encounter between a man with no importance and the mightiest sovereign on earth, a discussion that was to decide the fate of a large section of mankind. We know very little of what was said during that meeting in the rue Saint-Florentin. It is a shame that we do know so little, and yet it may be very fortunate. What we do know is that the next morning the people of Paris were confronted with the following proclamation, posted throughout the city:

The armies of the allied powers have occupied the capital of France. The allied sovereigns are prepared to accept the wishes of the French nation.
They declare:
That, although conditions of peace must carry the strongest

guarantees in order to restrain the ambition of Bonaparte, they will become more lenient when France, by returning to a wiser government, will herself offer security for peace.

The allied sovereigns therefore proclaim:

That they will make no treaty with Napoleon Bonaparte, nor with any member of his family;

That they will respect the integrity of French territory as it was under its legitimate kings. They can even do more than that, for they recognize the principle that it is necessary to the welfare of Europe that France remain large and strong;

That they will recognize and uphold the Constitution which the French nation decides upon. They therefore invite the Senate to appoint a provisional government which can carry on the administration, and draw up a Constitution acceptable to the people of France.

The aims that I have just expressed are those of all the allied powers.

ALEXANDER

The Emperor had understood the logic of his friend and had dared to promise France, Europe, and the world, in his name and in the name of his absent Allies, that the victors would not be afraid of their victory. He had understood, and he had made his decision because on the day of his interview with Talleyrand he had been in that state of exaltation—I am tempted to call it a "trance"—which sometimes transformed him into a genius. The acclaim he had received that morning was well in keeping with his superb self-confidence, and, instead of being frightened by his victory, he had gone back to the high ideals of 1804. The above proclamation was the joint masterpiece of the two rebels, and it was one of the greatest deeds in history because it was the first courageous act in a quarter-century of fear. The vicious circle of fear and violence had been broken. The great panic was defeated, the adventure finished. Reconstruction could now begin.[7]

[7] C. K. Webster, *The Foreign Policy of Castlereagh* (London: G. Bell and Sons, 1931), I, 243. There is a sentence on this page which reads as follows: "It was in Dijon [where Castlereagh, Metternich, and the Aus-

trian Emperor had been staying since March 24] that in the course of the next few days the fate of the Bourbons was decided." I cannot agree. The important decisions affecting the restoration were taken in Paris on March 30 and 31 by Talleyrand and Alexander. What took place in Dijon, besides the banquet on March 29, described by Mr. Webster, at which the illustrious guests toasted the restoration of the Bourbons? The only significance of the banquet lay in the fact that Metternich, the Emperor Francis, and Castlereagh, who up to then had been skeptical about the possibility of a Bourbon restoration, had changed their minds after the royalist coup in Bordeaux and were feeling very happy about an event which would facilitate the conclusion of peace. But the excellent Burgundy in which they toasted the Bourbons did nothing to help matters along. The only important initiative taken at Dijon which Mr. Webster can cite is the mission of M. de Bombelles, sent by the Austrian Emperor to the comte d'Artois with the conditions upon which the Allies would recognize the Bourbons. This was of little importance compared with the proclamation of April 1 signed by Alexander, the deposition of Napoleon, which Talleyrand induced the Senate to vote, and the direct contact which Talleyrand and Alexander established with Louis XVIII. Those are the actions which brought about the restoration of the Bourbons, and not the toasts at Dijon or the mission of M. de Bombelles.

VII

THE TREATY OF PARIS

It has long been a favorite pastime of writers and historians to attempt to provide an answer to the insoluble riddle of whether history is made by great men or by the interaction of great forces. It has been consistently ignored that, in no matter what type of state, during times of crisis those who decide the fate of peoples are always a very small group of individuals, who are not necessarily superior individuals. More often than not it devolves upon insignificant men to make great decisions. Whence so many catastrophes!

On March 31, 1814, the fate of Europe for the next century was decided by two men. In this instance they happened to be courageous and intelligent. Both sincerely wanted peace, the restoration of personal liberties, and the humanization of government. Because these factors were present, they did not fail. On April 1, reassured by Alexander's manifesto, the Senate named a provisional government made up of five men headed by Talleyrand, and entrusted him with drawing up "a plan for a Constitution which will be agreeable to the French people." On April

2, it declared Napoleon and his family to be dispossessed of the throne, and freed the people and army from their oath of fidelity. On the third, the legislative body in its turn voted the deposition, and Talleyrand gathered a score of people at his house to discuss the Constitution which the Senate had requested. All this encouraged the royalists to come out in the open. During the afternoon of April 3 and morning of April 4, the Cour de Cassation, the Cour des Comptes, the Paris *mairies,* and many officers of the National Guard came out in support of the Senate's deposition decree, some voicing their hopes for the restoration of the Bourbons. On the fourth, Talleyrand wrote to his niece: "I have good news for you, my dear. Marshal Marmont has just come over to us with his army corps. For that we can thank our proclamations and papers. He no longer wishes to serve Napoleon against the country." [1]

On the fifth, the plan of the Constitution was sent to the Senate, which, after adding a few amendments, unanimously approved it. Sixty-three out of one hundred and forty members were present.

All these events brought about by Alexander's manifesto resulted in the abdication of Napoleon on April 11. On the same day the Emperor's emissaries—Coulaincourt, Mac-Donald, Ney—came to Paris and signed the treaty which determined the fate of the Bonapartes. Napoleon ratified it on the twelfth, accepting seclusion on the island of Elba with the title of Emperor, and a civil list of two and a half million francs. The same day Monsieur, the comte d'Artois, brother of Louis XVIII, after twenty-five years of exile, returned to Paris as Lieutenant General to the King.

Principles resemble bones. They hold up society, just as the bones support the body, so long as they have life and elasticity. Like bones, they develop, grow old, and die, becoming like the *ossa arida* in the Bible—dead, brittle, breaking at the first blow, skeletal or parchment legitimacies. Besides legitimacies which are still alive and those

[1] *Revue d'histoire diplomatique,* I, 249.

which are dead there are also those which want to live yet
cannot, which are no more than mystifications and phan-
toms, forming with the others a triad into which mankind
is divided, for better, for worse. Talleyrand's legitimacy was
a living one, formed from the conjunction of the still
powerful monarchic and aristocratic principle and the doctrine of popular sovereignty. But no sooner did Talleyrand
invoke this legitimacy in France, than it came up against a
weird struggle which threatened for a moment to impede
its progress. This was the struggle between a ghost—the
Senate—and a skeleton—royalism. Although it had been
merely the instrument of Napoleonic despotism, the Senate
believed that it had deposed the Emperor and recalled
Louis XVIII, and that Louis XVIII might only become
King after having ratified and sworn to the Constitution.
Before he took this oath, the letters patent were nothing
but scraps of paper. But the royalists did not see it that
way. According to them, Louis XVIII had never ceased to
reign, for he had received eternal and immutable rights
from God; therefore the letters patent, which had named
the comte d'Artois, Lieutenant General of the kingdom,
were also sufficient to confer the sovereign power on him,
without any intervention from the Senate.

During the days which preceded the arrival of the comte
d'Artois in Paris, Talleyrand had not been able to bring
the Senate and the royalist party in accord; and on the
twelfth, the comte d'Artois had entered Paris, without anyone's yet knowing whether he came as the representative
of the King or as a private individual. But Paris greeted
him as the authentic representative of the legitimate King,
and enthusiasm for the Bourbons ran high—sincere enthusiasm and mercenary enthusiasm, which are always bound together during civil wars to hail the victor of the moment.
The marshals, the magistrates, the administration, the Academies, all rallied to the monarchy in a few days, as if they had
been awaiting it eagerly for twenty years. Even the old guard
of the Revolution—Barras, Carnot, the abbé Gregoire—

emerged from the obscure retreat to which it had been driven by Napoleon, in order to applaud. How could the letters patent be denied when both popular and official ratification had been obtained? With the assistance of Fouché and Alexander, Talleyrand got the Senate to confer the government of France on the comte d'Artois, who was given the title of Lieutenant General "until Louis of France, summoned to the throne of France, will have accepted the constitutional bill." On April 14, a delegation from the Senate presented to the comte d'Artois the act which conferred upon him the government of France. The comte d'Artois declared:

> I have taken cognizance of the constitutional act which summons the King, my august brother, to the throne of France. He has not given me the authority to accept the Constitution, but I know his sentiments and his principles, and I do not fear to be disclaimed when I assure you, in his name, that he will accept its basic facts.

The following day, on April 15, Francis I, Emperor of Austria, arrived in Paris; Metternich and Castlereagh had already arrived a few days earlier. Neither Metternich, Francis, nor Castlereagh had been satisfied with Alexander's manifesto to France. In a report sent on April 20 by Count Munster, minister from Hanover, to the Prince Regent, one reads: "I am tempted to believe that if the English, Austrian, and Prussian ministers had been in Paris, when the capital was taken, they would not have sanctioned the announcement of March 31, made by Emperor Alexander in the name of the Allies. This manifesto, drawn up by Talleyrand, is a veritable Pandora's box." [2] Yet Alexander's manifesto, the so-called Pandora's box, was the key to the situation, for it had assured the peace and safety of Europe in twenty-four hours. But Alexander's Allies thought that he had been too generous and conciliatory. What luck for France and for Europe that Talleyrand

[2] Quoted by Webster, *op. cit.*, I, 249, n. 1.

had found the Czar in one of his better moments on the thirty-first, and had managed to extract his signature! Hesitation at the last moment, a delay of a few days, might have jeopardized everything, and made possible a disastrous new attack of fear, the most dangerous and deadly of all fears: the fear of victory! But Talleyrand had acted in time and Alexander had been amenable. The Austrians and the English had found Paris all decked in white, and infatuated with Alexander, the Bourbons, the comte d'Artois, and Louis XVIII, whom nobody knew and who was still in England; royalty and the Revolution were embracing each other at every street corner; the Emperor of Russia was strutting around as the liberator of mankind and reaping the congratulations and the homage of everybody, from the highest to the meanest citizen.

Certain manifestations of this joy have been denounced as betrayals by indignant historians of later generations.[3] But one must admit that Paris had its excuse, even if it had gone a little beyond bounds. France had been at war and in chains for twenty-two years; until the thirtieth of March, everybody had thought that war and slavery would go on for another ten or twenty years, that they would never end, and that mankind would continue on a path strewn with never-ending hardships and leading to the black pit of universal ruin. And then, in a few days a mysterious hand had suddenly destroyed the nightmare which had terrified Europe for a quarter of a century! Now there was peace, the end of agony and horror, a beginning of freedom and an end to slavery—light, hope, a little bit of heaven, in other words! What was more natural than public sentiment should go to excesses in its joy and hope?

In short, when Metternich arrived in Paris, he found a blissful state of joyful expectation. Was he also going to be dazzled by so much light? But then he found Alexander, in the guise of a demi-god, riding the crest of this blissful wave, the fanatic with whom he had nothing in common

[3] Cf. Henry Houssaye, *1814* (Paris, 1914), pp. 570-572.

and whom he considered neither very serious-minded nor very intelligent, and in fact rather dangerous.[4] They had already done nothing but disagree during the war: about the command of the allied armies, for instance, and the invasion of Switzerland. No sooner did Metternich arrive, than they set to again, about the treaty of April 11, which had sent Napoleon to Elba, a few miles from the coast of Italy. "This treaty . . . will bring us back on the field of battle in less than two years," Metternich had protested. "One cannot doubt the word of a soldier and a sovereign without insulting him," Alexander had replied. Metternich, who would have had no qualms in offering this insult to Napoleon, had only signed the treaty because he had arrived too late to have it annulled.[5]

The incompatibility was in their different intellects and temperaments. The atmosphere of Paris, brought to a pitch by Alexander's contagious enthusiasm and the universal acclaim he received—the result of a general reaction against abuses of force, and of a confidence in the Bourbons, in universal reconciliation, in the resurrection of the law of nations, in the Constitution and the representative regime, which were to accompany the restoration of the dynasty— had very little appeal for the temperament of the young Austrian chancellor. Like Talleyrand, he was an aristocrat from head to foot, but of another stamp. One of those refined and humane *grands seigneurs,* who are nevertheless prudent and moderate, preferring whenever possible to yield to force rather than fight it, precisely because, although it is repugnant to their innate delicacy, they are convinced that it always has the best chance of winning. Since, in addition to this, he was one of those men who, the luckier they are, the less confident they become in their luck, and the less willing to take chances, he had been still

---

4 Metternich's true opinion of the Russian Emperor can be found in the remarkable portrait in his *Mémoires* (Paris: E. Plon & Cie., 1880-1884), I, 315 *et seq.*

5 Metternich, *Mémoires,* I, 195.

more weakened by the joys of an unbelievably happy life. What a contrast with Talleyrand, for whom life had been one hardship after another until his sixtieth year! Metternich had become chancellor of the Empire at the age of thirty-seven; he had unquestionably achieved the summit of human grandeur, with practically no opposition, and this at an age when most men are only beginning their careers. He, too, had a superior intelligence, but one of a different sort. Talleyrand was a philosopher, capable of co-ordinating reality with the principles which govern it; Metternich was an artist, capable of seeing through it intuitively. His description of countries, his personal portraits, his analyses of political or historical situations, his judgments of peoples and governments are veritable masterpieces. If literature had claimed him, he would have made a great novelist. In short, he was neither enough of a thinker nor daring enough to be guided by a principle, not even the principle of monarchy, and, like Talleyrand, to entrust it with his fate and that of the state he governed. But, though unlike Talleyrand he was not a constructive genius, his loathing for the spirit of adventure was even greater than Talleyrand's. He was far too civilized, far too cautious for that. But, if he was not a constructive genius and had a horror of adventures, what was he then? He himself could not have answered that question. Too weak to have principles, he became the victim of circumstance. Until the very end, except for an occasional prophetic gleam, he had thought Napoleon invincible. He had never believed in the restoration of the Bourbons. Metternich, the minister of one of the oldest monarchies in Europe, a monarchy held up, in spite of mediocre rulers, by virtue of strong principles and traditions, this man all his life was to hold the conviction that Napoleon could have founded a more permanent monarchy than the Bourbons because he possessed the quality of greatness.[6] He despised the Revolu-

6 In connection with this, see the significant passage in Vol. I of Metternich's *Mémoires,* pp. 196-198.

tion in all its manifestations—intellectual, spiritual, and political—but he believed it to be incurable because he had only a limited faith in the Church and monarchy, which should have fought it. He admired Talleyrand but was too much afraid of public opinion to ignore the enmity of the Church and nobility for the ex-bishop, and therefore doubted the permanence of the latter's achievements, the new France of Louis XVIII. He was suspicious of everything and everyone: Napoleon and the Bourbons, Talleyrand and Alexander, the Revolution and the Restoration.

Castlereagh's case is more simple. With his political views crystallized in and by the narrow, insular policy of his government, he was completely unable to understand the exalted frenzy and ideological transformation taking place in Europe. In the great drama of his age he saw only a balance of power that was injurious to England and must therefore be changed for forcing France to stay within her former boundaries—neither more nor less than that. In his opinion Alexander was too magnanimous and trusting toward France.[7] He distrusted both Talleyrand and his ideas, understanding the latter only up to a certain point, and smelling a trap.[8] His outlook was clear and uncomplicated as far as it went, but it did not go far enough and was too narrow.

An insular empiricist, a constructive genius, a brilliant fanatic, and a *grand seigneur* with a streak of Hamlet in him: these made up the quartet that was to put an end to a twenty-two-year war by the greatest peace treaty of history. A peace treaty is the most difficult to achieve of all human tasks because it is the most contradictory. Every peace treaty implies a coercion of the loser. But it is an elementary postulate of conscience that only free consent can create obligation. The result would be that a peace treaty, being by nature an imposition, would last only as long as the strength capable of imposing it. As

[7] Cf. Castlereagh, *op. cit.*, IX, 472.
[8] Concerning English distrust for Talleyrand, cf. *Ibid.*, IX, 436-437.

soon as that strength gives way, the loser will no longer have any moral obligation to observe the treaty and will therefore revolt. But under these conditions wars could only end with the extermination of one of the two adversaries; peace treaties would not be worth the paper they were written on; and the peace which human beings desire, a peace in which the adversaries are reconciled by a permanent settlement of their quarrel, a true peace which ends war for all time, would be impossible. Such a peace indeed becomes possible only by a contradiction. This consists of mitigating an action which implies coercion with a certain amount of liberty and offsetting the sacrifices exacted with certain advantages. Thus the treaty becomes a moral obligation and the loser will gain more by respecting it than by breaking it. But this contradiction presents tremendous difficulties. For these to be overcome, a great deal of courage is needed, for the victor must not be afraid that moderation will weaken him in the opinion of the loser and will encourage the latter to revolt.

Fortunately for the world, Paris in April, 1814, was carried away by a joyful excitement that inspired everyone with courage. In spite of their prejudices and jealousy of Alexander's great popularity, Castlereagh, Metternich, Hardenberg, and Francis succumbed to the atmosphere. Swept by one of those irresistible *élans* to which it occasionally gives itself up and which no other city is capable of emulating, Paris saved France and Europe during the months of April and May by showing to the great powers within its walls a glorious vision of the peace to be established. On April 16, the comte d'Artois officially set up his government, in the form of a grand Council of State, composed of the five members of the provisional government, marshals Moncey and Oudinot, and General Dessoles. Peace negotiations were begun immediately afterward. But, until Louis XVIII had come back and until the Constitution had been granted, the Council of

State created by Artois was no more than a shadow government which might later acquire body but might also disappear. Was it possible to negotiate a peace with a shadow? Yet the Allies not only opened negotiation; on April 23, they signed a preliminary treaty. By this treaty, France undertook the immediate evacuation of fortresses still occupied by French troops outside the boundaries of 1792; while the Allies, "in order to make definite the reconciliation between the allied powers and France and to allow the latter to enjoy the advantages of peace," undertook to withdraw their armies beyond the same boundaries. A momentous decision in view of the circumstances. France still had only a shadow government. No one knew whether the adherence of Napoleon's armies to the monarchy was sincere. Everything in France was in a state of uncertainty and fluctuation, as in all of Europe. And yet the Allies agreed to evacuate French territory before making peace. For this concession they received nothing; the fortresses given back by France would have been lost to her in any event.

Had the Allies lost their minds? Not at all; they were courageous. They were not afraid of their victory and did not feel the need of crushing their victim and binding him hand and foot. The preliminary treaty of April 23 constituted the second great act of courage after the proclamation of March 31, both of them prerequisites for a peace that would be genuine, honorable, and permanent. But for peace to be concluded, the consent of France was needed, and France had become Louis XVIII. Everything depended on him; why was he delaying his arrival? Fortunately it was no more than an attack of gout. Having recovered, he had already left Hartwell on April 20. On the twenty-first he had made a stately entrance into London. On the twenty-fourth he had left for Dover, and on the twenty-ninth he had arrived at Compiègne. There he had held Court for three days, receiving the provisional government, a deputation from the Legislature, and a great many people of high rank from Paris. He talked for a long time with Talleyrand and charged him with drawing up a declaration on the constitutional question, to be proclaimed before his entry into Paris. On May 1, Alexander arrived for a visit that lasted only one day. The youngest, the most energetic, and the most imaginative of the European sovereigns came to congratulate the French dynasty on its happy return to the throne, of which he flattered himself on having been the chief instrument, and at the same time to insist upon Louis XVIII accepting the Constitution of the Senate.

That same evening, however, Alexander returned to Paris in a rage, complaining to Pozzo di Borgo that the Bonapartes were more congenial than the Bourbons. Louis had given him a tiny suite; at dinner his host had been served first, seated in a comfortable armchair, while Alexander had been seated in an ordinary chair like all the other guests. As to his advice, Louis, coldly polite, had declined it and dropped the subject. The next day the Bourbon monarch proclaimed his own version of the constitutional declaration; the one drawn up by Talleyrand with the help of Alexander had been greatly altered.

After having carefully read the Constitution proposed by the Senate in the session of April 6, we acknowledge that its fundamental principles are good, but that a great many articles, bearing signs of the haste with which they were drawn up, cannot in their present form become the basic law of the state. Resolved to adopt a liberal constitution which shall be wisely drawn up, and unable to accept one which must indispensably be rectified, we therefore convoke for June 10 of this year the Senate and Legislature, undertaking to put before them the work which we shall have accomplished, assisted by a commission chosen from those two bodies, and to base that constitution on the following guarantees. . . .

The Senate's Constitution had been vetoed; but the guarantees promised were more or less the same as those embodied in that Constitution. Moreover, the Constitution of the King would differ from that of the Senate only in minor details. Why then was the latter spurned by the King? What was the reason for his running the risk of angering the men and the powers to which he owed his restoration—Talleyrand, Alexander, and the Senate? On May 2, Louis XVIII was still a King without a throne. For a century historians have wondered how anyone could have been so maladroit.

From the standpoint of politics alone, this was a blunder. But we must never forget that in 1814 the great drama of legitimacy was being played out. Every principle of legitimacy is a living entity, living not by itself alone but in the man who applies it. All power is an amalgam of two lives which never become identical, for the life of a principle is always different from the lives of the man or men in whom and by whom it becomes a practical reality, sometimes in opposition to them, and always stronger. What infinite tragedies are born from that contradiction! The restoration of Louis XVIII, for instance. Who was this fat, pompous old man who had come back to France at the age of fifty-nine, after an absence of twenty-five years? An exiled King whose palaces, wealth, and crown had been restored? He was more than that: he symbolized the age-old principle of legitimate monarchy, returning to France more alive than anywhere else because it was in France that it had received a mortal wound. An amazing paradox of history! In him and his family the Revolution had spurned, trampled under, imprisoned, exiled, and decapitated the principle of legitimacy which for centuries had been the source of authority in France and in most of Europe. As in the case of all the mighty who have fallen, his cup of bitterness had been full; he had been offended beyond forgiveness by the cowardice of his brother kings and emperors, who had all disowned him when he had fallen. He had suffered in silence. Alexander said that the Bourbons had not risked a scratch to recover their kingdom. But what could they have done, exiled, scattered, moneyless, abandoned by all Europe? Louis had restricted himself to waiting. And now, without having raised a finger or had a shot fired, he found himself King of France, recalled by the nobles, acclaimed by the populace, awaited with equal impatience by the repentant former revolutionaries and the allied sovereigns as the only man who could make peace. For he was the King, by virtue of an ancient law still recognized by the majority of the people.

An intoxicating triumph, and also a formidable trial! Would he lose his head and imagine that he had defeated the Revolution, subjugated Europe, and reconquered his kingdom single-handed? If that had been the case, he would have listened to the royalists surrounding him, refused the Constitution, and re-established absolutism, thereby ruining France and Europe. Would he show himself skillful and clever, in the worldly sense so admired by his historians? In that case, knowing that he was still only a shadow King without a vestige of power, he would have accepted the Senate's Constitution, courted Talleyrand, Alexander, the Allies, and the liberal and revolutionary opinion, of whose favor he might still stand in need. But he would have made a promise that could easily have been broken; once in power, he could have revoked the Constitution at the first opportunity on the grounds of illegality. The Senate was a creation of the Revolution, a phantom legality; now that the Revolution was dying, the Senate had no authority to grant the liberty to France which the militant and triumphant Revolution had never given her. The greatness of Louis XVIII lay in the fact that he did not attribute his return to his own efforts, to the Allies, or to Talleyrand, but to the resurrected principle of which he was symbol. By identifying himself with that principle, he became, during the two or three weeks needed to carry out the decisive steps, a unique figure in history, almost legendary, yet necessary to the safety of the world. His position was that of a shadow

King without power who treated the most powerful monarchs of Europe as though they were his subjects, and who accomplished the vital task which the Revolution should have done and did not succeed in doing. The young man who came to see him at Compiègne in the role of savior and adviser was in reality the petty ruler of a vast empire who had allied himself with the Revolution in the dream of sharing the world. And now he was pretending to be almost the protector of the French monarchy, which had returned because it alone could give Europe peace; and it alone could do that because he, brother of a decapitated king, without arms, money, or friends, had remained faithful to a principle. Only the minimum honors prescribed by protocol and an ordinary chair were enough for this petty monarch. The others, too, had betrayed the principle: the Austrian Emperor by prostituting his daughter to the Revolution, the King of Prussia by allying himself with it, the Pope by crowning it. The only ruler for whom Louis felt any gratitude was the Regent of England. England at least, except for the brief truce of Amiens, had always fought against the Revolution, win or lose.

Louis XVIII returned to the throne convinced that he owed the fact only to his own right—a right superior to circumstance. In his first meeting with Talleyrand at Compiègne, he had held a conversation with the Prince of Benevento which has come down to us in two different versions but of which the general sense was as follows: "You have far more need of me than I have of you."

He was even less willing to be the executor of the Revolution. He, too, was convinced that monarchy could no longer support itself by the monarchic principle alone; but he refused to accept Articles 2 and 29 of the Constitution decreed by the Senate. They were conceived as follows:

Article 2: The people of France freely and without restraint do call to the throne of France, Louis-Stanislas-Xavier of

France, brother of the last king, and after him the other members of the House of Bourbon, in accordance with the ancient law of succession.

Article 29: The present Constitution shall be submitted to the will of the people of France in the shape decided upon. Louis-Stanislas-Xavier shall be proclaimed King of the French as soon as he shall have sworn to and signed an act stating, "I do accept the Constitution, etc., etc."

Louis XVIII did not want to return to the throne as the choice of the people but as the legitimate successor of Louis XVII; nor to grant representative institutions to France as the executor of the deceased Revolution but as a sovereign entrusted by God with the development of his people's institutions. It was thus that on May 3 he entered his capital to the sound of bells and of cannon, in a carriage drawn by eight white horses; and his first act as King was to replace the provisional government with a definitive one. Talleyrand was included but only as the Foreign Minister in a cabinet headed by the King himself as President of the Council. It is significant that Talleyrand was beginning to see the fruition of his cherished theory of legitimacy, at his expense, however. As President of the Council, Talleyrand would not have been just an ordinary colleague and secretary of the King: he would have been the latter's acting counterpart, I am tempted to say his secular counterpart. Now, a degraded nobleman, an apostate and married bishop, a former minister of the Directory, the Consulate, and the Empire, could not be the secular counterpart of a King of France by the grace of God. Inasmuch as this apostate bishop had a great deal of experience, an unimpeachable political reputation, and considerable influence with the allied sovereigns, he could be made use of during the peace negotiations, but no more than that. It was impossible to expect more from a king who belonged to tradition and the Old Regime. The secret enmity of the royalists and the churchmen for the former bishop of Autun, which must have influenced

Louis XVIII, was merely the superficial manifestation of a fundamental incompatibility.

Be that as it may, on May 13, Talleyrand was Foreign Minister of France, charged with making peace with the Coalition made up of England, Austria, Prussia, Russia, Sweden, Portugal, and Spain. But to make peace was a question of reorganizing the European system, and the reorganization had to begin by giving half of Europe, still without governments, institutions that were capable of governing it. Truly a herculean, almost superhuman task! It would have been reasonable to foresee long, tedious, and difficult negotiations, complicated at each stage by the hates and fears of an inexpiable war and by the exultations of an unexpected and overwhelming victory.

This was far from the case. In four weeks the most difficult peace treaty in history was drawn up and signed. The discussions were so simple that very little trace of them is left. It is impossible to give a daily account of these discussions, which settled the fate of the world. The whole thing was a miracle. Even Metternich, even Francis I, even Castlereagh, who had come to Paris full of uncertainty and suspicion, were carried along. Alexander continued to play the part of the liberator to everyone he talked with, and to pass himself off in Paris as a great humanitarian. With his slightly obscure but undiminishing exaltation, he kept the fires of confidence and good will burning high in French and allied circles, fires which had been kindled by the almost miraculous end of the war and the general reaction against the abuse of force, by which Europe had been victimized for a quarter of a century. And with him Talleyrand, sure in his principles and his panoramic vision of present and future, formulated and brought into permanent accord the beneficial forces concealed beneath the general exaltation of the moment, destined to die with the passing of time. Both these men could depend upon a superb creation—perhaps the most superb—of the constructive mind: the eighteenth-century law of nations, the masterpiece of the Old Regime, which the Revolution had destroyed and which in 1814 had miraculously come to life again.

That is a point of the utmost importance in understanding what took place at Vienna. The law of nations of the eighteenth century must not be confused with international law, of which the nineteenth century made a particular branch of law studies in universities. International law in the nineteenth century derives from the law of nations under the Old Regime, but it has been desiccated by codification and jurisprudence. The eighteenth-century law of nations was not a system of more or less fixed juridical principles for which justice and enforcement were never found. It was a body of wise and humane rules, designed to prevent abuses of force in relations between states, which do more harm to the states committing them than to those upon whom they are committed—as the Revolution had just proved. The eighteenth-century conception of these rules did not necessitate their being imposed on any state through coercive methods; such methods no more existed then than they do now. In this absence of coercive methods, eighteenth-century political thinkers believed that every statesman worthy of the name was in conscience bound to apply these rules, knowing as he did that by doing so he was working for the best interests not only of his own state but also of other states and of mankind in general. One of the great writers of the eighteenth century—Montesquieu—clearly stated this precept for all civilized people: that in peace men should do each other the greatest possible good and in war the least possible harm.

In the law of nations formulated by the great thinkers of the eighteenth century there is far less of the juridical, in the strict sense of the word, than of a moral aspiring after an era of wisdom, of justice, of humanity in the intercourse between peoples and states, which would prevent, together with the abuse of force, all inexcusable wars.

A religion almost, which at certain times was capable of being transformed into ecstasy, into courage, and into prophetic vision, something which will never be possible for cut-and-dried juridical doctrine. A reading of Vattel [9] in this connection will be of help in understanding the Congress of Vienna, as well as the entire history of the Revolution.

It was largely due to this moral aspiring, which took hold of people's minds, that Europe acquired the courage and the intelligence which it needed if it was to save itself. The law of nations had always advised statesmen to mingle as little as possible the violent passions—hate, vengeance, cupidity, treachery, and cruelty—with warfare and peace-making; to be both generous and farsighted with the loser of a war, more concerned with the future and the permanence of peace than with immediate advantages. Released from their fear, the Allies applied these wise precepts in 1814, renouncing all reprisals, vengeance, and humiliating measures of safety which would have indicated fright on their part, and offering the same conditions they had offered at Châtillon when they had been uncertain of victory. They had conquered; therefore they no longer had any cause for fear and could seek reconciliation with the enemy. Besides, reconciliation was imperative so that the Allies could carry out their plan of reconstructing the European order. There could be no such order without France or with France against it; it was therefore necessary that a peace be found that would be acceptable to France.

All projects of partition or mutilation were abandoned. Furthermore, France received territorial gains beyond her boundaries of 1792: among others, Mulhouse, Landau, and Chambéry. Influenced by his marshals, some of Louis's advisers had at one point sought to obtain an important part of Belgium. Castlereagh had opposed this, and a lively exchange of words had followed. Thanks to Talley-

[9] Emmerich de Vattel, *The Law of Nations* (Philadelphia: T. and J. W. Johnson & Co., 1883).

rand's intervention, however, the difference was settled amicably.[10] England promised to restore the colonies, fisheries, factories, and other establishments which France had possessed on January 1, 1792, in the seas and on the continents of America, Africa, and Asia, with the exception of the islands of Tobago and St. Lucia, Ile de France and its dependencies, and that part of San Domingo ceded to France by the Treaty of Bâle, which was to be returned to Spain. On this point, too, the circle around the King and the influence of his marshals had created difficulties by proposing a plan that was even more favorable to France and by refusing to adhere to the suppression of the slave trade. But England had insisted that after having spent 600 million pounds on the war she was not being too harsh in demanding three small islands from France. Once again Talleyrand smoothed matters over.[11]

In his *Mémoires*, Talleyrand does justice to the peoples whose armies were then occupying France: "For twenty years they had seen their own territories occupied and ravaged by French armies; they had been forced to pay all sorts of levies; their governments had been insulted and treated with utter scorn; there was no outrage for which they might not have sought vengeance." [12] Restitution would have been a better word than indemnity for the Allies to demand. Yet they renounced any indemnity; at Talleyrand's request, they even agreed not to reclaim the works of art which Napoleon had collected *manu militari* throughout Europe. But making peace with France was only the prelude to the reconstruction of Europe; it was also necessary to determine what was to become of the immense territory which had been a part of the French Empire. One of the fundamental principles of the law of nations was that occupation by conquest could never con-

---

[10] Webster, *op. cit.*, I, 266-268. Charles Dupuis, *Le ministère de Talleyrand en 1814* (Paris: Plon-Nourrit & Cie., 1919-1920), I, 352 *et seq.*
[11] *Ibid.*, pp. 268-270. *Ibid.*, pp. 378 *et seq.*
[12] *Mémoires*, II, 174.

fer sovereignty on the invader, though the occupation lasted a hundred years. Sovereignty could only be acquired by the conqueror when it was ceded to him by the former sovereign. Consequently, it was necessary to differentiate between the various annexations of the Revolution, between those which had been accomplished by pure invasion and conquest and those which were legitimate because they had been ceded to France by treaty. Those territories which had been annexed by force had never ceased, according to the law of nations, to belong to their former sovereigns; and these had to be returned without any discussion, for the Coalition had no right to dispose of them. Next came the territories over which revolutionary France was the legitimate sovereign since they had been ceded to her by treaty. But France had agreed to withdraw inside her old boundaries, and therefore these regions, forming almost half of Europe, were left without rulers. It was from this enormous and inchoate mass that the new Europe was to be molded. The question was how? According to the law of nations, there was but one answer: France alone possessed legitimate sovereignty and alone could transfer it to rulers that would be legitimate. Any cessions, therefore, of this territory could only take place with the participation of France.

It was now a question of whether the victors were going to observe these principles of the law of nations. Obviously the principles considerably minimized their right of conquest, to use an unsatisfactory modern phrase. They were the masters of a large part of Europe by conquest; if they could agree among themselves, they could do anything they wanted. Why then bother to recognize that certain territories were completely outside of their jurisdiction, and why bother to discuss with France what could be decided among themselves? But the four allied powers bowed to the law of nations. In so doing they decreased their own authority but made their task easier, diminished their responsibility, and based their reconstruction from the beginning not on the arbitrary and changeable will of man but on universally recognized principles. The conquered territories had already been restored to their former rulers without any reservations. The Pope received back the lands which Napoleon had taken from him in 1808, but not the part which he had ceded to France in 1797 by the Treaty of Tolentino. To the King of Sardinia was returned that portion of his kingdom annexed without treaty by Napoleon in 1803, but not Nice and Savoy, which had been ceded to France by the Treaty of 1797.

During the month of May, the Allies had discussed various plans for the disposal of the territories which had been legitimately possessed by France. It was a difficult question. During the war the Allies had on several occasions stated their intentions of establishing a balance of power which would insure peace in Europe. They had touched on certain concrete plans, such as the substitution of a German confederation for the Holy Roman Empire, but they had never considered the matter in full. Naturally this would have been impracticable before Napoleon's abdication and the conclusion of peace with France. But now there could be no dissension. The dim vision of a reconstructed Europe had to become a definite reality on the map of the Continent.

But claimants were numerous, and it was not long before it was realized that all these solutions had been too hastily conceived. A great deal of time was needed to satisfy everyone and to guarantee a legitimate transfer by individual cessions to each state.[13] The difficulties could be solved by a gradual process of elimination. First, peace could be made with France at Paris and the question of her boundaries settled. With regard to her Empire, France would limit herself to the renunciation of her sovereignty over all territories to which she was legitimately entitled

---

[13] For a more detailed account of the partition plans discussed at Paris during May, see C. K. Webster, *Congress of Vienna* (London, 1918), pp. 42-44.

by treaty. The question of their disposal was to be post-poned until the Congress met in Vienna. But—and this is a factor of the utmost importance which historians have not yet realized—the Allies had been unwilling to defer the most important problem until they had determined without delay in Paris the principles along which it would be resolved. And these principles were all definite guar-antees given by the Allies to France and by each Ally to the three others, that they would not abuse their victory in Vienna any more than they had in Paris. Article 6 states that:

Holland, placed under the sovereignty of the House of Orange, will receive an increase of territory. The title and exer-cise of sovereignty over it can nowise belong to any prince bearing, or called upon to bear, a foreign crown. The German states will be independent and united in a Federation. Inde-pendent Switzerland will continue to govern itself. Italy, apart from the boundaries restored to Austria, will be composed of sovereign states.

What is the meaning of this article? That the Allies promised France to respect the independence of Germany, Switzerland, and that part of Italy not restored to Austria. In other words, that they would not expand in these countries to the disadvantage of France, by establishing outright or camouflaged protectorates.

Even more important were the secret articles. For ex-ample the second. It was drawn up as follows:

The possessions of His Imperial and Royal Apostolic Majesty in Italy will be bounded by the Rivers Pô and Ticino and Lake Maggiore. The King of Sardinia will remain in possession of his former lands, except for that part of Savoy ceded to France by Article 3 of this treaty; he will receive the state of Genoa as an addition to his territory. The port of Genoa will be declared a free port, the powers reserving to themselves the right to make arrangements with the King of Sardinia regarding this matter. France, in conjunction with the allied powers, will recognize and guarantee the political organization determined upon by Switzerland under the auspices of the said powers and according to principles fixed with their help.

Austria gave guarantees to France and to her own Allies that she would be satisfied with Lombardy and Venetia. After twenty years of warfare it was only natural for her to want some compensation.

No less important to France was the third secret article:

Inasmuch as the establishment of a just balance of power in Europe requires that Holland be so constituted as to enable her to maintain her independence by her own means, the lands bounded by the ocean, the boundaries of France fixed by the present treaty, and the Meuse, will be joined in perpetuity to Holland. The boundaries adjoining the right bank of the Meuse will be determined according to the military needs of Holland and her neighbors. Freedom of navigation on the Scheldt will be based on the same principle which regulates the navigation of the Rhine, in Article 5 of the present treaty.

The possibility of an annexation of the Netherlands by a great power had been removed, to the advantage of the House of Orange. Of all the solutions this was the least injurious and the most favorable to France. Finally the fourth secret article reads:

The German countries on the left bank of the Rhine, which have belonged to France since 1792, will be used for the aggrandizement of the Netherlands, and for compensation to Prussia and other German states.

This was still another guarantee for France. Prussia was to get part of the land on the left bank of the Rhine, but only in compensation for her former territory lost to her. Any expansion was forbidden. The words "balance" and "European order" were then, as now, indeterminate and could be perverted and turned to the advantage of ambitious and ruthless power. Dismemberment was not the only danger confronting France. Without mutilating France, by leaving her in possession of what she had before

1792, the Allies could nevertheless have made her a second-rate power by their own aggrandizement. Europe was theirs for the taking. England might have claimed Belgium and Holland. Vienna coveted Piedmont, the Legations, and unchecked expansion into Italy. The German states without rulers were ripe for an equal division between Austria and Prussia. What Europe might have been like if the conquerors of Napoleon had imitated him is anyone's guess; there was nothing France could have done in 1814 against such an access of violence.

At Paris, the four Allies jointly agreed to the articles in the treaty which limited their claims and ambitions. It is true, however, that the secret articles were preceded by an article—the first—conceived as follows:

> The disposal of the lands renounced by His Most Christian Majesty in Article 3 of the present treaty, and the agreements which are to establish a real and permanent balance of power in Europe, will be determined at the Congress in accordance with principles agreed upon by the allied powers among themselves and after the general dispositions contained in the following articles.

In the opinion of an extremely well-informed French historian, writing toward the end of the nineteenth century, this article was "an obligation on the part of the French representatives to ratify in advance all decisions taken by the other plenipotentiaries." [14] The article was unquestionably equivocal and mysterious. Later we shall see the captious interpretations which were put forth in Vienna and the difficulties it created. There is no doubt of its having been suggested by suspicion. The Allies wanted to make sure that France, after having obtained peace, would not try to hold out for more before putting her necessary signature to whatever they decided on for the states which had been part of the French Empire. But the French historian's interpretation of this article is too

[14] Henry Houssaye, *1815*, (Paris: Perrin & Cie., 1905), I, 122.

simple. France was not requested to accept the decisions
of the Allies without question; she was asked to accept the
principles on which the Allies would base their distribution of territory. The most important of these were enunci-
ated in the treaty France was to sign: the independence of
Germany, Switzerland, and non-Austrian Italy; the giving
up of her protectorates acquired under the Revolution; a
German Confederation; the conferment of Belgium on a
small power; the restriction of Austria's Italian claims and
Prussia's German claims. France was able to discuss these
principles before signing the Treaty of Paris, and after
signing it she was to accept them, not because they had
been imposed on her, but because they were wise and
could serve as the groundwork for an excellent plan to
reconstruct the European order, which was desired by
everyone. The European order which would come out of
the long discussion in Vienna, had its nucleus in the Treaty
of Paris, which had settled most of the questions of principle, essential to any reconstruction of Europe. The Congress had a great deal of hard work ahead of it to specify,
develop, and apply the principles, but the Europe which
was constructed during 1814 and 1815 and which was to
last for a century, had really been determined in Paris
during the four weeks of May, 1814. The reason that it
lasted a century was because its foundations had been laid
with courage, enthusiasm, good will, hope, sincere faith
in law, and equally sincere horror for violence. The fate
of generations is often decided in the space of a few moments of history. Thanks to a moment of wisdom, of
courage, and of nobility, Europe lived for another century.

That treaty of May 30, 1814, is a masterpiece of constructive thought, the finest model on which statesmen
seeking permanent peace after long war can base their
efforts. Both victors and vanquished collaborated in making it, the latter acknowledging that they had abused force,
the former not letting themselves become a prey to fear,
thereby abusing force in their turn. Alexander and Talley-

rand were the architects of this noble edifice. The others—
Francis I, Metternich, Castlereagh, Frederick William of
Prussia, and Hardenberg—seem to have been dragged
along, unresisting if not exactly enthusiastic. Where had
the two moving spirits of the treaty found such powers of
persuasion? Although a great tide of good will and
optimism had swept through people's minds, even those
of the mighty, fear, rancor, and greed still lurked in their
hearts. But for the moment Alexander was the idol and
the hope of Europe. The forces at his command, the risks
he had run, the manifesto of April 1, his youthful im-
petuosity for universal peace, the almost laughable humanity of his outlook, had all earned him the sympathy
of the masses. His name was on everyone's lips; in the
meanest hovel they spoke of him with reverence as the
man who would fulfill their hopes and bring them the
happiness which they had not known for so long. This
tremendous popularity gave him great authority even
though it provoked jealousy, for all the Allies were still,
as before, very conscious of changes in public opinion,
which they had used to good effect against Napoleon.[15]
Talleyrand enjoyed no popularity, and he did not even
have a very important position in the restored monarchy.
How could he, an ordinary minister to a new King,
manage to obtain so many concessions with such ease? The
"betrayal" of Erfurt had something to do with the phe-
nomenal success of Alexander's friend. To begin calling
for justice when one has become weak is easy but not
very persuasive. But Talleyrand was in the position where
he could say to the Allies: "I am not asking you to be
generous because France is defeated. When Napoleon
seemed master of Europe, I protested at my peril against
the abuse of force of which you were the victims. Show
France the same feeling that I showed you when you were
defeated." In that hour of destiny, so full of happiness for

15 Friedrich von Gentz, *Dépêches inédites* (Paris: E. Plon & Cie., 1876-
1877), I, 87.

the world, Talleyrand, the traitor vilified by historians, appeared to the allied sovereigns as the noble savior of Europe; his opposition to Napoleon after Austerlitz, as a credit upon which France could now draw, with moderation, from a victorious Europe. Before giving good advice, Talleyrand had practiced what he preached.

Europe paid its debt to Talleyrand in May, 1814. England, Austria, and Prussia had put their cards on the table by stating their principal claims in the treaty. It is impossible to deny, in view of twenty years of warfare, the abuse of force by the Revolution, especially during the imperial period, and a victory which put the Allies in possession of half Europe, that these claims were moderate. But what about Russia? The question of her claims was not brought forth in the Treaty of Paris. This silence was to be the tragedy of Alexander at the Congress of Vienna, now about to begin.

VIII

INTERMEZZO

———————————————————— >>> <<< ————————————————————

Alexander had also long been hatching a plan for the day of victory. Gentz has disclosed this in a dispatch which he sent to the Hospodars of Wallachia three weeks after the signing of the peace treaty.

The Emperor of Russia appears to have cherished a plan to form a separate yet dependent state out of the whole or greater part of what would be restored to him from the former Duchy of Warsaw, which would be called the Kingdom of Poland. I will not go into the various secret motives which might have suggested the plan to him. It is a fact that the Poles, always avid for anything that would give them back their former grandeur, count upon this project with great certainty; and, although the Emperor has never definitely declared his intentions regarding this matter, it becomes daily more obvious that the Poles are not mistaken in their hopes. It was at first believed that the Grand Duke Constantine would be given the throne of Poland, but for sometime it has seemed more likely that the Emperor himself would take the title. The execution of this plan, incompatible in more ways than one with the future tranquillity of Europe, would be particularly objectionable to Austria and Prussia, more so to the latter than to the former. The extension of the Russian frontiers is in itself disadvantageous and disquieting enough to her neighbors; when, however, this is accompanied by the resuscitation of a Polish monarchy, whatever its size or shape— that is, a center of ferment, of unrest, and of political intrigues —then it becomes doubly pernicious. I believe I am safe in saying that, in the Congress to come, the success or failure of this plan will depend entirely on the attitude of Prussia. If she is fully cognizant of her own interests and if she puts up a solid front with Austria against Russia's plans, it will not be impossible to persuade Alexander to satisfy himself with an outright annexation and to abandon his additional plans. If Prussia should yield, it seems unlikely that Austria will maintain her opposition singlehanded, at the risk of a quarrel with Russia.[1]

An amazing mystery! Historians will have us believe that Alexander wanted Poland rather than the liberation of Europe. But again this explanation is too simple. Russia's position after the war was different from that of Austria and Prussia in that she had no territory to recover. Far from having lost anything during the last twenty years, she had acquired Finland and Bessarabia. But in 1812 she had been invaded and frightfully devastated, while for a whole year her armies had been in pursuit of Napoleon across the whole of Europe. Rebel though he was against the responsibilities of his position and the traditions of his Empire, Alexander could not ignore the duty laid upon the Czar by the army, the chancellery, the administration, and the nobility after each victorious war—the duty to compensate for the war sacrifices of the Empire by an expansion of territory. This duty was supreme above all others for the Czar, whatever his personal beliefs. In his secret message of 1804, he had already considered it necessary to call England's attention to this point.

[1] Gentz, *op. cit.*, I, 80-82.

It is time to bring up the obligation which would devolve upon the two powers at the end of a costly war, to obtain advantages which would recompense them for their losses and which would be proof to their peoples that their interests have not been forgotten. In particular, Russia has the right to demand that, if her neighbors, such as Austria, Prussia, and Sweden, obtain advantages without which it would be impossible to get them to act, she in her turn receive similar advantages.[2]

This obligation on the part of the Czar was greater in 1814 than in 1804. The upper classes in Russia still failed to understand that the annexation of Poland had made Russia a European power and that the see-saw of war, alliance, and then again war with Napoleon had been Alexander's legacy from his grandmother and father. They had regarded this intervention in the affairs of Europe as a whim of their ruler's, and insisted that the sacrifices they had made be paid back in full by the only exchange they recognized—land. If the Czar had attempted to satisfy them with glory and prestige, which was enough for the rest of Europe, he would have met with his father's fate. Yet where was the Czar to increase his Empire but in Poland? Alexander might seem at that moment to be the master of Europe, but in reality he was a miserable captive of his Empire's greed and of geographical conditions. What he demanded was an absolute minimum.

It appears that the Allies became aware of his plans during the latter part of May, probably when, in order to give the guarantees to France and to each other that were contained in the three secret articles, each Ally had to state its maximum claims. It was then that Alexander was forced to reveal his secret. Up till then he had been busy arranging the peace and liberty of Europe, proclaiming to all the powers, including Louis XVIII and the French Court, the doctrine of liberalism and the necessity for propping up

[2] Czartoryski, *op. cit.*, II, 40-41.

the monarchic legitimacy with representative institutions and for allowing peoples to exercise the right of opposition. He had been so anxious about the Constitution which Louis was secretly drawing up, fearing that it would not be democratic enough for the times, that the Allies had been under the impression that Russia's only interest at the peacemaking in Vienna would be in the universal happiness of mankind. Feelings ran high in Paris when it was learned that Alexander, beside the freedom of France and the happiness of mankind, wanted also a large part of Poland. The Austrian leaders were furious. "Austria is raging," wrote Prince Czartoryski on May 20. "She has put in a claim for Cracow, and all peace negotiations have come to a halt." [3] Castlereagh and his colleagues were also annoyed. But Alexander was so anxious for peace that he retreated at once before the Austrian outcry and agreed to submit the matter to the Congress. Thus it was that seven out of the eight powers were able to sign the peace treaty on May 30 without any allusions to Russia's ambitions. Spain was the only absentee, and she was to sign it later, on July 20. But this opposition to his plans constituted the second disillusionment suffered by the savior of the world, the first having been his meeting with Louis in Compiègne. And what was more important, it was his first difference with his Allies. Dame Fortune is not apt to grace history with her presence for very long.

The first two disillusionments were soon to be followed by a third. On June 4, Louis XVIII came before the Legislature and presented his Charter. Fundamentally, this Charter resembled the Constitution of the Senate, but it was more precise, clearer, and more detailed. Montesquieu had been the inspiration and the American Constitution, the model, translated into the terms of an ancient European monarchy. The legislative power was divided between the King and the two Assemblies. In the Senate's Con-

[3] Cited by K. Waliszewski, *Le règne d'Alexandre* (Paris: Plon-Nourrit et Cie., 1924), p. 251.

stitution, the initiation of laws had been mainly the function of the Assemblies, while the King had only an accessory and indirect voice. In the Charter, the situation was reversed: the King had the initiative, and the two Houses had only the right to ask the King to initiate legislation. In both constitutions, the laws were sanctioned and promulgated by the King. The two assemblies had been called the Legislature and the Senate in the former Constitution; in the latter they were denominated the Chamber of Deputies and the Chamber of Peers. The Legislature and the Chamber of Deputies were to be elected. The Charter required that to be eligible a member must be forty years of age and pay a direct tax of 1000 francs, and to be able to vote one must be thirty years of age and pay a direct tax of 300 francs. This, then, was a Constitution qualified by the fact that only the wealthy enjoyed the right of opposition. The members of the second Chamber were to be appointed by the King, according to both constitutions. In the Senate's Constitution they were all to be hereditary appointments; in the Charter, they were to be either hereditary or for life, as the King saw fit. Both constitutions stated that no law could be promulgated, no tax could be levied and collected, without the consent of both Houses. The ministers were to be the secretaries and agents of the King. However, according to the Constitution of the Senate, they were to be responsible "for anything in the actions of the government that would be prejudicial to the laws, to public and individual liberty, and to the rights of the citizen." The Charter stated that they could be accused of treason or peculation by the Chamber of Deputies before the Peers. The Charter also stated that the nobility of the Old Regime would receive their titles back and that the nobility created by Napoleon would keep theirs. The King might create peers at will, but he could only bestow rank and honors, and the nobility were not to be exempt from the laws and duties of society. And, finally, the two constitutions guaranteed the freedom of the press, except in cases where this liberty was abused.

But, although the Charter was merely a better stated version of the Senate's Constitution, Alexander considered it almost a personal affront. He had left Paris the night before the Charter was presented, to go to London with Frederick William, and had been so furious that he had not wanted to see Talleyrand. He blamed him for not having prevented the proclamation of the Charter.[4] What could have been the difference between the two constitutions which drew such an outburst from Alexander? This was not to be found in their contents but in their origin. The Constitution of the Senate was a pact. Louis XVIII would become King of France through the will of the people and after the Constitution had been accepted not only by the King but also by the people. A plebiscite was therefore indicated, the nature of which "would be determined." On the other hand, the Charter was a concession made by Louis XVIII, King of France since the death of Louis XVII and successor to the throne in the long line of French kings. The King stated that with a vigor and clarity that left no doubt of his meaning.

In short, Alexander had almost come to blows with the French Court and with Talleyrand because Louis XVIII had refused to accept his crown from the hands of his people. He was sincere in his infatuation for democratic ideas; and, because he was sincere, he became irritated when he met opposition and deceit. Going everywhere as he did, he had found many secret enemies of the Restoration, especially many camouflaged Bonapartists, who had taken advantage of his anger to set him against Louis XVIII. They had called Louis an autocrat completely dominated by fanatical royalists, whispering that instead of giving France her liberty he would re-establish the Old

---

[4] All this came out in the letter which Talleyrand wrote to the Czar on June 13, an important document which Talleyrand included in his *Mémoires*, II, 210-214.

Regime in all its terror, and that by having favored the
Bourbons the Czar had fallen into a trap. Angered by so
much deception and taken in by these sly insinuations,
Alexander ended up in a complete fog about the policies
of Louis and Talleyrand and about the true situation
in France. As we shall see, in 1814 it was less imperative to
make a new and better constitution than the ones before,
than to put one into execution, even if it was mediocre.
Between 1789 and 1795, three excellent constitutions had
recognized the right of opposition, but not one of them
had ever been acted upon. The great question was whether
the Restoration intended to repeat the frightful recanta-
tions of the Revolution, and also whether it intended to
make a solemn promise regarding the right of opposition
and then fall into another 18 Brumaire which would abro-
gate this right. If, after a few half-hearted attempts to put
it into execution, the Charter had been replaced by a
despotism modeled on the Constitution of the Year VIII,
France would never have recovered from its great panic,
all Europe would have remained in the same state of panic,
no stable balance of power would have been obtained, and
the great wars of 1812, 1813, and 1814 would have achieved
a universal destruction. Would Louis XVIII have the
courage to apply his constitution to the limit? That was
what Alexander should have been anxious about, and not
the degree of liberalism contained in the text.

His infatuation with liberalism was the cause of another
project which was to bring about a great deal of commotion in the Congress. In May the Allies were already aware,
as Gentz tells us, that Alexander was proposing to transform the Duchy of Warsaw into a separate kingdom, and
they were extremely anxious. But Alexander wanted even
more: to endow the new kingdom with a liberal constitution. This plan, which has been considered a hoax by most
historians, appears to have been justified by more serious
reasons. Although contradictory, Napoleon's policy toward
Poland had awakened a latent nationalism, raised all sorts

of hopes, and fired the people's hatred of Germans and Russians. Therefore it was doubtful whether the new Duchy of Warsaw could be turned back into a Russian province except by force. It was no wonder that such an annexation was repugnant to Alexander, who was at the height of his sympathy for liberal ideas in the spring of 1814. At Paris he had been the ardent defender of these ideas; he would have served them to better effect if he had added the argument of example to the good advice he was giving his brother monarchs. But it was only too evident that if it was difficult to introduce representative institutions in France and Germany, it was doubly so in Russia. Alexander would not have dreamed of giving Russia a constitution. Absolute ruler in St. Petersburg and passionate liberal in Paris; the contradiction is obvious and somewhat ridiculous, although, aside from the excesses of imperial hysteria, it was neither absurd nor capricious. A constitutional monarchy in Poland might have minimized the contradiction by proving that the Russian autocrat had done something more than mere words to back up representative institutions, and in a country where they were hardly possible, a country as little westernized as Poland. True, the Kingdom of Poland was nothing but a dream: subsequent events were to prove it. But the dream was a noble one, and, in 1814, Alexander believed in it.

Be that as it may, three days after the proclamation of the Charter, on June 7, the Czar and the Prussian King arrived in London with their suites. They were hailed by huge enthusiastic crowds. In London that month, as in Paris during April, Alexander could well believe himself the liberator of Europe, the *restitutor orbis,* admired, loved, and glorified by high and low. On the one hand, he daily traversed the crowded sections of London, receiving frenzied ovations where the Regent dared not show his face for fear of being whistled at; on the other, he received a doctorate from Oxford as the "defender of the rights of Europe." After so much effort, anguish, and sorrow, he could afford to relax for a while in the sunshine of public acclaim. The brief visit of the two sovereigns was a happy round of banquets and celebrations, which took nearly everybody's mind off politics. But the four ministers of the allied monarchs found time to take several important decisions. The first concerned the Pope. The pontifical sovereign had sent Cardinal Consalvi to London in order to protest against the Treaty of Paris, which gave Avignon to France, and to say that he, the Pope, was not the sovereign but the trustee of the Church states. The sovereign was Jesus Christ; therefore, the Pope could not legally cede what did not belong to him, and all such cessions were null and void. On June 6, the four ministers came to an agreement:

... that His Holiness, in his capacity as a temporal power, should be treated on the same footing as the other states; that consequently, together with the Elector of Hanover, the Elector of Hesse, the King of Sardinia, etc., etc., he should be restored the possessions which had been taken from him without formal cession by him; that, nevertheless, the possessions which had been transferred by formal peace treaty between the predecessor of His Holiness and France should be considered by the allied powers as conquests on the part of France which these powers therefore became authorized to distribute so as to bring about a balance of power in Europe.

Thus, the law of nations, which the Allies wished to revive after the long period of revolutionary subversion, applied to all states, including the Church states. The second decision, taken on June 15, read as follows:

1st. What date shall be designated for the meeting of the plenipotentiaries of the powers in Vienna? It is agreed that a circular be sent to all the participating courts, bearing the invitation to send their plenipotentiaries on August 15 next.

2nd. What arrangement shall be made to work out the continental problems before Congress? Agreed to assemble the plenipotentiaries from the seven courts of Austria, Russia, France, England, Prussia, Spain, and Sweden in a committee

to be charged with presenting the scheme of adjustment for
Europe, according to the plan previously decided upon by the
four courts of Austria, Russia, England, and Prussia.

To this end, their ministers will assemble in Vienna not
later than the first part of August.

But on the day following this announcement, the Czar
declared that he was obliged to return to his Empire and
could not possibly be in Vienna on August 15. This was
a grave complication. A chaotic conglomeration of tempo-
rary situations, immobilized by military occupation and by
waiting for the Congress, Europe seemed threatened from
one day to the next by further catastrophes. The opening
of the Congress had to be hurried as much as possible. On
June 20, the ministers of England, Austria, and Prussia—
the Russian minister was absent—acquiesced to the wishes
of the Czar and decided to postpone the opening of Congress until September 1. But they begged the four great
courts "to enter into a formal and reciprocal agreement
to be in no way prejudiced nor to let anything be prejudiced concerning the intended ultimate adjustments in
Europe, between now and the next meeting of the sovereigns." Two days later, on June 22, Nesselrode sent a note
to Castlereagh giving formal assurance that the Czar would
be in Vienna before September 27, promising that matters would remain as they were until the opening of the
Congress, and requesting that the opening be definitely
fixed for October 1.[5] On the same day the Czar and the
King of Prussia left England.

The ministers remained in London until the thirtieth.
On the twenty-ninth, the Allies agreed to keep up an
army between them of 300,000 men, "in order to safeguard the decisions taken in Vienna and to maintain order
and peace until conditions in Europe have been firmly
established." [6] Keeping 300,000 men under arms during the

---

[5] The minutes of these discussions and negotiations were published by
Dupuis, *op. cit.*, II, 117-120.
[6] D'Angeberg, *op. cit.*, I, 183-184.

Congress, with so many countries occupied, amounted almost to a demobilization. The Allies judged that violence would no longer play a leading part in the events to come. They were in sight of a true and permanent peace.

July saw the return of the monarchs and their ministers to their own countries. Preparations for the Congress would be started in all the great capitals. But meanwhile the atmosphere in Europe was rapidly undergoing a transformation. June was not May, and London was not Paris. The discussion June 16 had elaborated the first secret article of the Paris treaty, the one which stated that the distribution of territories ceded by France would be arranged at the Congress *"in accordance with principles agreed upon by the allied powers among themselves."* The conclusions reached had been: first, that the four allied courts would draw up the final, detailed plan of distribution, filling in the rough sketch of the new European order which had been drawn in the Treaty of Paris; second, that this plan would then be put before the plenipotentiaries of the seven courts—Austria, Prussia, England, France, Russia, Sweden, and Spain—and that they would draw up the "scheme of adjustment." In this way, France, Sweden, and Spain would take part in the distribution, but the Allies would still have a majority vote in the discussions. This insistence on a majority vote probably explains why Portugal was left out, in itself an arbitrary oversight and under no circumstances justifiable.

On June 16, however, the discussions were about Congress procedure only. The most essential prerequisite to peace was the plan, for which the four great powers took on the responsibility and which they claimed the right to initiate. Yet nothing had been settled in London about this important matter. Instead, it had been postponed, and the ministers had agreed to meet in Vienna a couple of weeks before the opening of the Congress on August 15, in order to draw up the plan. The most essential part of the whole business, and it had been postponed. Even more serious had been the fact that the breach between the Allies, begun in Paris over the question of Poland, had considerably widened in London during June. In Paris, only Austria had set herself against Alexander's plans for Poland, but in London, during the celebrations, Metternich had succeeded in winning over the British government to his side and in changing the opinion of the upper classes.

On July 4, Gentz wrote as follows from Vienna:

The change which has occurred, I do not mean in the political principles of the British government, but in their direction and application, I believe to be a factor of the utmost significance. Up till now the exclusive preference shown Russia by England has made itself felt in all the important events of European politics. This preference, which has lasted for a century but which has been enormously strengthened during the last twenty-five years, has been on more than one occasion a great obstacle to any efficacious action against French hegemony. Now that this hegemony has been overthrown, the continuance of such a preference would endanger the balance of power in Europe from another direction. The British cabinet without compromising its relation with Russia, has finally abandoned this exclusive preference. The wisdom of Lord Castlereagh and his colleagues, together with the political virtuosity of Prince Metternich, have won the day, assisted by several personal elements. In my letter of the ninth, I told you about the personal relations between the Russian Emperor and the Regent. Everything I said is absolutely true, and, if you want to know what the mutual feelings of these two sovereigns were for each other upon parting, you have only to double what I said in that letter, and you will be nearer the truth.

The British government will take the same stand with regard to Poland as that of Austria at the Congress. In the English newspapers and even in Parliament, the question of Polish independence has been very favorably received. But this must not be misunderstood. The setting-up of a Polish state *in its entirety,* as before the first partition, is extremely popular with the English, and is one of the favorite themes of the Opposition. As we know, that is not the object of the Czar. He wishes to keep everything he had before the war, and add thereto the former Duchy of Warsaw, which, instead of incorporating it outright as a province, he will rule in some personal connection. As soon as the British understood *this* to be Alexander's scheme for Poland, they turned against him, for they had no intention of supporting such a plan which, without giving real independence to the Poles, would have absolutely no other effect than to make Poland's neighbors uneasy and endanger the peace of Europe. Since this discovery, Alexander has lost the favor even of the liberal party in England, and he will gain no support in this quarter.

At the beginning in London, both the people and the government of England had been well-disposed toward Alexander, recognizing that he had fought against Napoleon with far more energy and courage than Austria. But hardly had peace been declared when discontent, which a long war always provokes among the people, had broken out in England. In spite of victory, or perhaps because of it, the Regent and the Tory government were extremely unpopular. Everywhere a change in the Cabinet was demanded, and the people lost no opportunity to express their dissatisfaction. The presence of Alexander had something to do with this situation; he was acclaimed partly as a hero and partly as a superb contrast to the English Court. Already angered by his disillusionment in Paris and by the opposition his plans were meeting, the rebel Emperor did not have the patience to use tact against the mediocrity of the English Court and government. By a combination of faulty reasoning and an access of egoism, he had been carried away by the popular acclaim. Metternich had taken advantage of this by skillfully playing the irritation of the Regent and government circles against the ambitions of the Czar toward Poland. In this fashion Alexander, therefore, had lost the support of England for his cherished plans.

No less serious difficulties awaited him in Russia. His Empire was preparing to make amends to him, now that the war was over, for the opposition which his adventurous politics at Tilsit had provoked. But Alexander, who had blundered so in London, now gave proof of his contradictory nature by having a brilliant idea. He canceled the triumphal arches which were being put up in his honor, and made the humblest of entries into his Empire. He had won the war, but Russia was bathed in blood and suffering from a hundred wounds. Her finances were wrecked, her most fertile lands devastated, her holy city burned, while hundreds of thousands of graves marked the path of her armies from Moscow to Paris. Alexander might believe that he had saved Europe, but in the presence of so much ruin, he could not feel completely justified in claiming the credit for victory. Moreover, the conflict which had been caused by the war still continued with peace. The bureaucracy and the high nobility which had objected to the French alliance now began to clamor against Alexander's scheme for Poland. They were in favor of outright annexation but had no wish for a Kingdom of Poland outside of Holy Russia and governing itself by representative institutions.

Brief and fleeting are the happy moments of history. Exorcised for a short while, the specter of panic returned to haunt Europe. Vienna was afraid of Alexander's scheme for Poland; and it had managed to communicate its fears to London. And then an even greater dread began to stir the courts of Europe. The honeymoon of the Restoration was already coming to an end. Toward the middle of June, alarming rumors were rife among the Allies concerning the attitude of the French armies which were going home. Metternich, in a continual state of fear, had begun by doubting the success of the Restoration, while watching the entry of Louis XVIII from a window in the rue Montmartre, and ended up by despairing of it after the proclamation of the Charter and his first conversation with Louis a few days later. Metternich's intuition, as usual, was correct. The French King was in a quandary; it was impossible to return to the Old Regime, yet there were great dangers in the liberty he was forced to confer.[7] Article 75 of the Charter had renamed the Legislature but left it intact for the present. Under the Empire, the Senate had suffered from amputation and grafting, but the majority of the new House of Peers consisted of former senators under the Empire. Under Napoleon the two Houses had been the servants of despotism; an illusion of representative government had been kept up, in which the Houses had been commanded to give unanimous and unquestioning approval to every act of the government. But the need of liberty and dignity was so strong that the mutes in the palace had immediately found their tongues, once they had learned that the new ruler was asking them to deliberate. Without any more delay, the new Chamber of Deputies and House of Peers had begun to criticize the government and to clamor for everything that would make the right of opposition a reality in the New Regime, beginning with the freedom of the press. The example set by the two Chambers was followed by the whole country. During May and June a flood of political pamphlets—over two hundred—swept away the censorship, which had not yet been abolished, and the government made no effort to bring it back. In a few weeks the right of opposition became so overwhelming a reality that the Restoration was attacked from all sides by conflicting denunciations. The royalists made use of their freedom by spurning the Charter and maintaining that Louis XVIII should revert to the complete authoritarianism of his ancestors, that equal rights were a revolutionary doctrine, religious tolerance an impiety, the parliamentary system a deadly modernism, and freedom of the press a mistake. In their opinion, a monarchy which possessed a constitution, a parliament, and a Cabinet composed partly of Bonapartists and liberals, whose administration was directed by

[7] Cf. Metternich, *Mémoires*, I, 196-197. This is an extremely important passage.

former officials of the Empire, whose army was commanded by former marshals of Napoleon, a monarchy which allowed revolutionaries in the Chamber of Peers and regicides in the Court of Cassation—was no longer a monarchy. Former members of the Parliament of Paris denounced the Charter as illegal because it had not been recorded in Court of Parliament. An opposition was forming on the right, which called for nothing less than a general purge of the ministries, the dissolution of the armed forces, the re-establishment of the provinces and parliaments as before, and the suppression of all political freedom.

No more reasonable were the leftists. They condemned the Charter as an abuse of royal authority and denied the validity of a Constitution without a reciprocal contract between the King and the people. Besides these, there were also the admirers of what the Empire had done, of its transitory conquests and its theatrical despotism, all those whose interests, position, and future were compromised or threatened. They attacked the Restoration by protesting against the Treaty of Paris and comparing it unfavorably with the grandeur of the Empire. As though Napoleon had been victimized by the Restoration and not by his own fears and mistakes.[8]

The Restoration was passing through a crisis. Metternich was right. But his timidity allowed him to see no other solution but failure, and in this he was mistaken. France and Europe had been put in this dangerous position by the adventure of the Revolution and not by the mistakes of Louis XVIII. The Revolution had been afraid of the liberty which it had promised mankind; and, swept away by its fear to the perpetration of greater abuses of force, it had ended in tyranny—the Terror, the Directory, the Consulate, and the Empire. For twenty years it had been lost in a contradiction which it failed to understand, because its promises had resulted in too many hopes and

---

[8] Capefigue, *Histoire de la Restauration* (Paris, 1842), I, 187 *et seq.*

illusions and its violence had caused too many hates and fears. The shock of all these hopes, illusions, hates, and fears had so falsified standards, obscured the moral issues, confusing right and wrong, and so overthrown the social order and destroyed all logical thought, that for ten years France and Europe had been in a state of chaos. In order to prevent this chaos from exploding, the Revolution had found no other expedient than to put heavier and heavier shackles around it. Now that the Revolution had been overthrown, the constructive mind, whose task is to direct into useful channels the folly inherent in human nature, was faced for the first time with a problem which presented a frightful contradiction. In order to deal wisely and humanely with the frenzy let loose by so many adventures, it was first necessary to break the bonds with which the Revolution, in its terror, had bound it. But once these bonds had been broken, the frenzy would again be loosed upon mankind with even greater violence than before. The problem was whether the constructive mind would be able to canalize this new frenzy. Metternich maintained that it was impossible, that only failure could result. His lack of confidence blinded him to the one solution, which lay in the courage of a king, a great king, who was able to overcome the problem, at the risk of his own position.

That great king was Louis XVIII. He wished the monarchy to succeed where the Revolution had failed, giving France the right of opposition not only on paper but also in actual practice. He succeeded because he had courage; and he had courage, because, unlike Napoleon and the Directory, he refused to heed the sinister advice of fear: "By suppressing the opposition, you will stifle the discontent which causes so many fears and dangers and which proceeds from that opposition." The question rises: why did he have the courage which the Revolution and Napoleon lacked? The answer lies not in personal bravery, which alone would have meant little, but in the fact that his authority was a legitimate one. He was courageous because he was not afraid of his power, as Napoleon and the Directory had been afraid of theirs. He was not afraid of it because he had not usurped it either by a surprise attack or other violent measures, by a fraudulent election, or by a subterfuge. He had inherited it from his ancestors in accordance with a law which France had held sacred for centuries and which was still sacred to a majority of Frenchmen. He knew that he had a legal right to the throne and that this right was recognized by France. That was why he had treated Alexander, who on several occasions had dared to question that right, as an insignificant second-class sovereign. That was why he had not wanted to be the executor of the Revolution's will and had granted the nation a Charter in his own right. And finally, that was why, after having granted the Charter, he now had the courage, unlike the Revolution, to put it into execution. The blunders with which historians have reproached him and the tremendous service he rendered France and Europe after 1814, both come from the same source—the legitimacy of his authority. That is the one great lesson to be learned from the entire story of the Revolution: liberty is only possible under a legitimate government, whether it be monarchic or republican.

IX

THE FIRST CONFLICT:
PRINCIPLE VS. EXPEDIENCY

———————————————— ⇥»«⇤ ————————————————

The French monarch's plenipotentiary arrived in Vienna on September 23. His visiting cards informed Europe that Louis XVIII had not sent the prince de Benevento to Vienna but the prince de Talleyrand. The European aristocracy, which had been saved from the Revolution, was about to hold court; as a product of the Revolution, the principality of Benevento would have been considered a bastard in Vienna. The peace negotiators were all princes of the Old Regime; in such illustrious company, therefore, it was important that the representative of France should not lower the standard.

Prince Talleyrand was at the head of a delegation which included the comte Alexis de Noailles, the duc de Dalberg, the marquis de la Tour du Pin-Gouvernet, and Messrs. La Besnardière, Challaye, Formond, and Perrey. His niece, the comtesse Edmond de Périgord, accompanied him; she was to act as the hostess of his establishment in Vienna during the Congress. The Court of Vienna had prepared both a magnificent hospitality and an invisible surveillance for the emperors, kings, and princes who were coming to attend the Congress. Baron Francis Hager, Chief of Police, was to receive daily reports from his agents on what each illustrious guest said or did. Daily he was to read their correspondence. The French delegation in particular was subjected to a surveillance worthy of its importance. But the Vienna police, far from stupid, were not to be dazzled by the celebrities on this delegation. They lost no time in discovering a suspicious individual in the retinue. This was a certain Sigismond Neukomm, an Austrian from Salzburg, a composer and pianist, who since 1809 had been living with Talleyrand and whom the latter had brought along. A pianist attending a Congress convoked to reconstruct Europe? Metternich took fright: he smelled a plot somewhere. Orders were given for a strict surveillance of the musician.[1]

Talleyrand had received his instructions, contained in a long document drawn up by him in agreement with the King which Louis had signed. The title was: "Instructions for the King's ambassador to the Congress." [2] What were these instructions? They were an excellent plan to reduce the chaos in Europe and the order which was to replace it to three simple principles that were clear and coherent; and a plan to apply those principles to several vital interests of France. Of the three, two were already familiar. The other had been officially recognized in the decision taken in London on June 6 by the ministers of the four great powers concerning the claims of the Pope. They are formulated as follows in the Instructions:

The European nations do not live under moral or natural law alone but also under a law which they have invented and which gives the first law a sanction which it would otherwise lack; a law established by written conventions or by customs

---

[1] This curious story about Neukomm is taken from police reports, published by Commandant M. H. Weil: *Les dessous du Congrès de Vienne* (Paris: Payot & Cie., 1917), I, 114, 130, 135, 136, 352, 369, 372.
[2] These were published in his *Mémoires*, II, 214 *et seq.*

which are constantly, universally, and mutually observed, based always on mutual consent, whether expressed or tacit, and obligatory for all. This law is the law of nations.

This law has two fundamental principles. One is that sovereignty cannot be acquired by the simple act of conquest, nor be transferred to the conquerer, if the sovereign does not cede it willingly. The other is that no title of sovereignty, and consequently the law which proceeds therefrom, has any reality for other states, unless they recognize it.

In every case in which a conquered country possesses a sovereign, cession is possible, and it follows from the first principle cited that there exists no substitute or supplement for cession.

.   .   .   .

A sovereign whose dominions are conquered (if he is an actual person, not merely a title) does not lose his sovereignty unless he cedes his right to the throne or abdicates, but loses only the actual possession through conquest and consequently preserves the right to do everything not implied by possession. The fact that he may send representatives to the Congress is an indication of this right, for in so doing he may claim possession.

In other words, conquest is not enough to create sovereignty; the cession of the preceding sovereign is required; the countries annexed to France by unilateral action of the revolutionary governments had never lost their original sovereigns and must be restored at once. As a matter of fact, this had already been accomplished. But what was to be done with the countries which no longer had sovereigns, either because the sovereign had disappeared, as in the Republic of Genoa, or because the sovereign had renounced his sovereignty without ceding it to another sovereign? In this category were all the countries which the Revolution had annexed to France after regular treaties of cession and which France had given up by the Treaty of Paris without ceding them to another state. An unprecedented situation existed: half of Europe was without government. Since conquest did not create sovereignty, the allied powers could not transfer to a new sovereignty the sovereignty which they did not possess. It was necessary to create a new sovereignty out of nothing; yet who possessed this transcendent power? Here is the solution proposed by the Instructions for this novel case—the third principle, the law of nations, which is established as a preliminary to reconstruction.

But a conquered nation can be without a sovereign, either because the former sovereign has abdicated his rights, for himself and all his heirs, without ceding them, or because the reigning family has become extinct and no legitimate successor has been chosen. In the case of a republic, the moment it is conquered, the sovereign ceases to exist, for his nature is such that freedom is a necessary condition to his existence, and it is an absolute impossibility for him to be free for a single instant while the conquest lasts.
Cession by the sovereign in this case is therefore impossible.
Does it follow that the right of conquest can be prolonged indefinitely or can be converted by its own efforts into the right of sovereignty? Not at all.
Sovereignty is to the general society of Europe what private property is to a particular civil society. A country or a state under conquest and without a sovereign, as a piece of property without an owner, is a vacant estate, but forming part of territory which is not vacant; consequently it is under the jurisdiction of that territory's law and acquirable only under that law, namely: private property is regulated by the civil law of the particular state in which it is located, and the country or the state is regulated by the law of nations, which is the general law of the territory forming the common domain of Europe. It is one of the principles of this law that the sovereignty cannot be transferred by the mere fact of conquest. Therefore, when cession by the sovereign is impossible, it is of the utmost importance that it be supplied. Therefore, this can be done only by the sanction of Europe.

What is the meaning of this passage? Merely that the fate of the countries lacking a sovereign since the Treaty of Paris was to be decided by the whole of Europe met in

Congress. In these Instructions, Europe became what it had never been before: an almost mystical union of states which, like the pope and the emperor in the Middle Ages, had the power, when met in Congress, to recognize or create the right of sovereignty. This was a new law, one not covered by the law of nations. Where did it come from? What were its sources, foundations, limits? The Instructions do not go into details; they merely add to the two preceding principles, long familiar, the superior law of Europe, without either justifying or defining it.

There is no doubt but that Talleyrand, under cover of the law of nations, was executing a flank attack on the first secret article of the Treaty of Paris. We have seen how, unable to agree, after several weeks, on the division of territory recovered from France, the powers had tried to reconcile the law of nations, which required the signature and the consent of France to each individual cession of territory, with the wishes of the Allies not to let France take advantage of the freedom of action given her by the peace treaty and make too many difficulties. We saw what arrangement was made: France yielded her rights of sovereignty, suzerainty, and possession for all the territory; and she promised to accept "the decisions made in Vienna, according to principles agreed upon by the powers among themselves." But, according to the precise letter of the law, the arrangement was contradictory. As soon as France had renounced her rights of sovereignty, she could no longer transfer to the future sovereigns of her territories what she no longer possessed. The Allies in their turn could not transfer what they had never possessed. With the first secret article, the eighteenth-century law of nations had ceased to be applicable. Talleyrand, in agreement with Louis XVIII, was taking advantage of the contradiction by an attempt to put the countries in question in the same category as the countries without rulers, and to unify the whole of Europe into a superior authority that would decide their fate. The purpose of this attempt was obvious. The King and his minister wanted to wrest from the allied powers the exclusive decision on the distribution of this territory and to justify the intervention of France and the other states in the common and legitimate interests of France and Europe.

But beyond this political goal, which was in any case a legitimate one, Talleyrand and Louis XVIII aspired to a higher, almost metaphysical one. It is the task of the constructive mind to define and impose the principles which are to govern relations between states. But principles cannot be imposed unless they achieve some stability; and they cannot achieve stability unless they are based on something stable. Now principles only exist in and act through the human mind—its intelligence and will; the human mind is by nature eternally variable since it consists of a series of states of mind which follow each other without interruption. How can the eternally variable be fixed on at least a few essential points? That is the almost superhuman task which the constructive mind has to accomplish. Each state manages to fix roughly some rules and principles in its interior, by issuing edicts graven on stone or bronze, or written on paper, and to create an organization which compels their observance. In relations between states, everything is left to self-discipline of the passions, interests, and the strength which each state possesses—states of mind which are always mobile, and which can affirm and interpret principles with the unrestrained arbitrariness of their freedom. During the Middle Ages in Europe, there had been one stable point in the midst of all the confusion, and that was the pope. But Europe was no longer in the Middle Ages. Knowing that interests and passions, if given a free rein, would throw the Congress into a chaos of contradictory principles and their interpretations, Talleyrand and Louis XVIII wanted to constitute a superior authority, which might establish both the principles and their interpretation with a certain coherence and stability, might resolve the insoluble problem of stabilizing that which is variable by nature. And they had thought of a union of the European states, large and small, all of whom sincerely desired to effect the reconstruction of the European order.

An adroit maneuver and a noble vision, both of which, however, were vulnerable. Were the territories under discussion really vacant? The law of nations considered those territories vacant over which no state could claim any right, either of suzerainty, or sovereignty, or even of possession. The four allied courts had no more than a right of possession over these territories analogous to the right which France had exercised over territories annexed without cession. Moreover, would a law invented by Talleyrand and Louis XVIII, which was as new and vague as the law of Europe, have a chance to be recognized and applied in Vienna? If Talleyrand and his King were deluding themselves, their delusion did not last for long in the atmosphere of Vienna. The plenipotentiaries of Austria (Metternich), Prussia (Hardenberg and Humboldt), Great Britain (Castlereagh), and Russia (Nesselrode), who had preceded him to Vienna, had taken the following decisions the day before his arrival on the twenty-second of September.

1. That only the four powers can decide among themselves on the distribution of states (countries) which have become disposable as a result of the last war and the peace of Paris, but that the two other powers must be admitted in order that they may give their opinions and make, if they think it necessary, their objections, which will then be discussed with them;

2. That, in order not to deviate from this line of conduct, the plenipotentiaries of the four powers will not enter into conference with the two others on this subject, until they have come to a final decision, with perfect agreement among themselves, on each of the three points regarding the territorial distribution of the Duchy of Warsaw, Germany, and Italy.

These decisions were justified, in the protocol of the Conference, as follows:

The disposition of the conquered provinces falls naturally to the powers whose efforts have brought about their conquest. This principle has been sanctioned by the Treaty of Paris itself, and the Court of France has already consented to it; for the secret first article of the Treaty of Paris says in the most definite manner, "that the disposition which must be made of the territories will be determined at the Congress according to principles agreed upon by the allied powers among themselves." The terms "agreed upon" and "agreed upon among themselves," clearly show that there is no question here of simple distribution, or of discussions in which France would have a part. Nor is it stated where and how these principles are to be determined, and it would be an entirely arbitrary and unjust interpretation, if it should be maintained that this had been understood to refer only to the contents of the treaty already existing between the Allies.

But, since France is now under a legitimate government, the four powers do not mean to banish either her or Spain from all discussion on the distribution of the territories, inasmuch as these powers have a particular interest in it, or rather it is to the interest of all Europe, whereas they would have set France aside from it, had peace been concluded with Napoleon.

Thus, of the three alternatives which offered themselves on this point—not to be admitted at all, not to be admitted until the other parties have come to an agreement among themselves, or to accept in advance what the others would decide on —the second is obviously the one which France has a right to claim, but to which she must confine herself.

In any event, it would be extremely inconvenient to follow any other course of action. If France is not admitted until the four powers have come to a mutual understanding, she will nonetheless raise all the objections which she considers necessary to her own security and to the general interest of Europe; but she will not go beyond that.

If, on the other hand, she takes part in the preliminary discussions, she will take sides for or against each separate question, whether it touches her own interests or not. She will favor or oppose this or that prince, according to her own point of view; and the little rulers of Germany will take that as their cue to recommence the whole business of intrigues and cabals which in large part is responsible for the tragedy of the last few years.

That is why it is of the utmost importance not to confer with the French plenipotentiaries until the matter has been definitely concluded.[3]

The decisions taken at Vienna were therefore contradictory to those of Paris and London. In Paris, during May, the Allies had been satisfied with extracting a promise from France that she would accept the *principles agreed upon* by the Allies for the reconstruction of Europe. Spain, Portugal, and Sweden were to have a share in this determination. The reciprocal engagement had been rather vague and had left both France and the Allies a wide choice of action. In London, during June, the four allied powers had determined to decide upon a preliminary plan for the distribution and then communicate this plan to France, Spain, and Sweden—Portugal being left out. Whereupon these three would join the Allies in preparing the actual scheme of adjustment for Europe, basing it on the preliminary draft.

This arrangement still seemed to give France an important part to play. But in the resolutions of September 22, the following changes occurred: it was Sweden's turn to be completely eliminated; Spain was allowed to discuss only her own interests; while as for France, she was not permitted to present her views until after the four great powers had reached an agreement. During the three-months' interlude, France and the Allies had drifted in opposite directions. France had turned to Europe in an attempt to identify her interests with those of the Continent as a whole, while the Allies had drawn away from Europe into their own exclusive group. Even more serious

3 D'Angeberg, *op. cit.*, pp. 249-251.

was the sentence which read: "The disposition of the conquered provinces falls naturally to the powers whose efforts have brought about their conquest." By disposition is meant the attribution of sovereignty. The meaning is clear: the Allies assumed the right, through conquest, to dispose of the lands to which France had surrendered all claims. The eighteenth-century law of nations was contravened and the principle of sovereignty created by conquest adopted. Talleyrand had brought from Paris the idea of a superior law of Europe, which had yet to be defined and justified. To this, the Allies were opposing the pseudo law of *force majeure*, which the Revolution had abused to such an extent that the balance of power in Europe had been destroyed. What was the explanation for this sudden change?

Above all, the question of Alexander and Poland. If Alexander had been in the same frame of mind in September as he had been in May, it is unlikely that he would have assented to the resolutions taken on the twenty-second. He would even have been able to prevent them by aligning himself with Castlereagh, who had made certain reservations. But he wanted the Duchy of Warsaw, and Austria, along with England, stood in his way. Inasmuch as both his throne and his person would have been in danger if he failed to obtain for Russia a territorial gain of this magnitude, Alexander had sent Nesselrode to Vienna in August in order to prepare the ground. In the latter's instructions, the following passage occurs:

The Duchy of Warsaw is mine by right of conquest from Napoleon's Empire. The entire Continent of Europe had been in league against me, when I repulsed a most unjust aggression. Nevertheless, I did not hesitate to come to the aid of these same powers with an effort equal to that which had saved Russia. Now that victory has enabled the principal states of Europe to be reconstituted as they were before the last wars of Bonaparte and even enabled several of them to gain important acquisitions, it is only fair that my subjects be indemnified for so many sacrifices and that a buffer state guard them forever from the dangers of a new invasion.[4]

The rule of might as an excuse for sovereignty was there affirmed. Since he had conquered and was still in possession of Poland, his reluctant Allies did not contest his claim too vigorously, although the principle it invoked was the most dangerous of all for Europe. It was not surprising, therefore, that Nesselrode, seeing his master in such a frame of mind, voted for the resolutions of September 22, dragging along with him Metternich, Hardenberg, and Humboldt, over the reservations of Castlereagh. This suited Alexander's purpose with regard to conquered Poland.

But to the question of Poland was allied the problem of Saxony. In order to obtain Poland, Alexander had promised the Kingdom of Saxony to Prussia in exchange for that part of Poland which had formerly belonged to Prussia. Saxony, alone among the small German states which had supported Napoleon, had remained faithful to him until the bitter end. When the Congress convened, she was still occupied by allied troops, and her King was almost a prisoner. But, according to the law of nations, it was necessary to obtain the King's consent to the transfer of his sovereignty to Prussia. And what if he should refuse it? The Instructions of Louis XVIII to his plenipotentiaries peremptorily ordered them to demand the preservation of the King of Saxony and his kingdom.[5] In short, the law of nations was becoming a real threat to the Czar's plans for Poland. Alexander, in one of his abrupt changes, decided that he would resort to threats and even to violence, in the true Napoleonic manner, if his wishes with regard to Poland were not met in Vienna. The law of nations, which he had wanted to revive as far back as 1804 and which he had invoked in Paris before the peace treaty,

[4] K. Lutostanski, Le Partage de la Pologne et la lutte pour l'indépendance (Lausanne: Payot & Cie., 1918), p. 345.
[5] Talleyrand, Mémoires, II, 219, 245.

might go to the devil if it stood in his way. The resolutions of September 22 were a declaration to the world that the Emperor of Russia had changed camps.

The defection of Alexander was the more serious in that it was bound up with a general shift in the trend of thought. On going home, the allied sovereigns and their ministers had missed the exuberant atmosphere in Paris during the months of April and May—the atmosphere of wisdom, of confidence, and of courage out of which had come the Treaty of Paris. The ephemeral but dazzling victories of the Revolution had made a deep impression on the new generation. No more than a small minority of intelligent people remembered the law of nations of the Old Regime as a code of wisdom necessary to build a peace on firm foundations. In London, Berlin, and Vienna, not everyone had been satisfied by the Paris treaty. People who had not been in Paris during those two miraculous months considered it too lenient. Moreover, during the interlude between the signing of the treaty and the opening of the Congress, the vultures of covetousness and greed had been flocking around the bodies of the vacant countries. Every state, both large and small, had fond dreams of carving out for itself at no risk a good portion of rulerless Europe, after the fashion followed during the wars of the Revolution; and all these dreams were indulged in without restraint, for the secret articles of the Paris treaty were known only to a very small group of people. Europe as a whole was unaware that the Congress would not be in a position to dispose of vacant territories as it wished, and that certain questions of principle had been settled in Paris which brought the great powers together. And so, during the interlude, all sorts of impossible plans had been made, impossible because they contradicted the Paris treaty. At the Court of the Grand Duchy of Baden, a Kingdom of Helvetia was envisioned, modeled after the Kingdom of Westphalia. In Berlin, there was discussion of a plan to join Switzerland by a perpetual alliance to the German Confederation which was to replace the Holy Roman Empire. In Germany, the proposal was put forth to transfer the House of Württemberg to Switzerland. All sorts of projects were being fomented not only in the Court of Bavaria but also in the little courts which had escaped invasion by Napoleon. Turin, unaware that Lombardy had become the property of Austria, was beginning to hope that the Kingdom of Sardinia would be able to expand east, toward Lombardy, or south toward Tuscany.[6] The Archduke Francesco d'Este was looking forward to the recovery of Spezzia.[7] The former Grand Duke of Tuscany, Ferdinand III, although the brother of the Austrian Emperor, was not yet certain of recovering his former state, because of complications which we shall see later. But he had every intention of claiming it, with the addition of Lunigiana, Lucca, Piombino, and a number of imperial fiefs.[8] Even the Pope did not confine himself to claiming his former states, both the ceded portions and those not ceded, including Avignon: he was also considering whether he should not take advantage of the opportunity and lay claim to the Duchy of Parma.

In short, Talleyrand found a secret hostility in Vienna against the spirit which had seemed to triumph in Paris. On September 25 he wrote to his King: "In Vienna the language of reason and moderation is no longer to be heard from the lips of the plenipotentiaries...." Moreover, nothing was in readiness for the Congress, the responsibility for which Talleyrand seems to attribute to Metternich. On September 29 he wrote to Louis:

Unfortunately, the man who has charge of things in Austria, and who pretends to control them in Europe, considers the surest sign of superior genius to be an instability which, on the one hand, verges on the ridiculous, and, on the other,

[6] N. Bianchi, *Storia documentata della diplomazia europea in Italia* (Turin: Unione, 1865), I, 48 *et seq.*
[7] *Ibid.*, pp. 43-44.
[8] *Ibid.*, p. 38.

becomes, in the minister of a great state and under such circumstances, a calamity.[9]

This judgment is so severe that there must have been a more important reason for it than incompatibility of temperaments or clash of interests. Perhaps the developments of the Congress will reveal it to us.

On the twenty-fifth, Alexander made his entry into Vienna accompanied by the Prussian King, and no sooner had he arrived than he sent for Talleyrand. A private audience was arranged for October 1. Talleyrand was looking forward to October 1 more on account of his audience than of the opening of the Congress, which seemed to have been postponed indefinitely. Then, on the morning of September 30, he received a brief note from Metternich asking him, in Metternich's name alone, to be present at a preliminary conference at two o'clock in the latter's house, where he would find the ministers of Prussia, England, and Russia assembled. Metternich added that he was sending a similar invitation to M. de Labrador, the minister of Spain. Gentz tells us that the purpose of this conference was to make France and Spain accept the resolutions of September 22.[10] What took place at this first meeting has been described by Talleyrand in a long letter to Louis on October 4. As his letter has been confirmed by the splendid report drawn up by Gentz, who was present,[11] I reproduce it in the original text:

The words, "be present" and "assembled," were obviously intentional. I answered that I would be delighted to come and see him with the ministers of Russia, England, *Spain,* and Prussia.

The invitation received by M. de Labrador was conceived in the same terms as the one I had received, with the difference

9 Cf. *Correspondance inédite du prince de Talleyrand et du roi Louis XVIII* (Paris: E. Plon & Cie., 1881), p. 9.

10 Gentz, *op. cit.,* I, 108.

11 The twelfth of his *Dépêches inédites* (I, 107-118). It bears out every point in Talleyrand's letter and amplifies certain points.

that it was written in the third person and sent in the name
of Metternich and *his colleagues.*

As M. de Labrador had come to show it to me and ask my
advice on what reply he should make, I showed him mine, and
he drew up a similar one, in which France was mentioned *with
and before* the other powers. Both M. de Labrador and myself thus brought together what the others seemed to want to
separate, and we separated what they evidently wanted to keep
together in an exclusive group.

I arrived before two o'clock, and found the ministers of
the four courts already assembled about a long table. Lord
Castlereagh was at one end and appeared to be presiding;
at the other sat a man whom M. de Metternich introduced to
me as the secretary for their conferences: it was M. de Gentz.

.   .   .   .

The Portuguese ambassador, the Count of Palmella, having
been informed by Lord Castlereagh that there were to be
preliminary conferences at which M. de Labrador and I were
to be present, and to which he would not be invited, thought
himself obliged to protest against an exclusion which he considered both unjust and humiliating to the crown of Portugal.
Consequently, he wrote a letter to Lord Castlereagh, which
the latter produced at the conference. His reasons were strong
and well deduced. He demanded that the eight powers which
had signed the Treaty of Paris, and not only six of those
powers, should form the preparatory committee which was to
put into action the Congress whose assembly they had stipulated. M. de Labrador and I seconded this demand: an inclination to accede to it was displayed, but the decision was
adjourned to the next meeting. Sweden has not yet sent a
plenipotentiary, and consequently has not yet been in a position to make a demand.

"The object of today's conference," said Lord Castlereagh
to me, "is to acquaint you with what has been done by the
four courts since we have been here." And, addressing himself
to M. de Metternich, "You have the protocol." M. de Metternich then gave me a paper signed by himself, Count Nesselrode, Lord Castlereagh, and Prince Hardenberg. The word
"Allies" had been used in every paragraph of this document.
I remarked on the fact, saying that it caused me to wonder

where we were at, whether we were still at Chaumont or Laon, whether peace had not been made, and whether we were involved in a quarrel with someone. All replied that they did not attribute to the word "Allies" any meaning contrary to the actual state of relations between us, and that they had only used it for brevity's sake. Upon which I made it clear that however valuable brevity might be, it was not worth the cost of inexactitude.

As for the contents of the protocol, it was a web of metaphysical reasonings which attempted to assert the value of claims still based on treaties unknown to us. To discuss these reasonings and claims was to dive into a sea of dispute; I realized that it was necessary to reject the whole thing with a peremptory argument; I read several paragraphs and then said: "I do not understand." I read them again sedately, with the look of a man who seeks to penetrate the meaning of something; and I said that I did not understand any better. I added: "For me, there are two dates with nothing between them: May 30, when the assembly of Congress was stipulated, and October 1, when it is to meet. Everything which has been done in the interval is unknown to me and does not exist for me." The plenipotentiaries' reply was that they cared little about the document, and they did not in the last mind eliminating it, which led to an observation from M. de Labrador that, nevertheless, they had signed it. They took it back, M. de Metternich put it away, and there was no further question of it.

After having withdrawn that document, they produced another. It was the draft of a declaration which M. de Labrador and I were to sign with them if we accepted it. Following a long preamble on the necessity for simplifying and abbreviating the task of the Congress, and protestations that they had no desire to impinge on anyone's rights, the declaration asserted that the questions before the Congress were to be divided into two parts, for each of which a committee was to be formed, to which the interested states could address themselves, and that when the two committees had completed all the work, the Congress would then be assembled for the first time, and everything would be submitted to its sanction.

This declaration was obviously intended to put the four

allied powers in absolute control of all the operations of the
Congress. Assuming that the six principal powers would constitute themselves judges of questions relative to the composi-
tion of the Congress, to the problems it must settle, to the
procedures to be followed in settling them, to the sequence in
which they are to be settled, and assuming that these powers
would alone have the naming of the committees which would
have to prepare everything—then France and Spain would be
always two against four, even supposing that they would
always be of the same opinion on every question.

I declared that a first reading was not sufficient to form an
opinion on a project of this nature; that it required consideration, and that above all it was necessary to be certain that
it was compatible with rights which we all had every intention
of respecting; that we had come in order to guarantee everyone's rights, and that it would be unfortunate if we began by
violating them; that the idea of settling everything before the
Congress assembled was a new one to me—the proposal to
finish with what I thought it was necessary to begin with;
that perhaps the authority which it was proposed to confer
on the six powers, could only be given to them by the Congress; and that there were some measures which irresponsible
ministers might easily adopt, but that Lord Castlereagh and
I were in quite a different position. Here Lord Castlereagh
said that the opinions which I expressed had all occurred to
him, and that he appreciated their weight; but, he added,
what other expedient could be found to prevent inextricable
delays? I asked why the Congress could not be assembled
then and there, and what difficulties this would involve. Each
one thereupon brought up a difficulty and a general conversation ensued. The name of the King of Naples having been
brought up by someone, M. de Labrador expressed his opinion of him without reserve. As for me, I merely said: "Which
King of Naples are we discussing? We do not recognize the
man in question." And upon M. de Humboldt's remarking that
certain powers had recognized him and guaranteed his states,
I replied in a firm and cold tone: "Those who gave him his
guarantees should not and consequently could not have done
so." And in order not to prolong too much the effect that such
a manner had truly and visibly produced, I added: "But that

is not the point now." Then, returning to the matter of the Congress, I said that the difficulties they seemed to fear might be less formidable than they thought, and that by seeking one could surely find a way to obviate them. Prince Hardenberg announced that he was no more in favor of that expedient than of any other, but that one must be found to prevent the princes of Leyen and Lichtenstein from taking part in the general adjustments in Europe. Upon that, the meeting was adjourned to the second day after, and a promise made to send copies of the declaration and the letter of Count Palmella to me as well as to M. de Labrador.

Thus, at the very first contact, there was a clash between the Instructions of the King of France and the resolutions of September 22. The most striking thing about this first clash was the weakness of the Allies. They were the victors, they occupied the whole of Europe with their armies; yet, at the first objection, they withdrew their first proposal and produced a second, milder one; this one having been likewise rejected, they put everything off until October 2. Talleyrand was perfectly aware of this weakness, and he immediately took the offensive. On October 1, instead of waiting for the meeting appointed for the following day, he sent a note to the ministers of the five powers in which he maintained that only the Congress had the right to make decisions; the eight powers who had signed the Treaty of Paris were qualified to act only as a committee delegated to prepare the questions which Congress should decide, and to propose the formation of committees which it would be judged expedient to establish.[12] The pseudo law of force was emphatically denied, the superior law of Europe reaffirmed, but without any justification. After this he went to the audience which the Emperor had fixed. Here is the report of this historic conversation which he himself sent to the King.

When I approached him, he shook hands; but his look was not at all as affectionate as usual; his speech was curt, his

[12] *Correspondance inédite*, p. 17.

manner serious and even a bit solemn. I saw clearly that he was going to play a part.

"First of all," he said, "what is the condition of your country?"

"As good as Your Majesty could wish, and better than one would have dared to hope."

"Public sentiment?"

"It gets better every day."

"Liberal ideas?"

"There are more of them in France than anywhere else."

"But freedom of the press?"

"It is re-established with only a few restrictions imposed by circumstances; they will cease in two years and, until then, will not prevent anything that is good and useful from being published."

"The army?"

"It is completely behind the King. One hundred and thirty thousand men are in active service, and three hundred thousand more could join them at the first call."

"The marshals?"

"Which, Sire?"

"Oudinot?"

"He is devoted to the King."

"Soult?"

"He began by being a trifle moody; he has been made governor of Vendée and he is behaving beautifully; he has made himself liked and appreciated."

"Ney?"

"He misses his endowments a little; Your Majesty could remedy that."

"The two Chambers? It seems to me that there is opposition there."

"One always finds it in a deliberative assembly; opinions may differ, but feelings are unanimous; and in the difference of opinion, that of the government always has a great majority."

"But there is disaffection?"

"Who has been telling Your Majesty such tales? What more certain proof can one have that everything is aiming for the same goal, when, after twenty-five years of Revolution, the

King finds himself as well established in a few months as if he had never left France."

"What of your own position?"

"The confidence and kindness of the King surpass all my hopes."

"Now let us talk of our own affairs; they must be concluded here."

"That depends upon Your Majesty. They will be concluded promptly and happily if Your Majesty will show the same nobility and greatness of soul that you showed in France."

"But everyone must follow the rule of expediency."

"And everyone must obtain his rights."

"I shall keep what I have occupied."

"Your Majesty will want to keep only what legitimately belongs to you."

"I am in agreement with the other great powers."

"I do not know whether Your Majesty includes France among these powers."

"Yes, certainly; but if you do not want everyone to be guided by expediency, where do you stand?"

"I place rights above expediency."

"What is expedient for Europe is right."

"Sire, these words are not yours; they are strangers which your heart denies."

"No, I repeat: what is expedient for Europe is right."

Thereupon I turned toward the wall, which was near me; I leaned my head on it, and, striking the wainscotting, I cried out: "Europe! Unfortunate Europe." Then, turning back to the Emperor: "Shall it be said," I asked him, "that you have destroyed it?"

He replied: "Rather a war than to give up what I have occupied."

I let my arms fall; and, in the grieved but decisive attitude of a man who seemed to say, the fault will not be ours, I remained silent. For several moments the Emperor did not break the silence; then he repeated:

"Yes, rather a war." I kept the same attitude. Then, lifting his hands and waving them about as I had never seen him do before, in a manner which reminded me of the concluding passage of Marcus Aurelius's Eulogy, he shouted rather than said:

"It is time for the play; I have promised the Emperor to be there, and they are waiting for me." And he went off; then, with the door open, he came back and embraced me with both arms, saying in a voice which was no longer his:

"Good-by, good-by! We shall meet again." During the whole of this conversation, only the most important part of which I have set down for Your Majesty, Poland and Saxony were not once mentioned outright, but only referred to by circumlocution. The Emperor implied Saxony when he referred to those who have betrayed the cause of Europe. Which put me in a position to answer, "Sire, that is a question of date." And, after a slight pause, I was able to add, "And also the result of difficulties, into which one might have been thrown by force of circumstance."

Expediency makes right. There we have the unbalanced genius, of whom Talleyrand made such good use in the peace treaty, completely in the opposite camp. His defection was a universal tragedy. Talleyrand concludes his long account of the conversation on a pessimistic note: "Your Majesty must see that our position here is a difficult one; and it may grow even more difficult from day to day." He was right; there could be more hope of counting on Alexander. The Czar had arrived in Vienna furious against Metternich, whose fall he desired, and very distrustful of France and England, counting only on the Prussian King, who was more devoted and submissive than ever. And he had arrived in a kind of erotic frenzy—which would also have its repercussions. Vienna had become the headquarters for the loveliest women of Europe's aristocracy. A huge carnival celebrating peace was swelling the ranks of those come to attend the Congress. Alexander was thirty-seven. He expected to take advantage of the freedom which the peace carnival granted even to the most august crowned heads of Europe! Indeed, he had not wasted any time. He had arrived on September 25; on October 2, the police

were already informing Baron Hager that the Czar had
visited Princess Bagration the night of the thirtieth, and
that she had received him alone in her bedroom *en nég-
ligée*. *Honi soit qui mal y pense* was the classic remark
which concluded the secret report of the police on this interview.[13] *"Le bel ange un,"* as she was known in Vienna
because of her daringly low-cut gowns, was a morsel fit
for a king, and the Czar had only had a taste, though without any difficulty. In Dresden, the Princess had been the
mistress of Metternich, who had abandoned her for the
Duchess of Sagan. The Duchess was also in Vienna, along
with her lovers, among whom Metternich seemed to be the
only permanent fixture. The quarrel between Alexander
and the Chancellor, already serious, was to be aggravated
by the harebrained jealousies of the two fair ladies.

For the moment, there was nothing Talleyrand could do
but to wait for his note to take effect. The Prussians and
Russians had become angry and had accused France of
wanting to provoke a war so that she could recover the
left bank of the Rhine. Without going quite so far, Castlereagh had complained that Talleyrand's note had given an
official stamp to a purely informal conference. On the evening of October 4, Metternich delivered to Talleyrand, in
the parlor of the fair Duchess of Sagan, a revised declaration drawn up by Castlereagh. The new declaration stated
that the proposals made by the Allies were the direct result of the first secret article of the Treaty of Paris.[14] The
next day Talleyrand replied with a long letter, in which
he declared:

Nothing would be better than for the signatory powers to
the Treaty of Paris to form a committee of discussion, providing that the powers given this committee be within the bounds
of justice. That committees be formed to carry out the decisions would be most suitable; and, instead of two, I would
even suggest three: one for Italy, another for distributing ter-

13 Weil, *op. cit.*, no. 232, 233.
14 *Correspondance inédite*, pp. 26-27.

ritory in Germany, and a third for the latter's federal constitution.

But I still find it necessary for the committees to be chosen with the consent of the Congress. The reason that law and order are so much admired and respected in England is because they are native products.

It would be altogether different if they had been imposed from outside. In the same way, Europe will stand by the arrangements that are made, and these arrangements will be permanent only if they proceed from the general will.

If my plan is followed, a permanent solution will be reached. On the other hand, if the signatory powers to the Treaty of Paris take upon themselves to decide everything in advance, leaving the Congress nothing to do but to approve, then the accusation will be forthcoming that among the powers there were four who, by their union, formed a constant majority which had given them absolute authority in the preparations committee, and also that, by their individual and collective influence, they had then forced the approval of the Congress, so that it was their own will which had become the law of Europe.[15]

The superior law of Europe over the vacant territories, which in the Instructions had been so vague, began to take shape and to justify itself in this letter. It was specified and justified as a prerequisite to the stability of Europe, which everyone desired. Substantially, this is what Talleyrand meant: "Europe is a system of states which must exist together in harmony and balance. But these states are living entities. Stability among these living entities cannot be imposed externally by the strength of one more powerful state or group of states, according to their will. It must answer the vital needs of all the states. It is in order not to mistake these vital needs, that all Europe must concur in the establishment of the new order...." This was profound and incontrovertible logic; the Congress would accomplish nothing useful unless it followed Talleyrand's advice.

15 D'Angeberg, *op. cit.*, I, 271.

The same day, the fifth, the six plenipotentiaries assembled once more. Castlereagh communicated the contents of Talleyrand's letter, and he was asked to withdraw it, which he refused to do. A long discussion followed, and the prospect was faced of a postponement of the Congress. In the end, Talleyrand declared that, since nothing was settled, he would not object to the Congress being postponed for two or three weeks, but on condition that it would be convoked for a predetermined date and that the notice of convocation would establish the rule for admission. He even wrote down the rule, in accordance with the Instructions; it would have excluded the representatives of Murat from the Congress. No agreement, however, was reached, and the conference "evaporated rather than ended." Upon leaving, Talleyrand had a conversation with Castlereagh, which he recorded as follows:

Lord Castlereagh, who was one of the last to leave and with whom I was descending the staircase, attempted to win me over to their opinion by giving me to understand that certain matters which were of great interest to my government could be arranged to my satisfaction.

"It is not now," I told him, "a question of individual matters but of the law which must govern them. If the thread is once broken, how shall we bring it together again? We must meet the wishes of Europe. What shall we have accomplished for it if we do not honorably bring back the maxims, the abandonment of which has caused it so much trouble? The present epoch is one which occurs hardly more than once in the course of several centuries. We could not ask for a better opportunity. Why should we not rise to the occasion?"

"Eh," said he with an air of embarrassment, "there are difficulties of which you are unaware."

"Yes, I am unaware of them," I replied in a tone of voice which implied that I had no desire to be enlightened.[16]

Expediency? Interests? Talleyrand set aside the usual objects of diplomatic bargaining and attempted to bring

[16] *Correspondance inédite,* pp. 29-30.

everything down to a few questions of clear and simple principle.

Two days went by without a conference; on the first everyone was invited to a great fête, and the second was spent in hunting. A little entertainment was not amiss! On October 8, Talleyrand received a note from Metternich announcing a conference at eight o'clock, and asking him to come a little earlier, because there were some extremely important matters he would like to talk about. This is what took place between the two ministers, according to the account which Talleyrand sent the King on the following morning.

I arrived at seven o'clock, and was immediately shown in. He spoke first about a new declaration which he had had drawn up; it differed slightly from mine, he said, but was much closer, and he hoped that it would satisfy me. I asked to see it, but he did not have it.

"Probably," I said, "it is being read by the Allies."

"Let us not speak of the Allies any more," he replied, "they no longer exist."

"There are individuals here who should be Allies in the sense that, even without a formal alliance, they should think in the same way and desire the same things. How can you find the courage to place Russia like a girdle around your most important possessions, Hungary and Bohemia? How can you suffer the inheritance of an old and trusted neighbor, into whose family an archduchess has married, to be given to your natural enemy? It is strange that we are opposing such a move and you do not want us to."

He said that I had no confidence in him. I replied that he had not given me much cause to have confidence in him, and I reminded him of a few instances in which he had not kept his word to me.

"And then," I added, "how can I have confidence in a man who is full of secrets from those who are the most inclined to serve his purpose? As for me, I have no secrets, and I have no need of them; that is the advantage of those who are guided by principles in their negotiations. There are pen and ink.

If you care to write down that France asks nothing and would even accept nothing, I am ready to sign it."

"But you have the matter of Naples," he told me, "which belongs to you."

I replied: "No more than to the whole world. For me it is no more than a question of principle; I ask only that whoever has a right to Naples shall have it. Now, that is what everyone should wish for. If principles are followed, I shall agree to everything. I am going to say frankly what I can consent to and what I will never consent to. I realize that the King of Saxony, under the circumstances, may be obliged to make sacrifices. I believe he will be disposed to make them because he is prudent. But if the plan is to despoil him of all his dominions and give the Kingdom of Saxony to Prussia, then I will never give my consent. Neither will I ever consent to Luxembourg and Mainz being given to Prussia. No more will I consent to Russia's crossing the Vistula and having forty-four million subjects in Europe and her frontiers on the Oder. But if Luxembourg is given to Holland and Mainz to Bavaria, if the King and the Kingdom of Saxony are preserved, and if Russia does not cross the Vistula, I will have no objection to make about the division of that part of Europe."

Metternich then took my hand and said: "We are far closer than you think. I promise you that Prussia will have neither Luxembourg nor Mainz. We are no more desirous than you of letting Russia expand beyond reason. As for Saxony, we shall do our best to save at least a part of it."

It was only to know his stand on these matters that I had talked to him in that fashion. Coming back to the convocation of the Congress, he insisted on the necessity for postponing the announcement of the rule for admission which I had proposed.

"Because," said he, "everyone is afraid of it, and it is inconvenient for me too just now, since Murat, seeing his minister left out, would believe that his affair had been decided and there is no telling what he might do; for in Italy he is on his own grounds, and we are not." [17]

[17] *Ibid.*, pp. 32 *et seq.*

Here again, Talleyrand was attempting to put the discussion back on the ground of principles, pushing interests and expediency into second place. After this particular conversation, the two ministers went to the conference. Metternich read the two declarations—Talleyrand's and his own—on the convocation of the Congress: the only difference between the two was that Talleyrand defined the rule of admission and in such a way as to exclude Murat; Metternich confined himself to adjourning the opening of Congress to November 1, without adding anything further. He did not wish either to accept Talleyrand's ruling, excluding Murat, or to propose another admitting him. The Prussians, Nesselrode, Castlereagh, the minister from Sweden, who was present at the conferences for the first time, all declared themselves in favor of Metternich's project "because it was free from prejudice." This is what happened next:

Thus the difficulty was only being put off instead of resolved; but, since the original pretensions had been abandoned and it was no longer a question of having everything determined by the eight powers, and leaving only the right of approval to the Congress; since it was only a matter of preparing, by means of free and confidential communications with the ministers of the other powers, the questions on which the Congress would have to pronounce judgment, I decided that compliance, which would in no way interfere with principle, might help matters along, and I declared that I consented to the adoption of the plan, but only on condition that, where it stated that the formal opening of the Congress would be adjourned to November 1, an addition be made: *and shall be done according to the principles of the law of nations.* At these words, such a tumult arose as would be hard to imagine. M. de Hardenberg jumped to his feet, his clenched fists on the table, almost threateningly, and, shouting as is customary to men afflicted with his infirmity, uttered these broken words: "No, sir; the law of nations? That is useless. Why say that we will act according to the law of nations? That goes without saying." I replied that if it went without saying, it would go even better with saying. M. de Humboldt shouted: "What has the law of nations got to do with this matter?" To which I answered, "It has this to do with it, that you are here." [18]

The discussion was long and stormy; finally, when Gentz too intervened, Talleyrand's phrase was approved. But where to place it? A new discussion begun. Finally, they agreed, and the following declaration was signed by the plenipotentiaries.

The plenipotentiaries of the courts who signed the peace treaty of Paris, on May 30, 1814, have taken under consideration article 32 of this treaty, which states that all the powers engaged on either side during the last war, will send plenipotentiaries to Vienna, in order that in a general Congress they may settle the terms which are to complete the dispositions in the said treaty; and, after having seriously considered the situation in which they find themselves, and the duties which devolve upon them, they have realized that they could not better fulfill them, than by first establishing free and confidential communications between the plenipotentiaries of all the powers. But at the same time they are convinced that it is to the interest of all the intervening parties to delay the general assembly of their plenipotentiaries until the time when the questions on which pronouncement must be made will have reached a point where the result is in keeping with the principles of the law of nations, with the stipulations of the Treaty of Paris, and with the proper respect of our contemporaries. Therefore, the formal opening of the Congress will be adjourned to November 1, and the aforesaid plenipotentiaries feel certain that the work to which this delay will be consecrated, by defining ideas and conciliating opinion, will essentially advance the great labor which is the object of their mission.[19]

A few days later, Talleyrand was to write to the Department: "It is claimed that we have gained a victory by having forced the introduction of the expression 'law

[18] *Ibid.*, p. 35.
[19] D'Angeberg, *op. cit.*, p. 272.

of nations.' This opinion may given you a gauge of the spirit which pervades the Congress." But this opinion also is too simple. Actually, the discussion which had lasted eight days had been a battle between interest and principle, the like of which had never before been known in the history of diplomatic congresses. The representatives of Russia, Prussia, Austria, and England, who, in Paris, had seemed of one mind on the principles to be followed in order to reconstitute the European system, had, no sooner arrived in Vienna, disagreed on three questions which they considered of vital importance to their states: Poland, Saxony, and Naples. The Czar wanted the Duchy of Warsaw, and was disposed to let Prussia grab Saxony; Prussia accepted the bargain; Austria wanted neither Russia on the Vistula, nor Prussia in Dresden, but on the contrary she did want Murat in Naples; England, or at least Castlereagh, favored the views of Prussia on Saxony, but regarded the annexation of the Duchy of Warsaw by the Russian Empire as a catastrophe; she was, like Prussia and Russia, indifferent to the fate of Naples. Conflict of interests: in the atmosphere of Vienna—so different from that of Paris—the Allies sought to rid themselves of the question of principle, and of France, who invoked and supported it. Each Ally feared that the law of nations, which was helpful for the regulation of the European system, might be harmful to its interests in individual matters. This particularly explains Hardenberg's explosion at the meeting of October 8, for example.

France, too, had her point of view and her interests to defend in these particular matters, although hers were less immediate than those of the other powers. Like Austria, she opposed the Polish ambitions of the Czar, and Prussia's intentions on Saxony, but she wanted to clean up the Kingdom of Naples, in order to restore it to the Bourbons. Since the Allies were attempting to exclude France from future arbitration in Europe, Talleyrand, in order to break the Coalition, might also have let slide the question of principle, and sought to gain by the disagreements. Had he been a diplomat, he would have done so. But he was a builder. The more the Allies turned their backs on matters of principle and international law, in order to defend their real or imaginary interests, the greater energy he put into opposing their discordant interests not by more intrigue but by doctrine. A simple and coherent doctrine, hidden in the fog of diplomatic intrigue and subordinate to all these arguments, proposals, and counterproposals, which correlates and transforms into an ideological unity his conversation with the Czar, the letter of October 5 to Castlereagh, the suggestions made to the English plenipotentiary on the stairway the same day, the long conversation with Metternich on October 8, and his belligerent attitude at the conference which followed that conversation.

This doctrine can be translated thus in plain language. "Before the Revolution, what was called the law of nations was a body of rules and principles which canalized the actions of the European states, both in peace and in wartime, by making them predictable. Each state knew, at least up to a point, under what conditions war was to be feared and peace re-established in the event of war, because it respected these rules and knew that they would be respected by all the other states. Only the respect for these rules and the principles which justified them, used to make possible a certain confidence between the states, and consequently a certain order and balance in Europe, the balance being but the projection into their foreign policy of the reciprocal confidence between the states. Among these rules and principles, the principle that conquest, without cession of sovereignty, does not create sovereignty had been the cornerstone of peacemaking in Europe before the Revolution. Terrified by its fear, the Revolution had shattered it; and once this principle had been suppressed, the great panic had begun. Confidence was lost, stability and order became impossible; the world became lost in the vicious circle wherein fear provokes abuse of force and abuse of force intensifies fear. The only way to break this circle was to re-establish the law of nations. And for that to be done, it was necessary to preserve legitimate governments wherever they existed, as in Saxony; to eliminate illegitimate governments, as for instance in Naples, and to give legitimate governments to countries without rulers. Only legitimate governments possess the courage and vision that are needed to respect the canons of the law of nations; and only respect for the law of nations can exorcise panic, inspire confidence, and insure a stability of peace which will be acceptable to all states, large and small. The re-establishment of the law of nations, the peace and order of Europe, are therefore conditioned by the re-establishment of a legitimate government in each state."

Such was the doctrine of Talleyrand. If that doctrine happened to coincide with certain French interests, it was to the credit of an astute political philosopher who, by combining the doctrine of the legitimacy of authority with that of the law of nations, had succeeded by the end of the first week of Congress in stating the problem before Europe in the only way in which it could be solved, which will always be the only way as long as there is a question of freeing Europe from the great panic which is provoked by unrestrained wars and revolutions. It remained to be seen what effect this novel, determined, and philosophical attitude would have on a Congress composed of diplomats.

X

THE CONFIDENTIAL APPROACH

The ministers of the four allied powers were men of the
eighteenth century. Talleyrand's words on the law of nations, its principles, and the unity of Europe did not fall
on deaf ears. But, after twenty years of triumphant violence, they were not yet certain that principles had won a
definite victory, and they were distrustful of them. Was
France sincere? As guns had failed her, was she not making
use of the law of nations and the unity of Europe as
weapons to serve her ends? Principles and expedience;
Europe had come through the chaos of Revolution to find
herself torn apart and weakened by this insoluble contradiction.

This contradiction explains the weakness of the Allies
in the long discussion and the strange resolution of October 8. They had both given way and resisted: given
way, by recognizing that they could not alone direct
the Congress and dictate the affairs of Europe; resisted,
by refusing to allow the Congress to direct its own affairs.
A "semi-official article on the progress of the work
done by the Congress during the month of October,

1814," [1] gives a clear picture of this contradictory outcome of the diplomatic duel between the Allies and Talleyrand.

No great political insight is needed to see that this Congress could not be modeled on any which had taken place. Former assemblies which were called congresses met for the express purpose of settling a quarrel between two or more belligerent powers or powers on the verge of war, the issue being a peace treaty. On this occasion, peace has already been made, and the parties meet as friends, who, though differing in their interests, wish to work together toward the conclusion and affirmation of the existing treaty; the negotiation takes the form of a multiple series of problems, some of which have been settled by antecedent decisions and others which remain undecided. The powers which concluded the Peace of Paris had, certainly, the right to determine what interpretation should be placed on the decision of the Congress, an interpretation of a completely novel character, and, consequently, the right to prescribe the form which appeared to be the most expedient for attaining their ends. These powers made use of this right, to the equal advantage of each interested party and, therefore, to the well-being of Europe as a whole, by binding the plenipotentiaries gathered in Vienna to carry on their negotiations by the swiftest and most efficacious means, adopting the confidential approach.

Thus, the Congress was a spontaneous creation, without preliminary formalities, and without formal instructions, which no one should have had the authority to give. The council of powers which created it reserved to themselves only the general direction of the negotiations, without infringing on the rights of entirely independent parties. The presence of so many monarchs, ministers, and plenipotentiaries from great and small courts, eliminates the obstacles which distance and loss of time have so often opposed to the successful conclusion of complex negotiations. The European powers, gathered together in one spot, have between them many points at which they can meet on common ground and many methods of negotiating, which are lacking under ordinary circum-

[1] D'Angeberg, *op. cit.*, p. 362.

stances and which should facilitate a satisfactory settlement. The great European courts are taking advantage of this situation to negotiate directly with each other, summoning to their conferences one or more impartial mediators.

The "confidential approach" seems to have been Metternich's idea. It consisted of a compromise between the exclusive direction of the Congress by the four great powers, and the official organization of the sovereign and legislative Congress. The three weeks from October 8 to the opening date of the Congress on November 1, were engaged in a sort of preliminary Congress, during which the plenipotentiaries were invited to come to an agreement on the principal matters through "free and confidential communications," that is, through discreet, whispered negotiations held in corners. It is in these preliminaries, by means of these "free and confidential" communications, that the Congress opened on October 8, three weeks before its official inauguration. Starting from an insoluble contradiction between principles and expediency, it opened "without preparation or ceremony," to the tune of violins and in waltz time.

The parties of the Congress of Vienna are better known, but no better understood than its labors and vicissitudes. Carried away by the current of quantitative society, the twentieth century does not realize that in the qualitative society of that period, parties were not small private amusements, but a sumptuous ornament of society, supported by the state, the Church, the nobility, and the wealthy. Their splendor and magnificence always had to be proportionate to the importance of the political power, the religious authority, or the family who gave them, to the rank of the personages for whom they were given, and of the same import and significance as the events which occasioned them. The Emperor of Austria was playing host in his palace to an emperor and four kings, and in his capital to the political elite and the great nobility of Europe, who had all come to Vienna in order to put an end to twenty years of Revolution and warfare; and he was therefore under an obligation to provide an unprecedented magnificence of setting for such an occasion. His imagination and his pocketbook had to be equally inexhaustible. It seems that the Imperial table alone, from the beginning of the Congress, cost 50,000 florins a day—the expenses of a ministry! Since the imagination of one man would not have sufficed, the Emperor of Austria had entrusted a committee with the task of finding diversions and amusements. This amusement committee never stopped working; every day there was something new; banquets, concerts, masked and unmasked balls, hunting parties, tournaments, carrousels, military reviews, theatrical comedies and tragedies. The Emperor's example was imitated, on a smaller scale, by the princes of the imperial house, by the delegations of the various powers, by the great families who had come to Vienna from all corners of Europe for the occasion. In the salons of the comtesse de Périgord, Lady Castlereagh, the Duchess of Sagan, Countess Zichy, Mme. Fuchs, and a crowd of princesses—Esterhazy, Lichtenstein, Fürstenburg, de la Tour et Taxis, Bagration—Europe felt more at ease than in the Babylonian halls of the Burg. All Europe gathered together in various small groups and talked, flirted, gossiped, negotiated, sought information, deceived each other. Open house, balls, receptions, parties, gambling everywhere.

Nunc est bibendum! That vulgar wench—Revolution—had been subdued. But these festivities were less of a nineteenth-century following out of Horace's lyrical advice than the accomplishment of a duty, too pleasant not to be rather grim under the circumstances. Europe was hungry, afraid, hopeless about the future, raving; no matter, the Old Regime was celebrating what it believed to be its resurrection. Everyone, the Austrian Emperor first of all, would have thought that the Court of Vienna was lowering itself if it did not receive Europe with the magnificence worthy of its position, Europe, and the occasion. This illustrious example was to be followed by all the others. Every day they had to banquet, dance, dine, hunt, go to the theater and concert, while the money that had not been spent on powder and bullets was wasted on candles, flowers, and champagne. This senseless yet necessary carnival had at least one advantage: in the heat and tumult of the festivities, the strict formality of the Old Regime was being relaxed. A certain amount of freedom existed, thanks to which Europe would find herself more easily. A Frenchman, who had gone to Vienna on a nonpolitical visit toward the end of September, has given an eyewitness account of the first fancy dress ball given by the Court. It was a "brilliant tapestry of people" in which the experts sought to recognize in the crowd of dominos, by shape or carriage, the figures of the Russian Emperor, the Prussian King, the Bavarian King, the King of Württemberg, Eugène de Beauharnais. Leading off from the great ballroom were small salons in which kings and ministers, in domino but with masks removed, discussed the affairs of Europe, continuing the negotiations which they had initiated elsewhere.[2] Sovereigns and plenipotentiaries could meet each other unofficially in these various salons and carry on their negotiations while everyone was enjoying himself. This was a particularly useful method in the case of the soverigns, because during the festivities they could be sought out by the ministers without the latter going through the formality of asking for an audience. The art of accosting a sovereign on his way through one of the salons and engaging his attention, became an important factor in diplomacy during the Congress.

Such was the "confidential approach" thought up by the cautious and subtle Metternich. It was immediately applied by the four Allies to the problems of Poland and Saxony, but in the greatest secrecy[3] and to the total ex-

[2] De La Garde, Contes et souvenirs du Congrès de Vienne (Brussels, 1843), I, 29 et seq.
[3] On the secrecy of the negotiations between the great powers during this period, see the interesting account published by Weil, op. cit., I, 363.

clusion of Talleyrand from all negotiations. The use of the "confidential approach" was accompanied by a skillfully concerted attempt by the Allies to isolate the French delegation with its platform of the law of nations which Talleyrand had brought up before the whole Congress. The Spanish delegate was accused of ingratitude because he went too often to see Talleyrand. The Bavarian King confided to his intimates that he did not dare see as much of the ambassador of the French King as he desired. The small states were forced to make their visits to him in secret. The Allies were seeking desperately to reach an understanding among themselves, sheltering from the opinion of Congress, the law of nations, revived by France, and the objections of the latter's formidable spokesman. Castlereagh had already, on October 4, sent a memorandum to the other three Allies, in which the Polish claims of the Czar were firmly and irrevocably rejected as contrary to treaties, preposterous, and dangerous for Europe. The treaty signed on June 27, 1813, between Austria, Prussia, and Russia had stipulated that the Duchy of Warsaw be partitioned among the three Allies. How, then could the Czar, after signing such a treaty, dare to claim the whole of the Duchy of Warsaw? Castlereagh did not delay in answering that question, stating that the Czar had not seriously studied the matter and had acted unconsciously.

Since, therefore, it is understood that the measure is contrary to treaties, the situation takes on an even more serious aspect. For His Imperial Majesty, on examining the facts, must see that the policy which he has been induced to follow is a denial of the faith of his solemn engagements. Over and beyond the plan proposed by His Imperial Majesty to persuade Prussia and then Russia to join in fighting for the cause of Europe, was the fact that the time had come when "treaties would no longer be truces, when they could once more be observed with that religious faith, that sacred inviolability on which depend the respect, the strength, and the preservation of empires." Nevertheless, it is not to be doubted, after His Imperial Majesty has seriously considered his obligations, both in their outer form and in their spirit, but that he will be the first to recognize them and adhere to them, giving up any plan which is not in harmony with them.[4]

As for the Czar's plan, Castlereagh feared that a catastrophe would result from it.

The forcible annexation of almost the whole of a country as important and as populous as the Duchy of Warsaw, holding nearly four million people—such an annexation by the Russian Empire, already greatly augmented by the conquest of Finland, by acquisitions in Moldavia, and by her recent expansion toward Prussia, her extension of the Niemen into the very heart of Germany, her possession of all the fortresses of the Grand Duchy, thus completely exposing to her attacks the capitals of Austria and Prussia, left without any line of defense or boundary; the exhortation to the Poles to rally around the standards of the Russian Emperor in order to restore their monarchy; the awakening of new hopes, the opening of new scenes by the activities and intrigues of this volatile and restless people, the prospect of a renewal of those simultaneous conflicts into which the Poles have dragged themselves and their neighbors over a long period of time; the fear that this project will plant the seeds of another war; the extinction of all hope, rest, and real confidence and peace— all these considerations and many others occur to everyone and justify the fears which are agitating Europe. While there is a universal wish to recognize and commend the many virtues of the Russian Emperor, and also the tremendous benefits which his perseverance and energy have won for the general good, public opinion cannot understand why this dreadful union is adopted and even perhaps justified.[5]

The conclusion is a downright rebuke:

If His Imperial Majesty is seriously determined to ameliorate the lot of the Poles, without having in mind a territorial aggrandizement, it is suggested that the authority which he possesses is sufficient thereto, with regard to the numerous

4 D'Angeberg, *op. cit.*, p. 268.
5 *Ibid.*, p. 267.

inhabitants of the Russian provinces taken from Poland, together with a reasonable share of the Duchy of Warsaw, and that for an action of this kind, however useful it might be, it is not necessary to seek an acquisition to his empire as enormous and threatening as the one proposed (an empire today large enough for the purpose of good government), at the expense of the present position and future security of his Allies, and in contravention of his own obligations and of those principles of justice and moderation which he has so often declared to be the only rules of conduct and which so admirably governed his conduct toward France in the last peace treaty.

His Imperial Majesty should also consider how much against moral law it is to embark hastily on a venture which will raise fears and discontent in neighboring states and political unrest in his own. If moral duty requires that the condition of the Poles be ameliorated by a change as radical as the revival of their monarchy, then let this amelioration be carried out according to the high and liberal principle of re-establishing them as a truly independent nation, rather than transforming two thirds of it into a formidable military advantage in the hands of a single power.

Such a liberal action would be acclaimed throughout Europe without dissension and would be promptly accepted by Austria and Prussia. True, in the light of ordinary state-craft, it would be a sacrifice on the part of Russia, but, if His Imperial Majesty is not disposed to make such sacrifices to moral obligation on the part of his own Empire, then he has no moral right to make similar experiments at the expense of his Allies and neighbors.

More must be said. As long as His Majesty adheres to this unfortunate plan, it will be impossible for any plan of adjustment in the reconstruction of Europe to be suggested by the plenipotentiaries of the allied powers or for the present Congress to assemble formally to discuss and sanction any such plan.

Castlereagh entered the secret discussions with a real fear of the Russian plans. On the ninth, Prince Hardenberg took part in them. According to the note he sent

Metternich on that day, Prussia was primarily interested in "keeping closely bound up with the wise system of a European league, based on the most intimate union between Austria and England." [6] She was "ready to concur in all the measures which the two courts [Vienna and London] would consider appropriate to take in persuading that of Russia not to abandon the principles of the alliance and to modify accordingly her claims with regard to Poland." But the Prussian envoy demanded the whole of Saxony and Mainz, declaring that, as soon as Prussia had received the necessary guarantees, she would join with Austria "in the most complete agreement" on Poland. To begin with, he asked for the right to occupy Saxony with Prussian troops. The Prince enumerated the acquisitions which Russia, Bavaria, and Württemberg had received or were about to receive; and he asked: "Has not Prussia, who made the greatest efforts and the greatest sacrifices in the common cause, the right to claim acquisitions proportionate to those of her neighbors?"

Prince Hardenberg communicated the contents of this note to Castlereagh, asking for the latter's support. Castlereagh did not delay his answer twenty-four hours. On the eleventh, he replied, assuring Hardenberg that a Prussia which would be as strong as possible, was a necessary condition for European stability.

There is no principle, regarding European politics, which I consider more important than a substantial enlargement of Prussia. The glorious services which she rendered in the last war give her an outstanding right to our recognition. But an even more powerful motive lies in the necessity for recognizing Prussia as the only stable foundation in any and all arrangements come to for the security of northern Germany against the greatest dangers that might threaten it. In that crisis it is Prussia to whom we must turn. We must join our strength to hers; and, for this to be accomplished, the Prussian monarchy must be substantial and solid, endowed with all the

[6] *Ibid.*, pp. 1934-1936.

qualities of an independent state, capable of inspiring respect and confidence.

As for Saxony, he declared that she must be suppressed as an example for the rest of Germany.

As to the question of Saxony, I declare to you that, if the incorporation of this entire country into the Prussian monarchy is necessary to the accomplishment of so great a benefit to Europe, whatever my personal feelings are in seeing so old a family come to such profound misfortune, I could not harbor any moral or political repugnance against the act itself. If ever a sovereign has put himself in the position of having to be sacrificed to the future tranquillity of Europe, I believe it to be the King of Saxony, because of his perpetual evasions and because he has been not only the most devoted but also the most favored of Bonaparte's vassals, striving eagerly with all his might, in his dual role as ruler of the German state and of the Polish state, to extend the universal bondage into the heart of Russia.[7]

But he added that if he consented to give Saxony to Prussia, it was on condition that the latter did not consider Saxony as payment for her consent to the Czar's plans for Poland. To obtain Saxony, Prussia had to oppose the annexation of the Duchy of Warsaw. Castlereagh also gave his consent to the occupation of Saxony by Prussian troops.

The Austrian and Prussian delegates must have considered the English note of October 4 too severe and violent for a discussion with Alexander. Indeed, on October 12, Castlereagh wrote the Czar a letter full of compliments in a very friendly tone, accompanied by a new memorandum in which the arguments of the earlier note were repeated, but in a less brusque and severe manner.[8] It was obvious that the Englishman had been persuaded to mollify his tone in order to induce Alexander to diminish his claims.

[7] Ibid., pp. 274-275.
[8] Ibid., pp. 280-288.

Two days later, October 14, there was a surprise meeting attended by the following: Prince Metternich and Baron Wessenberg, representing Austria; Prince Hardenberg and Baron Humboldt, representing Prussia; Prince Wrede, Bavaria; the Counts Münster and Hardenberg, Hanover; Baron Linden, Württemberg; and the Aulic Councillor, Martin, as secretary. Altogether, nine men, who represented the five most powerful German countries. After having decided that it was necessary to form a committee to draw up a Constitution for Germany, they also decided that "this committee must only be composed of plenipotentiaries from the five courts of Austria, Prussia, Bavaria, Hanover, and Württemberg, *either because a larger number might hold up the proceedings, and in any case the five courts named above must be considered the most powerful, or because the other states had submitted beforehand to the arrangements which might be required by the order to be established for the preservation of German independence.*" The resolution promised that the Constitution would go into effect after it had been made known to the other German states, without, however, according them any opportunity to discuss or approve it. The resolution gave assurance that agreement among the five courts constituted the fullest guarantee.[9]

This was a kind of seizure, by the five most powerful Germanic states, of the future of Germany, to the exclusion of the smaller states and the Congress. This committee also began its work in the utmost secrecy. Fundamentally, the resolution of October 8 had only theoretically admitted Europe into the Congress. The small and medium states of Europe, as well as France, had been called to Vienna for the sole purpose of remaining outside closed doors, behind which the ministers of the four Allies argued, negotiated, and plotted. But, after several days of more or less peaceful waiting, this idle, badly informed crowd of spectators began to grow nervous as one alarming rumor

9 *Ibid.*, p. 289.

after another reached their ears: Germany was threatening to go up in flames; Murat was preparing an invasion of Italy; in Paris, the Restoration was tottering; in Vienna, the powers were unable to reach an understanding; the sovereigns were getting ready to leave; war was about to start all over again. On October 17, ten days after the "confidential approach" had been set in motion, Talleyrand sent Louis XVIII one of the most alarming letters on the situation, both in Europe and at the Congress.

Revolutionary discontent has broken out all over Germany; Jacobinism is rampant, not, as in France twenty-five years ago, in the middle and lower classes, but in the highest and wealthiest nobility—a difference which means that the course of such a Revolution, were it to break out, could not be charted in the same way as ours. Those whom the dissolution of the Holy Roman Empire and the enactment of the Confederation of the Rhine have lowered from a dynastic position to one of subjects, impatiently support for their rulers those whom they were or considered themselves to be the equals of, aspire toward the overthrowal of an order which their pride deems unworthy and toward the substitution of one government for all the governments in this country. With them are conspiring the academicians and the youth imbued with their theories, and those who blame the division of Germany into small states for all the calamities which have been caused by so many wars, of which she has been the continual theater. The unity of the German nation has become their battle cry, their dogma, and their religion exalted into fanaticism; and the fanaticism has even won over princes who are now reigning. Now, this unity, which France had no cause to fear while she was in possession of the left bank of the Rhine and of Belgium, would at present be of enormous significance to her. Who, moreover, can foresee the implications of disturbing a mass like Germany, when its divided elements are stirred up and merged? Who knows where such an impulse would end, once begun? The situation in Germany, a large part of which does not know whom it should have as a ruler; the military occupations; the annoyances which are the natural result of the occupations; new sacrifices required after so many past sacrifices; the present unrest; the uncertainty about the future—all these factors favor the plans for revolution. It is only too evident that if the Congress adjourns, if it fails to agree, if it comes to no decision, this state of affairs will be aggravated; and it is greatly to be feared that any further aggravation will cause an explosion. There is, therefore, the most urgent need for it to speed up its work and come to an end. But what is that ending to be? Agree to the demands of Russia and Prussia? Neither the security of Europe nor honor permit of such a conclusion. Opposing strength to strength? For that, it would be necessary for Austria, who, I believe, has such a desire, to find the will. She has immense forces under arms, but she is afraid of losses in Italy and dares not face Russia and Prussia by herself. She can count on Bavaria, who has declared herself very frankly and has offered her 50,000 men to defend Saxony; Württemberg will furnish 10,000 men. Other German states will support her, but that is not enough to reassure her: she would like to be able to count on our support, and does not believe she can. The Prussians have spread the rumor that Your Majesty's ministers have received duplicate instructions: one, on what they were to say, the other, not to make any promises. Metternich has informed Marshal Wrede that he believed this to be the case. One of his most intimate friends said to M. Dalberg a few days ago: "Your delegation talks very well, but you can do nothing on your own initiative." Your Majesty will believe without any trouble that I have no more love nor desire for war than yourself. But in my opinion it would be enough to threaten it, and it would not be necessary to wage it. Furthermore, I believe that fear of war must not prevail over the fear of something worse, which only war might prevent.

I cannot believe that Russia and Prussia would run the risk of a war against Austria, France, Sardinia, Bavaria, and a good part of Germany; or, if they would run that risk, all the more reason to believe that they would not retreat before Austria alone, supposing, what is not so, that the latter would want to fight alone.

Thus, Austria, deprived of our support, would have no other resource than to prolong the Congress indefinitely or to dissolve it, which would pave the way to revolutions, or to yield her consent to things which Your Majesty is resolved never to sanction.

In that case Your Majesty's ministers would be forced to retire from the Congress and give up obtaining what you most desire. Nevertheless, the state of things which will have been established in Europe, might render inevitable in a very few years the war which we would have prevented; and we might then find ourselves in a worse position to wage it.[10]

Talleyrand had ended his letter with a request for authorization and special instructions to reply to Austria, should the latter specifically ask to be supported against Russia, even to the extent of war. Thus, Talleyrand also, ten days after the "confidential approach" had begun to function, envisaged the possibility of another general European war. The police reports confirm these fears. A secret report to Baron Hager, dated October 20, says:

There is more and more talk about the approaching dissolution of Congress and the departure of the sovereigns and their ministers. Fear of war is growing stronger, and no one can see how peace will be preserved and everyone satisfied, in view of the divergence of opinion caused by the plans to cede the Austrian Netherlands and to partition Saxony, by the claims of Russia on Poland, and by the appetite of Prussia. The King of Bavaria wishes to leave and declares publicly that the partition of Saxony would be an infamy. Hardenberg also believes that a general exodus is near. And finally it is said that Metternich is striving to increase the confusion.[11]

Three days later, the twenty-third, another secret report states:

One no longer knows what or whom to believe. One moment it is Russia who gives in, the next it is we who give in to everything. Now we are being firm, Europe is with us, the King of Saxony is saved, Poland is only partly Russian. Now Murat has been sentenced, now he is more certain than ever

10 *Correspondance inédite*, pp. 55-59.
11 Weil, *op. cit.*, 340.

of reigning. The truth is that no one knows anything; it can at least be said that, if negotiations are going on, the secret is well guarded, for everything changes from one hour to the next, which proves that nothing is based on definite opinions.[12]

What was going on behind the closed doors of the real Congress? Only one thing—simple but unforeseen, and very dangerous—the "confidential approach" had run foul of Alexander's immovable resistance. Castlereagh had decided to adopt a soft tone, and, after having sweetened his note of October 4, he had had a long discussion with the Czar. Metternich had had five or six conferences with Alexander and had attempted to bring about the intervention of the Prussian King, who was Alexander's best friend. All in vain. Alexander had furiously and doggedly stuck to his guns, defying everybody, not only England and Austria, but also France, who remained apart as bystander and judge, not at all sympathetic. The papal legate, Cardinal Consalvi, relates how Talleyrand, during October, was carrying on a vigorous campaign of opposition in Congress against the Allies and referring to their negotiations on Poland and Saxony as *intrigues*.[13] It would have been to Alexander's advantage to let Talleyrand alone. But Talleyrand had told Czartoryski and Nesselrode that France would remain firm in the matter of Saxony but would be willing to yield on Poland. With regard to Poland, as long as it was not a question of restoring her complete independence, France would accept the solution upon which Austria, Prussia, and Russia agreed; as for Saxony, France would never accept her suppression.[14] Alexander, informed of this by his friend and minister, had expressed a desire to see Talleyrand and on October 23 he had made a violent scene. Talleyrand described it as follows in a letter to his King.

[12] *Ibid.*, I, 363.
[13] Rinieri, *Corrispondenza inedita dei Cardinali Consalvi e Pacca* (Turin, 1903), p. 51.
[14] *Correspondance inédite,* p. 74.

"In Paris," he told me, "you were in favor of a Kingdom of Poland; how did you happen to change your opinion?"

"My opinion, Sire, is still the same; at Paris it was a question of reviving the whole of Poland. I desired then, as I would today, her independence. But now it is a question of something entirely different: the question of Polish independence is subordinate to that of establishing boundaries which will give security to Austria and Prussia."

"They have no cause to be uneasy; besides I have 200,000 men in the Duchy of Warsaw, and no one is going to chase them out. I have given Saxony to Prussia, and Austria has consented."

"I am unaware," I said, "that Austria has given her consent. I would find it difficult to believe, as it would be so much against her interests. But can Austria's consent make her the owner of what belongs to the King of Saxony?"

"If the King of Saxony does not abdicate, he will be taken to Russia; he will die there. Another king has already died there."

"Your Majesty will permit me to disbelieve that; the Congress has not been convened to witness such an outrage."

"What? An outrage? Nonsense! Did Stanislas not go to Russia? Why shouldn't the King of Saxony go, too? The shoe fits! I see no difference." I was too angry to answer! I confess to Your Majesty that I did not know how to control my indignation. The Emperor was talking rapidly. One of his phrases was the following:

"I thought France owed me something. You keep telling me about principles; your law of nations means nothing to me; I don't know what you're talking about. What importance do you think I attach to all your documents and treaties? (I had called his attention to the one in which the Allies had agreed that the Grand Duchy of Warsaw would be partitioned among the three Courts.) There is one thing that is above everything else to me, and that is my word. I have given it, and I will keep it. I promised Saxony to the King of Prussia when we met again."

"Your Majesty promised 9 or 10 million people to the King of Prussia; you can give them to him without destroying Saxony." (I had a list of the countries which could be given to Prussia, and which, without overthrowing Saxony, would give her the number of subjects that her treaties guaranteed. The Emperor took it and kept it.)

"The King of Saxony is a traitor."

"Sire, the title of traitor can never be applied to a king; and it is important that it can never be applied." Perhaps I put some expression into the last part of my sentence. After a moment of silence:

"The King of Prussia," he told me, "will be King of Prussia and Saxony, just as I shall be Emperor of Russia and King of Poland. The favor shown to me by France on those two points will be the measure of mine for her on everything that can be of interest to her."

In the course of this conversation, the Emperor used no grand gestures, as in my first interview with him. He was firm and showed every sign of irritation.[15]

It was even worse the next day with Metternich. In a last interview, the Czar was so carried away that he went so far as to tell him that his remarks were *indecent* and that he was the only man in Austria who could take on *such a tone of revolt*. Metternich had left the audience in such a state of fury that he had declared he no longer wished to see the Emperor of Russia in private. Alexander was no longer in control of himself. After he had faced so many dangers and taken on so many responsibilities, the unexpected opposition of his Allies, who were recompensing him by upsetting his throne, sent him into a furious rage. But neither did the Allies expect to strike such a stumbling block; there it was the last part of October, and they were in consternation. What to do? Metternich seemed to Talleyrand like a pilot without a compass. He accuses him of seconding, through blindness and timidity, the game of Russia and Prussia, of thwarting the efforts of the Court to make an alliance with France; [16] and of being prepared to sacrifice Saxony to Prussia for

[15] *Ibid.*, pp. 76-78.
[16] *Ibid.*, pp. 66-67.

Poland—which was true enough.[17] He gives credence to an anonymous informer who told him: "M. de Metternich, who prides himself on giving an incentive to everything, himself receives it without being aware, and, plaything of the intrigues which he believes he is directing, lets himself be fooled like any child." [18] But, if Metternich's weakness made Talleyrand anxious, Castlereagh's inconsistencies and obstinacy were just as bad. During the last half of October, Castlereagh began to realize that he had over-rated his strength and that it would have been better to oppose to the Czar not England alone but all Europe, assembled in Congress, as Talleyrand had suggested.[19] But he was more relentless than ever against the Kingdom of Saxony—an inconsistency and a complication that presented grave difficulties. To destroy Saxony was to help the Czar gain Poland; and the fate of Saxony was stirring up the whole Congress, especially the crowd of medium and small powers. To despoil a king of his dominions in the name of punishment! But that was to throw over the whole eighteenth-century law of nations and imitate the French Revolution and Napoleon! The feeling was so strong that Prussia herself let it be understood that she was asking for Saxony because there was no other compensation to be given her for her Polish territories. And there, when even Prussia was hesitating, stood England with sword unsheathed, ready to execute the Kingdom of Saxony—the greatest service it could do for the Emperor of Russia, whose plans it was fighting! Talleyrand used all his eloquence to persuade Castlereagh that by suppressing Saxony they would be destroying the foundations of the building to which they were already adding a roof. But this was Greek to the nobleman! As a last resort, they made use of Princess Bagration and pinned their hopes

---

17 *Ibid.*, p. 81. Cf. Metternich's reply, on October 22, to Hardenberg's letter of the ninth. D'Angeberg, *op. cit.*, p. 316. This letter bears out Talleyrand.
18 *Correspondance inédite*, p. 65.
19 *Ibid.*, pp. 79-80.

on a visit which the Czar paid her during the night of October 31. The police had noticed that the visit was prolonged from 10:30 till 2 A.M. There had been plenty of time to discuss politics. But the next morning the Princess confessed to an agent of the police that the boudoir had been no more successful than the salon or the ballroom.

He will not listen to reason on this subject. He considers it a question of his honor and says he has given his word to the Poles and that he owes it to himself to keep it, that the whole world can fall on him and he will not yield; he intends to go to Munich, then to Berlin, then to Warsaw to be proclaimed King of Poland, and if anyone wants to oppose him, he is ready.[20]

November 1, the day of the official opening of the Congress, finally arrived in an atmosphere of general uneasiness. On that day a secret report for the Emperor to Baron Hager paints it in brilliant colors. Here it is, the work of an intelligent and conscientious observer:

Public opinion with regard to the Congress is still bad. Everywhere it is said that there is no agreement, that it is no longer a question of re-establishing order and justice but of forcing the issue and each taking what he can, and that things are pointing toward a general war which will not long delay in breaking out.

The affair of Saxony is deeply felt by everyone. That of Murat ... is no less displeasing. It is said openly that Alexander cannot bear Metternich; that Talleyrand is the only one talking sense now and that the Gospel, if preached by the devil, would still be the Gospel, and it is true, for Talleyrand asks nothing for France. He wants only justice, stability, moderation, and peace, erected on the sacred principles of right and reason.

In general, the public, and especially the Vienna public, possesses good sense and makes a true appraisal of how matters stand. . . . This places the French at the top in the opinion of

[20] Cf. Weil, *op. cit.*, I, 461.

society and the middle classes, while the Russians, the Prussians, and our own minister have lost favor in the public eye. People are tired of so many amusements, worried by so much expense, the only results of which will be that we shall have brought Russia into Hungary, lost Galicia within a few years, dethroned the most ancient family in Germany, established a perpetual hatred between Saxons and Prussians, and placed the latter at the mercy of Russia, who, as mistress of Poland, will be within four days' march of Berlin and within easy striking distance of the heart of Germany.

Besides all this, we shall have, if we can, sanctioned the usurpation of Naples, rewarded in Murat the crimes we punished in Bonaparte, and horrified the world by the most infamous politics ever practiced, which the Russians, English, French, Spanish, Italians, and all Europe, will lay exclusively to our door and especially to that of Prince Metternich, who, I am sorry to say, is losing more and more the favor of the people, to the point where I had to defend him against people who were saying that he had been bought by Murat, which proves to what extent people are angered at him.

As for Alexander, it can be said that he is well understood in Vienna. He is thought to be a schemer who practices philanthropy with honest people but who also wants to stay in good with the rabble, so as to have everyone on his side. People call him deceitful, lacking in moral sense but preaching good will like a saint and keeping up appearances. This monarch is not only disliked here but also despised and hated.

The Prussians have no more liking for him than the Viennese, but they conceal their feelings in public and talk frankly only in small groups.

Last Friday, the twenty-eighth, the English ambassador visited Mme. de Sagan during the evening. All of a sudden this eccentric turned to her and said: "What do you think of Alexander? For my part, I consider him an ambitious lunatic and an imposter. That is my opinion. What do you say?"

The Duchess, startled and embarrassed by this disclosure made before ten other persons, at first smiled, and then said: "I find, Milord, that you are taking the bit between the teeth like the horse which you gave my sister Dorothea this morning, who came within an inch of breaking her neck on the Prater."

Whereupon she got up and went to talk with someone else. I heard this story from someone who was there.

Nor is there much hope for this German Confederation without a head. People are certain that it will not work, that the Congress will come to an end, because it must end some time, but that it will leave matters in a greater tangle than they were when it convened.

What I find most painful is that the peoples, who, because of the successes, the sincerity, and the nobility of such a fine Coalition, had conceived a great esteem and affection for their rulers, now that they see these forgetting what they had solemnly promised—justice, order, and peace founded on stability and legitimacy of possession—will end up by no longer liking their rulers nor having confidence in their principles or their promises. And then where will we stand?

The outlook is very sad. Only loyalty, firmness, and justice can save us now.

The Prussians, for their part, are trying to make excuses for their King, whispering to everyone that he is very sorry to be forced to take Saxony; that he would prefer to take back Poland, although he has no reason to love the Poles.

That is the substance of what I have heard from morning to night, now that I am so in touch with the public that during a single day I see no less than a hundred people of different classes and nationalities.

The Princess of Wales has been extremely generous and lavish with her company in Milan, but very sparing with her purse. She has given nothing to anyone, although she has made herself a nuisance to a lot of people and visited all sorts of places where a stranger is generally expected to give something.[21]

Three weeks of the "confidential approach" had been enough to awaken in Congress the great panic which had been stifled for a while in Paris during the first days of April. Fear was creeping up on everyone. England and Austria were frightened by Russia's Polish ambitions.

[21] *Ibid.*, p. 445.

Prussia was terrifying all the small German states by her attitude toward Saxony. All four Allies were afraid of the Restoration, of the dangers which threatened it in France, and of the resistance which Talleyrand was putting up against their "intrigues." The Czar, seeing his plans in danger, was beginning to see in Austria, England, and France his most dangerous enemies and no longer trusted anyone but Prussia. Talleyrand, even he, had almost been convinced, by some mysterious exegesis of English policy, that Castlereagh was trying to create a gigantic Prussia and unite it closely with Austria, for the sole purpose of isolating France on the Continent, making her dependent on her own strength alone, and preventing her from ever having a powerful navy.[22]

Though the five greatest powers in Europe had assembled to make a lasting peace, by the end of October they were as frightened of each other as if they were at war. Furthermore, by their fright they were demoralizing the delegates of the smaller states and also the lesser representatives of the important delegations. This crowd of overlooked individuals, who made up the real Congress, watched, spied upon, criticized, and hated the active and secret inner circle of the Allies. Shoved aside, condemned to idleness, informed of only part of what was happening, and that at random, frightened by the universal unrest, the Congress took revenge for its fears and humiliation by tearing apart the Allies, their ministers, and their sovereigns. They were the ruin and the curse of Europe, all of them together! Metternich, as the Chancellor of the Austrian Empire and chairman of the Congress, was the favorite target. He was accused of indolence, cowardice, incapability, instability, duplicity, and venality. He was bold only with women; he was incapable of fixing his attention on anything; he treated serious matters as though they were trifles, and vice versa; he had taken half a million from the Prussian King, and a million from the

Republic of Genoa. The exchange was falling, living expenses were rising, the Congress was dragging, war was threatening, and he was the man to blame for it all. He was accused of postponing the most urgent matters in order to run off to amorous rendezvous. People laughed at his partiality for the Duchess of Sagan, who openly changed her lovers from day to day. The story went around that he had told the Russian Emperor that he was the lover of Countess Julie Zichy and that the Emperor had repeated his indiscretion to the Countess, whereupon a series of violent scenes had resulted between the Countess, the Prince, and the Emperor.

All exaggeration and calumny. But they were the daily fodder of a Congress preyed upon by terror and of a Germany preyed upon by despair. The mediatized princes, the smaller courts, Stein and the patriots, the clique of Stadion's friends, the strictly nationalist Austrians, were all united in hating this Rhenish nobleman, this stranger, who was neither an Austrian traditionalist nor a German federalist. The Prussian Court and chancellery, Talleyrand and the French delegation, maintained proper relations with him; but in his bad moments, Frederick William did not hesitate to treat him as a scoundrel while Talleyrand did not spare him in his letters. As for Alexander, he was more than ever eager for Metternich's resignation, even at the risk of upsetting the Congress. He used every possible means of discrediting him with Austria, the Allies, and the Congress; treated him like a servant; announced to everyone that the Chancellor was the best master of ceremonies and the worst minister in the world; played all sorts of savage tricks on him. There is no other way to describe the strange story of the Duchess of Sagan, which has been preserved for us by the secret reports of the police. The Duchess had most of her fortune in Russia. It seems that, toward the end of October, the Czar demanded her to break off relations with Metternich if she wanted to draw on her income. For a while, at least, the

Duchess had given in. She gave her lover the gate; and in a letter she wrote about him as follows: "A minister who has lost the confidence of foreign powers can no longer retain his position."

Toward the end of October, the rumor was abroad in Vienna that Metternich was going to resign. Just when its official work was about to begin, the Congress was in a state of frenzied confusion, which prevented anything constructive being attempted. In the midst of this general disorder, where could they establish the foundations on which the constructive mind might base its decisions? Would the constructive mind once more be lost in the vast chaos of interests and passions which had been let loose twenty-five years ago by the spirit of adventure? On the eve of Congress, everyone in Vienna was trembling, terrified by the impossible task which it had to perform, but particularly one man, a Cardinal, the legate of the Pope. On October 30, representatives of the eight powers which had signed the Paris treaty assembled and decided that a committee of three delegates, chosen by lot, would first examine their credentials, after which the delegates of the other powers would be asked to submit their credentials to the same inspection. The choice fell on Russia, England, and Prussia. After these resolutions had been taken, Talleyrand proposed that, once the credentials had been examined and verified, the Congress should be convened, and a general committee and three special committees be formed. The general committee would be composed of the delegates from all the imperial and royal courts, from the Holy See, and from the crown prince of the united provinces of the Netherlands. According to Talleyrand, the Pope should be the chairman of this committee. Talleyrand obviously wished to give proof of his regard for the Pope; with this intention, he communicated his proposal to Cardinal Consalvi, thinking the latter would be pleased.[23] The legate, however, considered this

[23] Rinieri, *op. cit.*, pp. 51-56.

a terrible blow. If the proposal was accepted, the Pope
would have to give his opinion on all the difficult problems
before the Congress. With all the discord that had already
divided the Congress before its opening, with no principle
or doctrine to go on, this was the quickest way to get em-
broiled with everybody. The Holy See, which desired to
regain all its former territories, whether ceded or not, had
need of powerful friends in the Congress. "God preserve
us from the acceptance of M. de Talleyrand's proposal,"
wrote the legate in a letter to the Secretary of State, in
which he revealed his "painful position"! Another anxiety
confronted him: should he submit his credentials as minister to the Congress committee, or should he remain in
Congress merely as the spokesman for the interests of the
Holy See? In the latter case, he would only have to plead
for the See, without mixing in the quarrels of others, and
would be able to seek the good will of everybody!

During the constant political changes in the Middle
Ages, the Pope had remained the one fixed point—God's
representative on earth—on which the constructive mind
had always been able to find support. As supramundane
guardian, he had specified, established, interpreted, and
defended peacefully, by the spiritual power of the sacred
word, the principles of legitimacy which justified temporal power. And now, at the beginning of the nineteenth
century, the Pope's legate in Vienna neither wished nor
dared to be anything more than a petty applicant for
territory, lost among all the others. But we have already
seen how the greatest achievement of the Revolution had
been to complete the overthrow of papal theocracy, begun
by the Renaissance and the Reformation. The proof was in
Vienna, where the vicar of Christ, through his representative, was showing himself an apt pupil of the immortal
Pontius Pilate. The Pope's role in Vienna, that of guardian and defender of principle, was taken by a churchman,
but he was an apostate and married bishop. Talleyrand
was the real pope at the Congress. Nothing gives a clearer

idea of the spiritual chaos into which the Western world had sunk at that time, and of the terrible blow which had been dealt the papacy, Italy, and the Old Regime during the adventure of the Revolution.

XI

THE SECOND CONFLICT:
LIVING LEGITIMACIES VS.
DEAD LEGITIMACIES

――――――→»»«←――――――

At the meeting on October 30, Talleyrand had not only proposed the creation of a general committee, but had also added three special committees: one for Germany, one for Italy, and one for Switzerland. The Congress was to choose the members of these three committees.

Talleyrand was returning to his idea of making the Congress the absolute authority for nineteenth-century Europe.[1] But the allied powers were afraid of Europe. A decision was postponed till the next day; and in that meeting, Russia's representative, Nesselrode, declared that he was not sufficiently informed to enter into a discussion on these proposals. In short, he proposed their adjournment. The adjournment was approved after an argument which seems to have been rather violent.[2] Always the same

[1] On this important question, on Talleyrand's attitude, and on the opposition which he met, cf. the significant intercepted letter from Löwenhielm to Engeström, published by Weil, *op. cit.*, I, 475.
[2] D'Angeberg, *op. cit.*, pp. 358-362. Cf. Weil, *op. cit.*, I, 441.

irresolution and evasion; the door of the Congress was left neither open nor closed, but ajar.

The "confidential approach" was still in use. But this time the Allies realized that, due to the general confusion created by their disagreement and their inability to get anything done, France could no longer be shut out with the small states. Talleyrand's opposition would have become too dangerous. On November 5, Talleyrand was invited by Metternich to come to see him at 4 o'clock. He found Castlereagh and Nesselrode there. Metternich frankly admitted that the Congress had reached an impasse, and begged Talleyrand, on the part of Castlereagh and Nesselrode, to lay aside all personal feelings and help them reach a solution.[3] This was obviously an advance. Talleyrand replied that they were in distress because they had not convened the Congress. "It will be necessary to convene it sooner or later. The greater the delay, the more apparent it is that there are designs which are being concealed."[4] Castlereagh agreed with Talleyrand, but added that "the very mention of the Congress terrified the Prussian delegates, and that Hardenberg in particular was obsessed with fear."[5] Metternich agreed that the Congress should be convened, but said that it would be preferable to wait "until an agreement had been reached, at least on all the important questions." He assured Talleyrand that the work of the committee on German affairs was proceeding in an extremely satisfactory manner, and informed him that the Allies intended to settle the affairs of Switzerland with the help of France; and he proposed to begin the immediate discussion of Italy's affairs. Talleyrand's inclusion was an amicable compromise. For the moment, Talleyrand accepted it.

The question of Italy came up for the first time. The Italian problem was closely related to the German prob-

---

[3] *Correspondance inédite,* p. 99.
[4] *Ibid.,* p. 100.
[5] *Ibid.,* p. 101.

lem. In both countries, the armies of the Revolution had destroyed the Old Regime and superimposed on its ruins military dictatorships that were hastily organized and maintained by force. What was to fill the void in Italy and Germany caused by the shattering of the French Empire? That was the problem. At first sight, the solution for Italy appeared relatively simple. Nowhere else did the Old Regime possess such ancient and sturdy roots, nowhere else had the Revolution met with such success in looting the treasure vaults and breaking the laws, and with such failure in penetrating minds and institutions. In 1814, no sooner had the revolutionary governments fallen in northern and central Italy, than the vast majority of the country had returned to the past with a vengeance. The King of Piedmont and the Pope had reoccupied their states and brought back the Old Regime in full force. The government set up in Genoa by Lord Bentinck had planned to revive the Republic as it had been before the Revolution, and had sent to Vienna a youth of twenty-eight, Marquis Brignole-Sale, to ask the Congress to perform this miracle. There were only a few groups of young men, belonging to the upper classes, who wanted to take advantage of the catastrophe to plan a glorious future for Italy. But what sort of a future? Unity? Independence? Their aspirations were rather vague; their strength and influence so insignificant that they had found no support in the Italian governments represented at the Congress. This youthful faction was represented in Vienna by several nobles of Milan—Confalonieri, Somaglia, and Litta—who were there as tourists and observers. But all the official and semi-official representatives of the Italian states admitted to Congress, headed by the papal nuncio and legate, demanded the complete restoration of the Old Regime. Francis I, Emperor of Austria, had taken on the role of liberator and savior for them, when, in May, he had told a delegation from Lombardy in Paris that after the victory of the Allies there could no longer be any question of unity or constitutional government in Italy; and when, in October, he had instructed Metternich to tell the Count of San Marzano, minister of the King of Sardinia, that he was going to insure the tranquillity of the peninsula by smothering all ideas of federation and constitution.[6] Led by the Church, the upper and middle classes in Italy were united in their hatred for the Revolution, and wanted no more talk of constitution, liberty, or unity.

Nothing would have been simpler or easier than to apply the law of nations to the Old Regime in Italy. And yet, even in Italy, the law of nations came up against unforeseen obstacles. In 1801, Bonaparte had managed to obtain the Duchy of Parma and the Grand Duchy of Tuscany, through cession by their rulers. He had annexed Parma to France and had indemnified the Duke of Parma with Tuscany, giving it the high-sounding title of Kingdom of Etruria. The Duke of Parma's father-in-law, Charles IV, King of Spain, had paid for this classical title with no less a sacrifice than Louisiana. The Grand Duke of Tuscany, Ferdinand, had in his turn been recompensed in Germany, with the Duchy of Würzburg. But in 1807, Napoleon had transformed the Kingdom of Etruria into a *département* of France, promising in exchange to the Queen of Etruria, who had become regent after the death of her husband, a hypothetical kingdom of Lusitania, which he intended to create in Portugal. By the Treaty of Paris, France had ceded to the Allies the *départements* created out of the former Duchy of Parma and the former Grand Duchy of Tuscany. What was to be done with them?

As to the position of Parma, there could be no doubt. It had been ceded by formal treaty; a legitimate possession of France from 1801 to 1814, it was now vacant territory. The Congress could legally dispose of it. But Tuscany was a different case. The Grand Duke had ceded it by a formal treaty to France, who, by formal treaty, had ceded it to the Duke of Parma. The latter and his widow

6 Bianchi, *op. cit.*, I, 10-11.

had therefore been the legitimate sovereigns of Tuscany until 1811, when the widowed Queen of Etruria had in her turn ceded it by formal treaty to Napoleon, against the promise of the future kingdom of Lusitania. As the promise had not been kept, the cession was null and void. Therefore, the Queen of Etruria had never ceased being the legitimate ruler of the former Grand Duchy of Tuscany; the Congress had only to restore her dominions.

That was the thesis of Louis XVIII in his Instructions. But at this stage an unforeseen complication arose. The former Grand Duke of Tuscany, Ferdinand, who in 1801 had consented to exchange his Tuscan garden for the bleak Duchy of Würzburg, had in September, just before the opening of Congress, without any authorization, *motu proprio,* returned to the Palazzo Pitti and resumed the government of Tuscany. The population had welcomed him and obeyed him as their legitimate sovereign. And so he was, if not by letter of the treaty, by virtue of the "ancient law of posession," which Talleyrand had acknowledged to be one of the foundations of legitimacy, comparing it to the interpretation of common law. An absence of thirteen years had not made the people of Tuscany forget their ancient dynasty and the peaceful prosperity which they had enjoyed under its government. Everyone in Tuscany knew the latter, and no one knew the treaties and the distant powers which, since 1801, had twice changed the regime without in the least troubling to find out what were the desires and interests of the people.

Add to that the fact that Ferdinand was the brother of the Austrian Emperor. This explains why the Neapolitan army, which in September was occupying Tuscany, saluted him as lawful overlord, when he introduced himself. If the Congress had decided in favor of the Queen of Etruria, it would have been necessary to persuade or to oblige Ferdinand to get out—an insult to the House of Hapsburg and its ruler, of which the Vienna Congress would never be guilty! Louis XVIII had foreseen the difficulty, and he had thought, "if the restoration of Tuscany proved too difficult," of giving the duchies of Parma, Piacenza, and Guastalla to the Queen of Etruria. Being vacant territories, they could be restored to their former owner. But the treaty signed on April 11 by Napoleon and the Allies, which had been confirmed by the French government, had promised these lands to Marie Louise. For some time, a way out of these difficulties had been sought. One solution proposed to give the Queen of Etruria part of the Legations. These could be disposed of by the Congress, as the Pope had ceded them to France by the Treaty of Tolentino. But the Etruscan Queen refused to accept them. Cardinal Consalvi was threatening with hell fire any sovereign who touched one clod of the former pontifical territory.

Although a government can only be a government when it is legitimate, there are different principles and forms of legitimacy which come into collision. The Queen of Etruria might claim Tuscany by virtue of her treaties; while Ferdinand might claim it on the ground of "the ancient law of possession," which, for people weary of revolutionary anarchy, might have more value than treaties. And there are not only living legitimacies, but also legitimacies that are dead or dying, that remain only in skeleton form—parchment legitimacies. The living legitimacy which Talleyrand was attempting to introduce into the Congress carried along with it a host of dead legitimacies: aristocratic republics, absolute monarchies, and the little vassal sovereignties of the Old Regime which had vanished in the revolutionary cataclysm and which could no longer be resuscitated, such as Berne, Genoa, and the mediatized and immediate princes of the Holy Roman Empire; or which aspired to being restored just as they had been when they disappeared, such as the House of Savoy and the papal states. It was not easy to distinguish between the living and the dead legitimacies in the midst of the celebrating in Vienna, where they were all dancing, feasting, intriguing, quarreling, and arguing together. And finally, just to make things more difficult, Murat was in Naples. In January, Austria and Naples, despairing over their future, had made an alliance. Now, in October, with victory behind her and all fear removed, Austria found this alliance very troublesome. It was difficult to fit this leftover from the Revolution—Murat's kingdom—into the new European order; Vienna was perfectly aware of this. But the treaty of January 11 was a clear reminder that the Austrian Emperor had guaranteed Murat's domains. At that time treaties had not yet become scraps of paper. Besides, it would have taken force to dispossess Murat. Vienna was unwilling to resort to that and did not want France to do so. Under no circumstance were French troops to enter Italy again. There was an even greater danger. Murat might put himself at the head of all the turbulent and discontented elements which had supported the revolutionary regime, and attempt to create a separate and independent kingdom of Italy. This was Metternich's chief worry.[7] That is why, on November 5, during the first discussion of Italian affairs in which Talleyrand participated, Metternich proposed to withdraw the question of Naples from the Congress and postpone it to some future date. This is how Talleyrand summarized, in his correspondence with Louis, the discussion which this proposal started.

"The press of circumstance," he told me, "will inevitably bring about the return of the Bourbons to the throne of Naples."

"The press of circumstance," I replied, "seems strongest to me right now; the Congress must settle this question. From a geographical standpoint, the question should come up the

---

[7] For an understanding of Metternich's ideas on the subject of Murat, Cardinal Consalvi's letter to Cardinal Pacca (September 8, 1814) is extremely important. Cf. Rinieri, *op. cit.*, pp. 7-8.

last of the Italian problems, and I consent to our following a geographical order. Further than that I am unable to go."

M. de Metternich then spoke of Murat's partisans in Italy.

"If you organize Italy, he will lose them all. Put an end to this odious makeshift; establish the succession in Sardinia; send an archduke to administer Milan; recognize the claims of the Queen of Etruria; restore to the Pope what belongs to him, which your troops are occupying; then Murat will have no more hold over the people; he will be considered nothing but a brigand by Italy."

It was agreed to take up the Italian questions in their geographical order, from north to south, and to start the next conference with Sardinia. The difference between the attitudes of Metternich and Talleyrand is obvious. Metternich wanted to postpone or to get around difficulties; Talleyrand wanted to take them by assault without any delay. Metternich, who distrusted principles, wanted to gamble with fate and lost himself in fear and indecision. "The word 'complication,' Talleyrand wrote to the King, "is one which M. de Metternich constantly uses in order to cling to the vagueness which his weak policies require." [8] Secure in the principles he followed, Talleyrand never hesitated. But the resolutions of November 5 on the Italian question had a deeper and more universal significance. To be understood, they must be interpreted in light of the principle of legitimacy, which is the basis for all Talleyrand's actions at the Congress. Talleyrand's thoughts on this subject might run as follows: A unified state of Italy could not be justified by the principle of monarchic legitimacy, because there is no royal family which is recognized by the whole of Italy, as the Bourbons were by the whole of France. Nor could it be justified by the principle of democratic legitimacy, because the Revolution had made the principle of popular sovereignty objectionable by distorting it; the majority of the people either do not understand it or reject it. A unified Italian

[8] *Correspondance inédite,* p. 101.

state today could only be a military and revolutionary dictatorship without legal justification, such as the Cisalpine Republic, the Kingdom of Italy, and the Kingdom of Murat; one of those violent artificial states, of which we are trying to rid Europe because they are unable to live in peace. The complications which you, Metternich, fear in Italy have no other cause or origin; and you will not eliminate them by evasion and guile or by letting events take their course. In order that Italy may not become a permanent source of trouble for Europe, she must be governed by legitimate governments; and the only regimes in Italy which have preserved their legitimacy are those which were overthrown by the Revolution. If you restore some of those regimes and permit a military and revolutionary dictatorship to exist alongside, you are making war inevitable. In order to legitimize his throne, Murat will try to gain possession of the whole peninsula. The stability and peace of Europe will again be in danger.[9]

The same reasoning is applicable to Germany. It seems obvious to me that when Talleyrand wrote the King that "German unity would at present be of enormous significance to France," and when he alluded to the "disturbance of a mass like Germany," he was thinking of similar dangers. More generally, Talleyrand's thesis on the unity of Germany and of Italy may be summed up as follows: "In order that the two countries may be united without exposing Europe to the gravest peril, they must be united by governments whose legitimacy is of a substantial and acceptable nature, which will free them of the obligation to take chances." The history of Europe up till now has been a striking confirmation of this opinion. But at the moment, Talleyrand's profound judgment caused fresh discord in the Congress, and the struggle between the great powers became sharper. At the beginning of November, Alexander succeeded by a rather strange maneuver in

[9] Cf. on this viewpoint the opinion of Capo d'Istria, revealed in a secret report to Baron Hager, Weil, *op. cit.*, I, 593.

winning Prussia back to his side, just when Metternich and Castlereagh believed they had weakened her resolution. The political gambler was becoming bolder as the knight errant disappeared. He invited the Prussian King to dinner and easily convinced him that he should declare himself wholeheartedly in favor of the Polish scheme. At the end of the dinner, the Czar summoned Hardenberg, the Prussian chancellor; no sooner had the latter appeared than Alexander, in the presence of the silent and impassive King, informed him in no uncertain terms of the definite and unshakable agreement he had reached with the King regarding Poland. When the unfortunate Hardenberg attempted to raise objections, the Czar ordered him to say outright whether he was going to obey the commands of his King. Hardenberg declared that he would execute the letter of the King's orders without discussion.

If it is true that Hardenberg said later that he had never been in such a position in all his life, we may well believe him. The result of this conversation was a secret memorandum handed to Castlereagh by Hardenberg on November 7. Hardenberg declared that all resistance to Alexander's plans must be abandoned, and that future discussion must be confined to determining the boundaries of the Polish Kingdom and to the approval of its establishment under a constitutional government. He endeavored to show that a constitutional Kingdom of Poland would weaken the Russian Empire and possess certain advantages for Prussia and Austria.[10]

At the same time, Alexander wished to be reconciled with Talleyrand; and, a few days before his dinner with the Prussian King, he had asked to see him. Talleyrand had avoided the interview, fearing that an audience under such abnormal conditions would cause too much suspicion.[11] After the capitulation of the Prussian King and

[10] This memorandum was published by Lutostanski, *op. cit.*, pp. 358-360.
[11] *Correspondance inédite*, p. 117.

Hardenberg, however, Metternich, furious at the Czar, bethought himself of a *rapprochment* with Talleyrand. On November 11 he took a definite step in that direction. He had assembled Talleyrand, Castlereagh, and Nesselrode for a discussion on Italy. The question of Genoa was brought up and gone over thoroughly in a very friendly fashion. In the end, they decided to have Metternich convoke, on the following day, the delegates of the signatory powers to the Paris treaty and the representatives of Genoa and the King of Sardinia, in order to decide the fate of the former republic. After Castlereagh and Nesselrode had departed, Metternich vowed Talleyrand to secrecy and proceeded to read him his letter to Hardenberg of October 22, in which he had promised Hardenberg the whole of Saxony in exchange for Prussia's support on the question of Poland. Metternich assured Talleyrand that he was through with such illusions and that Austria would never again abandon Saxony.[12] But, although this part of the conversation pleased Talleyrand, what followed pleased him a great deal less. He wrote to Louis:

As for Poland, he gave me to understand that he would yield a large part, which signifies that he will yield everything if Alexander abandons nothing.

And he added:

I was still with him when the report was brought to him showing the condition of the Austrian army. He allowed me to see it. The present strength of this army consists of 374,000 men, 52,000 of which are cavalry, and 800 guns. Yet, with all these forces, he still believes the Austrian monarchy has no other choice than to submit to everything, and resign itself to the inevitable.

Once more Talleyrand was astounded at Austria's trepidation. Was the Court of Vienna more afraid than anyone else of the powerful army it could muster? There was an enigma which even the astute mind of Talleyrand could

12 *Ibid.*, pp. 112-114.

not grasp. Nevertheless, Talleyrand was not dissatisfied with Austria's sudden change of policy, which made him hopeful of breaking up the allied Coalition. He became more and more reserved with Alexander. The latter, seeing that his advances were futile and that Talleyrand would not be persuaded to ask for an audience, had been seeking him out for several days in the various salons. But Talleyrand avoided him as much as possible. The day after his conversation with Metternich—Saturday, November 12— Talleyrand was at a large reception given by Count Zichy. Alexander was there. Talleyrand had spent almost the whole time in the game room in order not to encounter him, and had taken advantage of the moment when the guests were sitting down at table to make his escape. But just as he reached the door of the anteroom, he felt a hand on his shoulder. Turning around, he saw Alexander. After reproaching him for his inaccessibility, the Czar asked him to pay a visit on Monday in ordinary clothes instead of court attire, as a friend. This time Talleyrand could not get out of it, and he had to accept the invitation for the fourteenth.

On the thirteenth the delegates of the eight signatory powers to the Paris treaty met to deliberate on the convening of the Congress and the setting-up of committees, as they had decided to do in the last meeting on October 31, and on the question of Genoa, as planned in the conference called by Metternich on November 11. Metternich, who was presiding, moved that they open with the application of the second secret article of the Paris treaty, which was conceived as follows:

The King of Sardinia will receive an addition to his territory in the state of Genoa; the port of Genoa will remain independent; the powers intend to come to terms with the King of Sardinia regarding this matter.

But did these powers have the right to establish the indemnity for the King of Sardinia? Only the Congress had the authority to do that. It was necessary to choose a committee on the affairs of Italy, similar to the committee on those of Germany. This thesis was held by the Spanish delegate, M. de Labrador. Metternich replied that the indemnity for the King of Sardinia had been established by the Treaty of Paris; and he opposed a subtle distinction to the formation of a committee on Italian affairs. Germany was obviously a political entity, since she was to be united in a federation. Italy neither was nor was it planned to make of her a political entity; she was a peninsula made up of a number of independent states. Her problems were, therefore, all individual and separate problems, to be treated separately, beginning with Genoa.

M. de Labrador had spoken as a disciple of Talleyrand's. Genoa was a vacant state; neither the conquerors nor the eight signatory powers had any right to dispose of it. But this time the master did not bear out the disciple; and he agreed with Metternich that the question of Genoa had been settled by the Treaty of Paris. It is possible that he decided it was useless to defend his position on this subject, which would have led to a kind of revision of the Paris treaty. He was content to propose that formal notice be given to the Marquis of Brignole, the delegate from Genoa, that "The powers will concede the most liberal conditions for the union of Genoa to Piedmont and will take into full account the interests, wishes, and needs of the Genoese." This was approved. The question of Genoa having been settled, Metternich put forth the question which had been postponed by the last meeting: should a general meeting of all the delegates be convened immediately after the credentials had been verified? It was decided that "in view of the present state of individual negotiations, this general meeting would be of no use, and that it would be better to postpone it to a future date.[13]

Another postponement! The Allies could not bring

[13] Cf. the minutes of this meeting in Angeberg, *op. cit.*, pp. 425-427.

themselves to acknowledge the sovereign law of Europe, and yet dared not assert their own sovereignty. Everything was vague and uncertain. This was proved the next day, November 14, when the Swiss problems were taken up, and another collision occurred between conflicting legitimacies.

Switzerland had revolted when the Revolution had attempted to force a republic on her. But at the same time she had also welcomed the flood of new ideas which had overwhelmed Paris at the beginning of the Revolution and had later continued in a feeble trickle, interrupted by accesses of panic. The regime of mediation had been the product of two forces: armed resistance to invasion and a welcome acceptance of the nobler ideals of the Revolution. Whereas the Italian Republic proclaimed at Lyon bound northern Italy to France, to the exclusive interests of the dominant power, the mediatory government gave Switzerland substantial compensations for the disguised protectorate which it imposed on her. Among these were the suppression of the *baillages;* [14] the liberation of Vaud and Argovie; the democratization of a number of cantons, beginning with the most powerful—Berne. The government of mediation, unlike the Italian regime, had not been an outright imposition. It had been imposed on the aristocracy, which wanted to preserve the Old Regime, and on that part of the population which sought complete independence; it had been accepted by that part of Switzerland which for a generation had aspired toward a greater degree of liberty and of equality. Also unlike the Italian regime, it had not fallen with the Revolution, although it had experienced a number of vicissitudes. When in 1814 the Allies had entered Switzerland, the former aristocratic party had come out from seclusion and demanded the restoration of the Old Regime, including the *baillages.* The new cantons of Vaud and Argovie had threatened to defend themselves by force of arms. On January 3, the Allies had asked the cantons to draw up a constitution.

14 Tribunals who were responsible only to the sovereign.

The aristocratic cantons had set up a Diet at Lucerne, while the democratic cantons had set one up at Zurich. In the spring of 1814, the outlook for Switzerland was bad: war between the cantons over boundaries; civil warfare in many cantons between the old aristocracy and the new classes favored by the mediatory regime. Fortunately for Switzerland and for Europe, one small group of men had not despaired; they had been aided by the fantastic plans of the European ministries—a return to the old Empire, a Kingdom of Helvetia—and by the pressure of the Allies. Very wisely, the latter had declared that they would uphold the integrity of the nineteen existing cantons, but made it a condition for Switzerland's admission to the Congress that she draw up and approve a constitution. On September 12, the Diet had in principle admitted the three cantons of Valois, Neuchâtel, and Geneva to the Confederation, and on the twentieth the Diet had approved the new federal pact. This pact showed signs of having been drawn up in haste, but it sufficed to give a juridical basis for the Confederation. It was all the more urgently required in order to put an end to the chaotic conditions in Switzerland and to enable the Vienna diplomats to determine the real legitimacy of the restored independence.

It was for the purpose of giving a legal standing to the new regime that the representatives of the allied powers "intervening in the affairs of Switzerland"—as they were officially described—assembled on November 14. The French representative was not present. We have already seen that, on November 5, Metternich had promised Talleyrand to include France in the discussions on Switzerland. What, then, had happened? I have not been able to find the answer. Complications of some kind must have arisen. The fact remains that on November 14 the Allies had returned to their original plan—at least in the matter of Switzerland—of settling things themselves. But they immediately found themselves up against a claim by Berne which threatened the destruction of the Confederation, as it had been constituted by the federal pact of September 12. Berne claimed the restitution of Argovie, which had been recognized by the pact as one of the twenty-two cantons making up the Confederation. What was even more serious, Berne justified her claim by a principle of the law of nations which Louis's Instructions had declared fundamental; this was the principle that force can never create sovereignty. The demand of Berne could be stated thus: "The territories of Vaud and Argovie have been taken from us by force; we have never ceded them, therefore they have never ceased to belong to us. We do not reclaim all that has been taken from us; we will be satisfied with Argovie and with certain indemnities from the canton of Vaud. But Argovie must be returned to us."

The Congress could not reply that Berne, like Genoa, was vacant territory, because of its dynasty having died out when the ruling aristocracy had collapsed. For the Allies had supported the restoration of the former government; the sovereign power had been resuscitated and, though mutilated, was alive; therefore its rights were indefeasible. But the Allies neither wanted nor were able to grant the claims of Berne. The new order which Berne declared illegitimate had not been created and imposed on Switzerland by force alone; it had been made at least partly legitimate by consent and necessity. If it was imperfect, then declaring it a complete usurpation would not improve it. In order to satisfy Berne, force would have to be used: either foreign intervention or civil war, or both. Could Europe be given peace, while at the same time Switzerland was put to fire and sword for the sake of restoring the former grandeur of a few noblemen in Berne? The Allies had no intention of doing this. But how were they to reject the claims of Berne without contradicting the principle on which they were painfully seeking to establish the reconstruction of Europe, upset by so many wars and revolutions?

"We are guided by principles as by railroad tracks. Thanks to them, we may advance without looking," wrote Leo Ferrero. They guide us like tracks because they, too, are rigid and straight. But the earth's crust on which the tracks are laid and human existence to which principles are applied, are both uneven. That is why it is so difficult to construct a railroad, even on a plain, and to govern human society by means of principles.

The problem raised by Berne was so serious that the Austrian and Prussian delegates, Wessenberg and Humboldt, had come to the November 14 meeting with written opinions in order to justify their votes. Wessenberg's statement declared that the intervening powers had pledged themselves to uphold the political existence of the nineteen cantons; therefore, they could not "support the canton of Berne in her claims on Vaud and Argovie." He suggested offering Berne "a part of the bishopric of Bâle, which the intervening powers may dispose of as a conquest." The Prussian delegate had drafted a longer note which went into the matter more thoroughly and was based on the principle formulated below; it was necessary

. . . only to propose a settlement acceptable to all the parties which would establish a state of possession in Switzerland based on mutual consent, rather than on actual or rightful possession, which is contested. This is all the more necessary since the position of the four allied powers would make it equally difficult and painful for them to force acceptance of their decision.

Applying this principle, Humboldt concluded that it was impossible to retrocede Argovie to Berne, and that it was necessary to offer Berne a part of Bâle, "carefully abstaining from using the term indemnity." After these two notes had been presented, it was decided that Russia and England would also give their written opinions at the next meeting on the morrow, and also that the Swiss delegation would be invited then in order to declare its mission.

That same day, instead of attending the meeting, Talleyrand had kept his promise to visit the Czar. He had, however, first taken the precaution of informing Castlereagh and Metternich of what had happened, "so as to allay any suspicion of trickery which they might feel." After the long audience, Talleyrand wrote Louis that "everything went smoothly and peacefully." The interlocutors stated their viewpoints frankly, but in the most cordial fashion; both remained unconvinced, and they parted as old friends. Talleyrand received the impression that the Czar had made the interview in order to inform himself about the armament which had been attributed to France; to discover whether France, if the case should arise, would be disposed to conclude an alliance with Russia; and to sound out France's real intentions with regard to Saxony.[15] The political gambler was playing his cards with incontestable skill. Talleyrand saw in Russia, too, the possibility of carrying out the plan which he was pursuing: to split up the Coalition of Allies. It was evident that Alexander no longer counted on obtaining what he wanted through the support of his Allies; and, like Austria, he was beginning to lean toward France.

When Talleyrand returned to his own lodgings after the audience, he found the minister of Saxony, who conveyed to him, with a protest from his King, a grave piece of news. Prince Repnin, the Russian governor general in Saxony, had proclaimed in a circular to the Saxon authorities that, as a consequence of an agreement between Russia and Prussia to which Austria and England had given their consent, he was turning over the administration of the Saxon kingdom to the representatives of the Prussian King. This was another blow. Alexander was repaying his friend's support of his own plans, and making a twofold attempt to force the hand of the Congress and compromise

15 *Correspondance inédite*, pp. 119-127.

Austria and England. Metternich and Castlereagh protested that this was an abuse of their consent, by making it absolute when it had been purely conditional.[16] The more the Allies attempted to form a Coalition against France, the further apart they got.

The following day, November 15, Lord Stewart, the English delegate, brought his written opinion on the claims of Berne, and read it aloud. Capo d'Istria declared his intention of reading his own opinion at the next meeting. Lord Stewart also put forth a question of principle, perhaps in less subtle fashion than Humboldt, but nevertheless very clear:

This settlement, to be efficacious, must, if possible, be unanimous on the part of the intervening powers; it must appear to conform, as far as possible, to all previous declarations by them. Finally, it must be of a nature to disturb as little as possible the state of possession which has existed for several years and which the allied powers, whatever the justice or injustice of its origin, have no right to change and construe as a conquest, inasmuch as their armies entered Switzerland as friends, on the heels of a declaration announcing her neutrality; consequently, their right to intervene should be strictly confined to that of necessity.

Starting from this premise, the English delegate concluded that it would not be possible to restore Argovie to Berne or even to indemnify her with a portion of this territory. He declared himself ready to study the question of sufficient compensation to "preserve Europe from the evils which might result from the confusion of Swiss affairs." After this reading, the Swiss delegation was brought in, and its head, M. de Reinhard, made a long speech. He thanked the powers for everything they had done for Switzerland: he presented the new federal pact and asked for the solemn recognition of the liberty and independence of the Confederation, recognition of Swiss neutrality by all the powers participating in the Congress, and the terri-

16 *Ibid.*, p. 130.

torial reconstitution of Switzerland, with defensible military frontiers. He declared that in his opinion civil war in Switzerland could only be prevented by the intervention of the Allies. However, on this point, the delegation was not in accord; M. de Montenach declared that Switzerland should resolve her domestic problems "independently of any foreign intervention." Upon the request of the Russian and Prussian plenipotentiaries, he specified arbitration as the most efficient method, a procedure which had been used by the cantons for centuries. At this point, an argument arose between M. de Reinhard and M. de Montenach on the possibility and efficacy of arbitration under the present circumstances. M. de Montenach finally admitted that, although he found foreign intervention repugnant, the Allies would perform a great service to Switzerland by recommending arbitration to the cantons. After the Swiss delegation had withdrawn, the committee deliberated on whether they should send a message to the Diet asking it to uphold the peace in Switzerland, but came to no decision. Instead, they determined to invite the deputy from Berne to the meeting on November 17. The matter would be taken up then.

On November 16, the two Russian delegates, Stein and Capo d'Istria, drafted and signed their report on the claims of Berne. The Russian opinion was longer and more detailed than the three others had been. In it, the two questions of right and of expediency were carefully differentiated; the former was set forth in this manner: Has the act of mediation, to which the cantons of Vaud and Argovie owe their existence, been completely annulled by the Diet's decree of December 29, which abolished it?

Such is the general state of the matter before the Committee. It presents for discussion questions of right and questions of policy or expediency. The most important of the former is the one on the validity of the act of mediation, and on the rights which it gives to the interested parties. The act of mediation cannot be considered as originally and essentially worthless. It was drawn up under a dominating influence, but not one which would make the consent of the deputies who accepted it fallacious. It was created by the mediator with full knowledge of Switzerland's interests. Its influence, according to the word of almost every inhabitant, has been beneficial to the nation and has been accepted as law for eleven years.

If the act of mediation was not worthless in its origin, by what right do some persons demand the return of aristocratic institutions, monopolies, and the subjection of their compatriots? It is true that the act of mediation has been abolished by the Diet's declaration of December 29. But certainly this implied no retroactive and unlimited effect; on the contrary, it preserved quite expressly the existing cantons, etc.

The foreign powers invited these same cantons to draw up a Constitution (January 3), and later expressed their wish (March) to preserve the absolute integrity of the cantons. The rights of the claimants are therefore founded neither on the act's unlimited abolishment, nor on the will of the powers. Since Berne and the claimant cantons took no part in the war, there can be no question of *jure postliminii*.

In this text, the distinction between living legitimacies and parchment legitimacies is clearly understood.[17] It is obvious that the hesitant policy produced in the Allies at the beginning of the Congress by the opposition of Talleyrand, was crystallizing more and more, as the Congress became more involved and protracted, into a living drama of human weaknesses. If they had imagined for an instant that they could re-establish peace and balance in Europe by combinations of power and interests, of which they would be the sole arbiters, the Allies had soon perceived their mistake after seeing the demands, ambitions, and aspirations which had been making havoc of the Congress for a month and a half. Their leaders and ministers were still men of the eighteenth century, and they had suffered too much under the Revolution, not to realize that order

[17] For this period of Swiss history, it is well to read the first six chapters of M. Rappard's important work, *L'Individu et l'Etat dans l'évolution constitutionelle de la Suisse*, Zurich, 1936.

would reign in Europe, confidence would live again, and peace would be established by confidence only if they adhered to certain principles and laws which were universally understood and accepted. But which? Talleyrand's principle of legitimacy? The eighteenth-century law of nations? At first, both sovereigns and ministers had feared that all these fine doctrines would prevent them from safeguarding the interests of their states. A conflict between interests and principles had broken out. Now that they were making up their minds to reconstruct Europe according to certain principles, an even more complicated and obscure conflict was breaking out between living legitimacies and those which were either dead or dying. How were they to resolve the dilemma? It was not easy to lay tracks over the mountain of ruins which covered Europe after twenty-five years of revolutions and wars without rules.

The Russian note on the demands of Berne was to be communicated to the committee of intervening powers at the meeting on November 17. But this meeting never took place. On the sixteenth, the very day on which the Russian plenipotentiaries were drawing up their note on Swiss affairs, Count Vinzigerode and Baron Linden had addressed a note to the committee on German affairs, to notify it that the King of Württemberg was withdrawing from the committee, and refused to take any further part in the discussion. The same day the plenipotentiaries of twenty-nine sovereign princes and free cities of Germany addressed a note to Prince Metternich and Prince Hardenberg, asserting that the future Constitution of Germany should be discussed and approved by all the German states. It amounted to a declaration that the committee was illegitimate and its labors worthless. This thunderbolt suspended the operations of the Congress for several days. What had happened in the committee?

XII

GERMANY

By the end of the eighteenth century, the Holy Roman
Empire had become little more than a vast, dilapidated
Gothic structure in the last stages of decrepitude, threatening to collapse at any moment. But its crumbling arches
still offered, like the Old Regime in France, shelters against
the abuse of force and the innate folly of man: laws, customs, individual rights, legal organization of the great
bodies of the state, tribunals, Diets, and the imperial constitution. In any case, its former power was so reduced that
it could do neither much harm nor much good. The earthquake of 1806 had demolished this ancient edifice and
thrown Germany into a revolutionary confusion, which
had been the German echo of the French Revolution. The
juridical and political crystallization of the Holy Empire
had been replaced by a permanent state of war, and by
the militant concentration of power in the service of contradictory interests, ambitions, and ideologies; Germany
had been hurled into a chaos where the spirit of adventure,
force, and the frenzy of fears which its abuse provoked, had
exploded. Everywhere, governments had become more

active, arbitrary, and demanding. By comparison, the Empire, like the Old Regime in France, had been in a state of quiescent debility. For several years, Napoleon had tried to substitute his revolutionary Empire for the Holy Roman Empire, by establishing his protectorate over the Confederation of the Rhine, and by forcing an uncertain vassalage on Prussia and Austria. All he had accomplished had been to provoke a terrific revolt in Germany. Now, the Holy Roman Empire and the French Empire were both resting in their graves; Germany was no longer anything but a shapeless and quivering mass of small and large states juxtaposed without any link or line of conduct. Talleyrand had already made Louis XVIII understand that this mass, left to its own destiny in the center of Europe, might become extremely dangerous for Europe and for France.

It was necessary to put chains around it, but not by force, against which it had just revolted; it was even necessary to begin by freeing it of the chains with which force had burdened it, during the Revolution and the war. Thus it was necessary to find a liberating chain in Germany, even as in France; a contradiction *in adjecto,* as a philosopher would say. During the war, the Allies had considered a Germanic Confederation which might replace the old Gothic unity of the Holy Roman Empire. The Congress was to translate this generic project into a written and practical constitution; this was the task which the committee of the five great German courts—Austria, Prussia, Hanover, Bavaria, Württemberg—had arrogated to themselves on October 14, in a rather arbitrary manner. Two days later, the representatives of the five courts gathered together in order to begin the work. The meeting opened with a protest from the representative of the King of Württemberg, who declared that he was not able to sign the protocol of the previous meeting because (I quote the official text of the protocol):

... not only in the heading, but also in the text itself, Hanover was named before Württemberg and the signatures were placed in such a way that there was no space for him to put his name between those of Bavaria and Hanover, whereas he had to insist that the King of Württemberg rank above the King of Hanover.

The King of Hanover was the Regent of England; but he had only been King for four days. On October 12, he had transformed into a royal title the electoral title which he had kept until then, although since 1806 the Emperor whom he was supposed to elect had ceased to exist. Württemberg had ceased to be a Duchy and had become a Kingdom in 1806. The question of which had the right to sign first, the infant kingdom or the child kingdom, was to be of immense importance to the peace of the world, since it took up the greater part of the meeting. Six men possessing a high degree of intelligence strove for several hours to find an expedient "by which this difference may be settled without prejudice to either of the two parties"; many proposals and counterproposals were offered and rejected; finally they managed to persuade the representatives of the King of Württemberg to accept a compromise solution *ad referendum.* This decisive question having been eliminated, a plan for a federal constitution, presented by Austria and Prussia, came up for examination. The plan called for a confederation of all the German states, great and small, under the direction of the Diet, but they were to be a part of the Confederation only so far as their German possessions were concerned. The German sovereigns were to renounce warfare among themselves, and to submit to the federal tribunal; all the states which had no possessions outside of Germany were to promise not to make war against foreign powers, not to take part in the wars of these powers, and not to conclude, without the agreement of the Confederation, any treaties of alliance, of subsidy, or of cession of troops. Finally, Article 2 of the Constitution declared that the aim of the Confederation was "The guarantee of external security and independence, as well as that of the constitutional rights of every class in the nation." Article 11 was formulated as follows:

The federative act establishes the necessity for a system of estates [1] in each state of the Confederation, and fixes the minimum rights of the estates, relying on the members of the Confederation not only to accord wider prerogatives to their estates but also to give them an organization conformable to the customs and character of the inhabitants and to the law.

The text is a little involved, but its meaning is clear; the new Germany will no longer exist under the arbitrary absolutism imposed by the wars of the Revolution: the peoples will have guarantees. Nothing is definite in the nature and extent of these guarantees; the use of the word "estates," *Stände,* indicates a certain leaning toward the representative forms of the Old Regime, which only recognized the people in the political and juridical organization of its better classes: the nobility, the clergy, and the bourgeoisie. But the right of the people to take an active part in the government was recognized in principle and on the suggestion of Prussia and Austria. The opposition came from the courts of Bavaria and Württemberg, the two kingdoms created by Napoleon, who, by having allied themselves to France and the Revolution against Germany, had been able to establish absolute governments more or less patterned on the revolutionary model of Paris. From the very first, at the meeting of October 20, the Bavarian representative declared that he could not accept the obligation of the purely Germanic states not to conclude, without the consent of the Confederation, treaties of alliance or of subsidy with foreign powers, and in particular with Prussia and Austria, for wars in which the Confederation would

[1] Translator's note: This has been chosen as the most exact translation of the word, *états,* and refers to the three estates of the realm in the Old Regime; that is, those classes which were invested with political powers and were represented in the government.

take no part. Bavaria was the third most important German power; to let herself be bound by this condition meant that she would never be able to play any part in Germany or in Europe.[2] Besides, with respect to Article 11, the Bavarian representative stated that the King had already "decided to grant his estates a Constitution in keeping with his dignity as well as suited to the locality." His Majesty, therefore, considered that it was "unsuitable to allow the future Federal Council to determine the maximum and minimum of the rights to be given this and that estate." [3] Württemberg in her turn protested against Article 9, claiming that it reduced the sovereign rights of the kings to less than those which had been enjoyed by the electors; she demanded an explanation of the allusion by the second article to "the guarantee of the constitutional rights of every class in the nation"; and she declared herself firmly opposed to Article 11 because it was harmful to sovereignty.[4]

At the meeting of October 16, the committee had split up into a majority of three—Austria, Prussia, and Hanover —and a minority of two—Bavaria and Württemberg. During successive meetings this opposition became accentuated. At the meeting of October 20, the three German states which had not been under Napoleon's rule, came out with a vigorous reply to Bavaria and Württemberg. The official protocol was as follows:

The plenipotentiaries of Austria, Prussia, and Hanover declare unanimously, regarding this matter, that they consider it absolutely necessary, in order to fulfill the purpose of the Confederation, to insist on the principle that the purely German states of the Confederation may take part in no war nor contract any alliance with foreign powers, without the consent of the Confederation. Only in this way will it be possible to attain an objective which is so important and essential to

2 D'Angeberg, op. cit., p. 305.
3 Ibid., p. 310.
4 Ibid., pp. 311, 315.

the peace of Germany. This objective is to insure that Germany, in the form of a large body of federated states situated between France on one side and Russia on the other, may not find itself, because of action taken by individual members, in a compromising position; nor become engaged in war; nor be deprived of the benefit of general neutrality, so important for Europe; nor, finally, be a witness to Germans fighting against Germans, which would come to pass if, for instance, in a war between France and Austria in Italy, one of its states could come to the assistance of France, and another to that of Austria.

It must have been quite a shock to Bavaria, so eager to take a prominent part in future events in Europe, to hear Austria and Prussia declare that the Germanic Confederation must be a peaceful and neutral bulk between France and Prussia, the purpose of which was to maintain stability and balance in Europe. But that was not all. At the same meeting, Metternich in person refuted the absolutist doctrines of Württemberg.

On the occasion of a statement against the necessity of establishing the rights of subjects belonging to the German nation—a statement contained in a declaration by the plenipotentiary from Württemberg which was read by him (Annex C)—Prince Metternich said that, nevertheless, the establishment of rights was absolutely necessary; that in the former constitution certain rights had been guaranteed to German subjects; but that recently, in a few states, repressive measures had been introduced, against which the subjects should, in the future, necessarily be guaranteed.

Several days later, the representatives of the King of Hanover vigorously entered the debate, submitting to the committee a written opinion in which it was expressly stated that:

...the term, sovereignty, in no way signifies the idea of despotism. The King of Great Britain is indubitably as much of a sovereign as any European prince; and the liberties of his people, far from upsetting his throne, serve the purpose of keeping it stable.

A representative system has functioned in Germany, without need of sanction, since time immemorial. In several states it was based on individual agreements between prince and subjects; while in the countries where there were no longer estates, the subjects enjoyed important rights which had been legally established by the Empire and which were under the protection of the laws.

His Royal Highness, the Prince Regent of Great Britain and Hanover, cannot assert that the changes which have taken place in Germany have given to the princes absolute or despotic sovereign rights over their subjects.

From these premises, the opinion drew the specific and clear conclusion which follows:

Starting from these premises, the undersigned feel themselves obligated to demand:

1. That the rights which, from time immemorial, have belonged to German subjects, be clearly defined;

2. That it be declared that the territorial constitutions based on laws and conventions be upheld, excepting necessary modifications;

3. That, even in the event that Austria, Prussia, Bavaria, and Württemberg, whether on account of their position or because of alleged treaties, should seek exemption, it would be proclaimed as law in those countries where there have been no estates but whose sovereigns wish to submit to all measures necessary for the well-being of Germany, that,

a) The consent of the estates to taxes (being understood that they are obliged to contribute to the needs of the state) is required;

b) That they must participate in making new laws;

c) That they must co-operate in the supervision of the use to which the taxes they have voted are put;

d) That they be authorized, in cases of embezzlement, to demand the punishment of the guilty officials;

It is only by putting into effect liberal principles such as these that, in view of the present trend of thought and the moderate claims of the German nation, we may hope for the re-establishment of peace and general satisfaction.

What was going on in the German mind? Had the world turned upside down? It was not surprising to find the King of Hanover—Regent of England—standing up for German liberties. But it was surprising to see Prussia and Austria, in the early meetings of the committee, posing as the godparents of a free and peaceful Germany against the specious and equivocal arguments of Bavaria and Württemberg. Yet the key to this puzzle was in Vienna. In the story of the Revolution there was one figure, Napoleon, who was always on stage and who seemed to control everything. And there was another figure who remained behind the scenes, apparently no more than an official cipher, ageless and anonymous, a kind of abstract sovereignty setting itself up against power incarnate. Yet, this invisible abstraction was no less important than the tangible incarnation. It was Francis II, who had become Emperor of the Holy Roman Empire in 1792.

He was hardly more than a child in politics, having acceded to the throne at the age of twenty-four. And he was not even a German, but an Italian, a Florentine born in the Pitti Palace in 1768, who owed his astonishing good fortune to an accident of monarchic heredity. If his uncle, Joseph II, had produced any children, Francis would have had to be satisfied with the modest title of Grand Duke of Tuscany; if his father, Leopold, had not died young, he would not have ascended the imperial throne until much later, with a great deal more experience. And yet the accession of this child was the turning point in the progress of the Revolution and of Europe. Up till then, the relations between revolutionary France and the Austrian Empire had been confined to an exchange of diplomatic notes and to mutual distrust. Although Vienna wanted to help the endangered French monarchy and to defend the interests of the Empire, threatened by the Revolution, neither

Emperor Leopold, nor Chancellor Kaunitz, nor the government circles in Vienna had any thought of war. They were only interested in negotiations. Francis II came to the throne on February 28, 1792; seven weeks later, on April 20, war broke out, a general war which devastated Europe for over two decades.

In 1792, when Francis became Emperor, Germany was in a ferment. The rich and the poor, the nobility and the bourgeoisie, people who complained of Joseph II and the reforms passed by his enlightened despotism and people who admired him while regretting that his reforms had not been even more radical—in short everyone—demanded liberty, universal happiness, invigorating reforms, rights hitherto undreamed of, the palingenesis of mankind. Out of this ferment rose a sympathy for the French Revolution which filled Germany with joyful and chimerical hopes. One year later a complete change had occurred. The police, censorship, totalitarian reorganization of education and culture, legal persecution, farcical trials, cruel sentences—all the terrible machinery of reactionism had been set in motion to stifle every trace of "Jacobinism." This degrading term was used to designate the hopes and aspirations which the romanticism of the eighteenth century and the events in France had raised in Germany.

An unfortunate coincidence? Was there a tie between the accession of this child to the Empire and the beginning of a cruel repression? Let us seek out this mysterious figure in the obscurity which has hidden him from the very beginning; let us place him under the pitiless microscope of history; let us tear off the imperial purple which covered him all his life and try to understand him as he really was.

In spite of his efforts to remain unknown, we have a direct and valuable testimonial to his character by Joseph II. This is how the latter summed up his nephew, while he was still at the Pitti Palace.

Of a dull and sullen disposition, but at the same time insensible and thereby showing few strong emotions. . . . He nevertheless appears to be energetic and systematic. . . . It seems that he is working assiduously in the field of science and he has acquired numerous attainments; it even appears that he knows a great deal of factual and scientific knowledge for one of his age. . . . But there is more of a mechanical aptitude in his exercises, an ability to copy, to take dictation, etc. Thoughts are lacking; there is nothing of himself. He does not seem to have acquired characteristics of thought or planning, whether in his speech or in his writing, which are essential. . . . I found him not without knowledge or application, but having a slow, cold judgment, though at times right. Moreover, he exhibits a singular indifference for everything in the way of entertainment and distraction. Although intellectually lazy, he is physically healthy, even sturdy in spite of his small stature. And, though I doubt whether this boy will ever possess mental or physical accomplishments, I do not despair of his showing resolution some day and a mind well-fitted for the duties which await him . . . but in that country and in such company it is impossible for my brother's sons to grow up capable of some day serving the state, in whatever position it may be. The mind shrinks into itself and the body is weakened in that climate and with that way of life.[5]

Joseph II was no more satisfied after his nephew had spent seven or eight months' intensive training at the Hofburg:

I have the greatest proof of it in my nephew Francis, whose apathy and indifference, and misled stoicism, you well know, this in spite of all I have done to put him at ease, to make him sincere, frank, and natural, to lead him to think and act for himself without embarrassment; I am far from having accomplished anything in that direction; on the least excuse he relapses, stands rooted to the ground, absent-mindedly, with his arms and legs dangling, and would not move from

5 Viktor Bibl, *François II* (Paris, 1936), pp. 11, 12.

that position until the next day if someone did not tell him to get along.[6]

Joseph II complains of his nephew's laziness. But Francis II was to be neither a lazy nor a stupid emperor; he was even to astonish his contemporaries by his indefatigable and meticulous activity. Joseph II seems to have denounced as laziness in the child what was to become, in the man, the extreme curtness of a distrustful temperament, a resistance to enthusiasms, illusions, flights of fancy, dreams, to all the seductions of imagination and passion. He was a man who distrusted both imagination and passion because they were too strong, and reason because it was too weak. Thence, his incurable repugnance for and distrust of the spiritual effervescence of the *Aufklärung*, and the encyclopedism which, since the second half of the eighteenth century, had been agitating part of Europe. The Pitti Palace, and Poggio Imperiale, where he had lived until his seventeenth year—he had been transferred to the Hofburg in 1784—had still further chilled and stiffened him against the passionate breaking-up of his century. The warm rays of the *Aufklärung* and of encyclopedism had fallen powerless on the immense glacier of the Italian Counter Reformation. French books had penetrated into Italy and had been read by a small part of the elite; but they had provoked no collective enthusiasm, no great intellectual movement. The lethargy which possessed Italy, asleep in her fair garden and untouched by thought, coincided much better with the cold, distrustful temperament of the new emperor than did the dreams, the dissatisfactions, the need to reform everything, the aspirations toward an imaginary future, with which part of Europe was seething. In other words, he was not a sovereign of the *Aufklärung* like his uncle and his father, but a crowned disciple of the Italian Counter Reformation. And this crowned disciple of the Italian Counter

[6] *Ibid.*, p. 13.

Reformation had become emperor at the age of twenty-
four!

The world has been, is, and can only be, governed by
old men. Gerontocracy is the natural political structure
of humanity. Youth desires and fears with equal ease; that
is why it is the predestined instrument of the spirit of
adventure, of its unthinking temerities and of the vast
collective fears in which these temerities always end. When
an accident of history gives power to youth, the spirit of
adventure and fear seize upon the world. It had happened
in 1792; hardly had he ascended the throne, than Francis
II, against the advice and protests of the aged chancellor,
Kaunitz, had taken a position clearly hostile to the Revolution, and had provoked war in less than two months.
The universal war which began in 1792 and ended in
1815, the universal war which was to let loose the great
panic of Europe, had its origin in the dual adventure of
a twenty-four-year-old emperor, and of a party—the Girondists—the greater majority of which were "under thirty."
But the young Emperor, like the Revolution, was not long
in losing his head, in the fearful chaos which the combination of war and the Revolution unleashed on Europe. The
Revolution was a monster to him; driven by hatred and
fear of the monster, he began, after the decapitation of
Louis XVI, a ferocious persecution of Jacobinism. But if
the Revolution was a monster, it was also a formidable
one. It was impossible to deny that the frightful destruction of the Old Regime which it accomplished both at
home and abroad, greatly increased France's strength. It
was he, the young emperor, who, by precipitating war, had
let loose this latent and unknown force; and the longer
the war went on, the more he feared this force.

And so it was that in 1797, at the age of twenty-nine, he
had met on the road to Vienna another young man of
twenty-eight, who came from Ajaccio. At a certain point,
the two young men, equally imprudent, inexperienced,
and impressionable, had scared each other. Francis had

been frightened to see Bonaparte at the gates of Vienna;
Bonaparte had been frightened at having come as far as
Leoben. And they had both sought safety by hurling
themselves into an adventure before which the more
mature courage of a statesman would have recoiled: the
partition of northern Italy between France and Austria,
between the Revolution and the Old Regime. At first the
Directory had balked, a momentary gleam of prudence,
which, however, was in vain. With Venice destroyed,
France and Austria, the Revolution and the Old Regime,
had found themselves face to face in the partitioned north
of Italy; again they had frightened each other, and again
they had come to blows. They were to fight each other,
save for brief truces, for seventeen years. Seventeen long
years, during which the young Emperor's fear of the Revolution was to grow while a new and terrible problem
was to rise before this disciple of the Italian Counter
Reformation who loathed the Revolution with every pore
of his body. Should he borrow from the Revolution, in
order to conquer it, its most formidable weapons, at the
risk of revolutionizing the whole of Europe? At court,
his younger brothers, the majority of the cabinet and
chamberlains, a considerable portion of the civil service,
and even several high churchmen, were in favor of the
reforms which would enable him to fight the Revolution
on its own ground. They cried that upon these reforms
depended the safety of the Empire, the dignity of his
throne, and the peace of Europe; they decried the dangers
of a delay, pointed out his mistakes, and emphasized the
responsibilities which he had taken on—all with an
acrimony which was little in keeping with royal etiquette.
Everyone was lecturing him, everyone was giving him
advice, everyone was urging him on with more and more
vehemence, as defeats and unfavorable treaties piled up
behind him. And the Emperor bowed his head and listened
to them, took all the criticism and the reproaches, sought
the advice of his brothers and ministers; but he never

made up his mind until the last minute, often too late, and then his reforms were half-hearted, and were almost immediately revoked in part. His whole policy seemed to be a perpetual groping, now and then interrupted by some stupefying piece of daring. Thus, three months after the French Empire was proclaimed in Paris on August 11, 1804, he declared himself hereditary Emperor of Austria —a piece of political and legal nonsense which scandalized the Old Regime. It was a patent violation of ancient imperial law, for Austria was an imperial province by right of investiture. By proclaiming himself Emperor of Austria, the head of the Holy Roman Empire was revolting against himself. Why had he taken this step against the interests of his own position? For once, he had been persuaded by the Revolution that a hereditary empire could be created in one day by force, and that a hereditary emperor, partly originating in the Revolution and modeled on Napoleon, would have more power than the elective Emperor of the Holy Roman Empire.

And so, sometimes imitating, sometimes fighting, but always fearing the Revolution, Francis, full of fresh fears, allowed himself to be dragged into the Coalition with England and Russia. And then what a series of disasters! Austria loses her spoils in Italy, acquired at Campo Formio; the Empire begins to break up; southern Germany, like all Italy, becomes a French protectorate; on August 6, 1806, Francis, threatened by the French Emperor, relinquishes the crown of Charlemagne. At this point, Francis II, now become Francis I of Austria, finally realized that, in order to fight the Revolution, he had to borrow certain ideas and sentiments from it; and he began the reform of his Empire for which his family and advisers had been clamoring for so long. Count Stadion had the field, and he set to work. Conscription and the beginnings of a popular army were introduced for the first time in Austria; a study was made of various reforms; attempts were made to incite mass reactions of enthusiasm and hope which would weld together the different classes in the face of danger; even patriotism, that revolutionary poison which Francis considered the greatest enemy to order and religion, was fed to the Austrian people. Francis made a desperate attempt, one completely foreign to his whole make-up, to become a modern ruler. But the attempt came to an end with the Battle of Wagram. Francis committed liberalism to the devil and on August 4, 1809, appointed Metternich as Chancellor.

Metternich, like Napoleon, has been regarded by historians as a solitary figure in the Revolution. Appearing suddenly out of thin air, he seemed to have no visible means of support. But, even if historians have not perceived it, there was a point of support for both men. In the case of Napoleon, it was the Directory; in that of Metternich, the Austrian Emperor. Metternich was a minister in the exact sense of the word—the executor of the policy definitely chosen by his master after the liberal experiment with Count Stadion. In 1809, Metternich was thirty-six, the Emperor was forty-one. Until that time, Francis had always had ministers who were much older than himself, who never hesitated to treat him and even scold him, as a backward student. He had become fed up with this guardianship, which, moreover, had only led to disaster. He was now a man; he had governed the Empire for seventeen years, and his apprenticeship was finished. Now he wanted to put his own ideas into practice, and for this he possessed a chancellor who, younger than he and owing him everything, would not be in a position to set his own experience against the inexperience of a youthful Emperor. He had chosen well. Appointed Chancellor at the age of thirty-six by a sovereign who was forty-one and was neither stupid nor incapable of action, Metternich did not dream of forcing his own political philosophy on the Emperor, if indeed he had one, which is doubtful. Before this, he had filled various diplomatic posts, important ones, but executive rather than administrative. He must have felt fortunate and honored to execute the orders of his sovereign and relied purely on his own ability of execution to insure himself a high position, with the good will of the Emperor. If at times his opinions did not coincide with those of his master, it was a proof of his fidelity and a duty for him to yield. In any event, it is certain that the young Metternich was careful not to irritate his sovereign, as his predecessors had done with their plans for reform, to which he had turned a deaf ear. It was only in 1816, after seven years of his administration and with the war terminated, that he handed the Emperor a memorandum. Francis put it away in a drawer, like all the others, and the prudent Metternich did not insist.

Austria's policy after Wagram was that of Francis rather than that of Metternich. With the help of this extraordinarily able minister, Francis freed himself from the tutelage of his family, his other ministers, his court, and the administrative heads, and began to rule in his own way. The novel policy initiated by Francis consisted of solving the difficult problem presented by his dual fear of the Revolution, by destroying all liberal thought within his Empire, recognizing it as the dominant force in Europe, and allying himself with it. It would be preposterous to believe for a moment that a young minister could have had the audacity to advise the head of the oldest dynasty in Europe to bring about the marriage of Marie Louise and to ally himself with revolutionary France against Russia. These two actions were the most momentous taken by Austria after the partition of Italy in 1797, for they were a betrayal of the principle and the tradition of monarchy —a betrayal perpetrated by the European dynasty which was the most hostile to the Revolution, at a time when the French Empire was beginning to waver. To recognize the Revolution as the most dominant power in Europe in 1810, on the eve of its downfall; to give it a helping hand in its last desperate attempts to retain the hegemony of Europe; and by that help to sacrifice the prestige of the

monarchy and all the institutions of the Old Regime,
which Francis wished to preserve in his own Empire—
could a more absurd and more dangerous policy be imagined? So senseless was it that only the will and the
prestige of a legitimate monarch, reduced to despair by
the complexities of an impossible situation, were able to
impose it on the feelings and thoughts of his subjects.

But this dangerous and absurd maneuver had won a
most amazing success. That is one of the secret keys to
the history of the nineteenth century. Napoleon's mistakes, the fearful confusion in Europe, the superior skill
of Metternich, had made it possible for Austria to abandon
Napoleon and put herself at the head of a coalition
against him, at the very moment when so dangerous a
maneuver could be executed with the greatest chance of
success. Francis had succeeded, in spite of all his mistakes,
his weaknesses, and his inconsistencies; and the outcome
was extraordinary, even incredible. He had kept intact
the Old Regime in Austria, he had made not one concession to revolutionary thought in his own dominions,
while at the same time he had carried out various adventures in company with the Revolution, chief among
which had been the marriage and the alliance, made *in
extremis;* in spite of this alliance he had helped to destroy
the Empire which the Revolution had created in Europe;
and now he was about to regain everything he had first
won during his revolutionary exploits and then lost—
Italy, the Adriatic coast, and the church principalities
which had been annexed. Could a more dazzling success
be imagined, as a reward for so many defeats and so much
confusion? While his opponent of Camp Formio, his conqueror at Austerlitz, Pressburg, and Wagram was about
to be shut up on St. Helena, Francis had become powerful
and Vienna had regained its position as the political
capital of Europe. Now he was the real master of his Empire; all resistance, beginning with his family, had evap-

orated at his success. And he had become one of the masters of Europe.

How would he use his paradoxical grandeur? Adventure? Or construction? He had shared in adventures with the Revolution, he had been the most active accomplice and collaborator; of all the European sovereigns, none had worked as hard as he to destroy in Europe the Old Regime which he wished to preserve in his own Empire, and to throw Italy and Germany into chaos. Was he also to become, with Talleyrand and Louis XVIII, one of the architects of the new Europe? No; after his paradoxical triumph he became again what he had always been basically, except during the years of adventure—a sovereign of the Italian Counter Reformation, as hostile to the spirit of adventure as he was incapable of understanding the constructive mind. In Vienna, in 1814, he became at last what he was to be until the end of his life, not a builder, but a preserver. Conqueror of the Revolution and master of the Continent at the age of forty-six, Francis I intended to make Austria and Europe over on the model of his fair garden of Tuscany, as it had been before the Revolution. The lava spewed up by the Revolution had, during his youth, devastated Italy and most of Europe, but no matter! The grown man hoped that it would cool off in Europe as in Italy, his Italy, the lava of medieval anarchy and the religious wars had cooled off; and that with this lava one might be able to build in Austria and all of Europe an order similar to the one into which he had been born, an order at the center of which there would be an indisputable but legitimate, paternalistic government inimical to despotism. In 1814, Francis I was not even opposed to the re-establishment of the Diets or estates which had existed during the eighteenth century in a great part of the Empire, and which the war had more or less overthrown; they were institutions of the Old Regime which were in accord with his plans for a general restoration. The Court and the Diets, at the head of an administration which would be watchful, rather narrow, but honest and zealous, would prepare for each individual or social group a system of ideas, a code of conduct, and a place in the sun, just as in the Italy of the Counter Reformation; constantly preoccupied with the security and well-being of all classes, this superior government would give them *panem et circenses,* work and amusement, at the price of a minimum of discussion; it would regulate commerce, industry, the professions, so that wealth and labor, too, instead of inciting the spirit of adventure, might stabilize, with luck, the spiritual orientation of society.

The Italian Counter Reformation had a strange revenge in Vienna; buried in the graveyard of history, it became the model on which one of its destroyers wished to reconstruct Europe. In order to have a clear understanding of the Congress of Vienna and its results, we must never forget that one of its guiding geniuses was an eighteenth-century Florentine and as such was practical, intelligent, prudent, timid, narrow, astute, unfit for great enterprises and constructive thought, distrustful of ideas, doctrines, principles, but recoiling from the spirit of adventure and its false grandeurs. Whatever may have been the extent of his attempt, one must admit that he was rational; he knew that a totalitarian regime is a damper, and he did not wish to use it, as do the modern dictators, to kindle the fires of war and revolution in the masses, but to extinguish them. He wanted no more wars. His horror of war, that explosion of the spirit of adventure which provokes the great panics of humanity—his horror of war, that subversive and revolutionary force, was to become the key to his whole strange system of government, which no longer had anything in common with the Hapsburg policy of the seventeenth and eighteenth centuries. No more wars, no more wars for any reason; although she had become the most powerful state on the Continent, Austria was to abandon the imperialistic Hapsburg traditions, and to limit herself to defensive measures, becoming a state whose boundaries were fixed. And, in order to obtain peace, Francis I was willing to pay a suitable price. After the victory, he had been very moderate; apart from what the treaties signed after 1796 had already assigned to him, he had asked only for Lombardy; part of it had belonged to Austria before 1796, and there was no way of determining who else should receive it. But he would not hear of the imperial crown of Germany, and he detested those who offered it to him, as though they were public enemies of his imperial crown of Austria. He feared, as much as Talleyrand, the movements which might be produced in the German mass, if one day it should come under the direction of a single, ambitious ruler; he wished to unite Germany in a Confederation which would make her at the same time unassailable and unable to attack others; he wished to place at the head of the Confederation, not one emperor of Germany, but a diarchy, the Austro-Prussian diarchy. In this diarchy the uncertain aggressive ambitions of the two powers would counteract each other. Under a dual and pacific guidance, all the German states would have to keep the peace among themselves, and with non-German states. Having come through twenty-three years of wars set in motion by his fatal imprudence of 1792, his horror of war was so great that he not only wished to numb the spirit of adventure, of revolution, and of war in Germany with totalitarianism; he wished also to chain her with a Confederation so constructed that it would make war impossible.

This was the secret of the weakness and indecision of the Austrian policy, which was puzzling Talleyrand so much. Talleyrand held Metternich responsible, but Metternich was merely the instrument, albeit a willing one. The real instigator hid behind him, higher than he and invisible; the one actually responsible was the Emperor, the cautious and hidebound Florentine, who, scared once and for all by the interminable tempest of wars which he had helped so much to let forth, wanted nothing more but peace, peace, peace; peace at any price; peace forever, even if it were to be the peace of the tomb. So as to have perpetual peace, he was ready to embalm the whole world with the ointments of the Counter Reformation.

Prussia, which, in 1814, was a state worn out by an accumulation of misfortunes, had accepted without too much resistance this preservative plan which a grand duke of Tuscany, in the travesty of an Austrian Emperor, had promulgated. But Bavaria and Württemberg were fighting it with every ounce of strength. Why? Because they were two hybrids born of a monstrous union between the Old Regime and the Revolution. Their kings were not false kings, like the Bonapartes, the Beauharnais, and the Murats; their sovereign authority had long been recognized in the territories they had governed, one as prince-elector of the Holy Roman Empire, the other as duke. But neither were they authentic kings, like the kings of France or England. They had enlarged their dominions and received the royal title by allying themselves to the Revolution and the French Empire against the Holy Roman Empire and Germany; they had established an active and arbitrary despotism in their dominions, imitating the example of the false monarchy in Paris; actions which had involved some advantages but which were irregular and adventurous, and had aggrandized the power of the two kings while falsifying its legitimacy. Therefore, the two kings were uneasy and full of fear. The King of Württemberg was the great curiosity of the Congress because of his corpulence. People said that it was necessary to cut a hole in the tables at which he sat so that his paunch might be accommodated. Even at the masked balls, he was immediately identified by his circumference. A ridiculous figure of a man, a limited intelligence, and a doubtful royalty—this triple coincidence had resulted in a monarch who was distrustful, touchy, preyed upon by a persecution complex, obsessed by fear of having his title and his authority as revolutionary king slighted, and very fearful of his subjects. The idea of providing them with a Constitution, by means of which they might legally protest against his government, terrified him. The King of Bavaria feared his subjects no less; he was very distrustful of Austria, against whom he had fought, and of Prussia, whose ambitions on Saxony he dreaded; bold and cunning, he intended to continue his double dealing with Germany and France, with the Old Regime and the Revolution, which had assured him such handsome profits. One of his chief occupations, at the moment, was to find a place for the illustrious but unemployed revolutionary sovereign who was his son-in-law, Eugène de Beauharnais. He had not the slightest desire to have his actions restricted, either inside or outside his dominions, by a German Confederation under the direction of Austria and Prussia.

In short, Austria and Prussia were able to carry on a preservative if not a reconstructive policy in Vienna, because they were two legitimate monarchies; Bavaria and Württemberg could not, because their two royalties had a doubtful legitimacy. It was another confirmation of Talleyrand's doctrine. Bavaria's and Württemberg's opposition, first begun at the meeting of October 16, had become livelier during the next four weeks. Bavaria had asserted with increasing vehemence that the Confederation had no business interfering in the political constitutions of the different states, as each state had the right to make the constitution it wished. She had stated that she was able to defend herself alone; thus the Confederation in itself held no interest for her; she was disposed to enter it out of a feeling for German solidarity, but only on the condition that she would not be forced to make excessive sacrifices. She demanded for every member of the Confederation the right to conclude any sort of treaty, even alliances, provided they were not directed against the Confederation. If Prussia and Austria, with regard to their dominions situated outside of the Confederation, saw fit to make war on a third power, Bavaria had to be free to

side with Austria and Prussia; if Austria and Prussia went
to war, Bavaria had to be free to join either side, even
though the Confederation remained neutral. If Prussia and
Austria made war on France, independently of the Confederation, Bavaria had to have the right, not to declare
herself on the side of France, but to dissuade Prussia and
Austria from making war, or to preserve her neutrality
and prevent the Prussian and Austrian troops from passing
through the territory of the other states of the Confederation.[7] Finally, Bavaria demanded that she, also, have two
votes in the Directory of the Confederation, or else that
Prussia and Austria have only one.

The discussions got rather heated. The five German
states got along no better than the eight European powers
which had signed the Treaty of Paris. Four weeks had gone
by; amendments, proposals, counterproposals had been
discussed; influence had been brought to bear, but no
agreement had been reached. The Prussians had not been
content with mere discussion. More up to date than the
Austrians, they had anticipated a twentieth-century cus-
tom by instigating a violent attack against Bavaria and
Württemberg in the Coblentz newspaper, *Rhine Mer-
cury,* in the hope of frightening the two smaller states.
The latter had made an equally vigorous protest to the
Congress. Stein had lashed out against the small and
medium-sized states, accusing Bavaria and Württemberg of
wanting to see all Germany under the rule of governments
as arbitrary and tyrannical as their own. Austria and Prussia had then asked Russia to intervene. After November
11, the two powers had a confidential note from Russia
read before the entire Congress, in which Nesselrode, in
the name of the Czar, gave his wholehearted blessing to the
plan proposed by Austria and Prussia, emphasizing the
liberal motives which inspired it. The plan appealed to
him because it was intended to protect the rights of all
Germans by "strong, wise, and liberal institutions."

[7] D'Angeberg, *op. cit.,* p. 331.

But Germany, unfortunately, did not know what she wanted. Discussion and maneuvers had no other effect than to stir up a hornet's nest of the smaller states, which up till then had been shut out of the Congress by the Allies with the promise that they would form a critical audience to judge what the Allies had decided. As this was a question of Germany, it was only natural that all the little German states should be the most excited. Suddenly, on the sixteenth, the latent crisis came to a head in both the committee and the Congress. The Württemberg delegate flatly declared that it was useless to discuss the statutes of the Confederation, and the rights and duties of its members, when these members, the extent of their territories, the geographical and political boundaries of the Confederation, were yet unknown. Consequently, he would take no more part in the discussion. On the same day, a far more serious event occurred. The delegates from the twenty-nine sovereign princes and free cities of Germany delivered a memorandum to Metternich and Hardenberg which was nothing less than revolutionary. They did not only demand Germany's right to decide her own fate; they also condemned both the Austro-Prussian proposal and the opposition put up by Bavaria and Württemberg. The memorandum denounced the feeble dualism of the proposed Constitution and demanded a single head of the government, as had been the case with the former Emperor—a demand which was not calculated to please either Austria, Prussia, or France, who had developed a healthy fear of single rule. Thus the whole Austro-Prussian plan was upset right at its foundations. But the memorandum was no less vigorous against the opposition of Bavaria and Württemberg. It had this to say against them:

They are especially agreed that all arbitrary authority must cease, generally speaking by the establishment of a federative constitution, and particularly in each state by the setting up of estates which should have the following prerogatives:

1. The right to approve and fix taxes required by the government.

2. The right to take part, by their approval, in the promulgation of new laws.

3. The right to inquire into the uses of money spent for public needs.

4. The right of protest, especially in cases of embezzlement by ministers or sovereigns and of all kinds of abuse.

Leaving each sovereign, however, the right to organize the estates in his own country, according to the character of the people, the place, and the customs.

These are no longer the Diets, estates, or *Stände,* of the Old Regime which the smaller states and cities of Germany were demanding, but the right of opposition, essence of the modern state and chief point in the program of the Revolution. Europe was beginning to take on an active reality in the Congress.

broidered like the bodice, but with gold and colored gems. On the head is a small toque, also in velvet, and encrusted with precious stones.

The other quadrilles have chosen costumes which differ in cut and shape but were equally splendid. The twenty-four beauties have crossed the arena under the concentrated gaze of thousands of eyes, each wearing a long transparent veil figured with gold which, fastened to her headdress, floats to the ground. Now they are sitting motionless beneath their veils in the tribune, and countless glances are cast at these living flowers of beauty, wearing more than thirty million francs in jewels. Another flourish announces the sovereigns. Everyone rises; the twenty-four beauties throw back their veils. To thunderous applause, the Austrian Emperor seats himself in the center of the tribune facing the beauties, with the Empress beside him. The other sovereigns and reigning princes arrange themselves in order of precedence. Half the sovereigns of Europe are here tonight. For a while, it was believed that Marie Louise and the little King of Rome would come; but at the last moment she had preferred not to leave Schönbrunn.

The monarchs and spectators have been seated. Immediately the hall resounds to the shattering strains of martial music. The twenty-four paladins are at the gate. They are the flower of the Empire's nobility. They, too, are divided into four quadrilles corresponding to the colors of the women's quadrilles, and they are all in the costume of the day: close-fitting velvet doublet with puffed sleeves and satin lapels, the front ornamented with gold buttons and braid; tight breeches; yellow half-boots with gilded spurs; gauntlets of the same color, embroidered with gold; a large hat turned up in front, where a white plume which curled to one side was fastened with a diamond clasp; and a sword held up by a belt encrusted with diamonds. Each lady has given her knight a magnificent scarf embroidered with silk and gold; this is worn on the opposite side from the sword. It is the only expense which has been incurred by the ladies; all the costumes—for both men and women—have been provided by the Court.

The paladins are astride beautiful and richly caparisoned Hungarian horses. Twenty-four pages holding aloof their banners precede them; they are followed by thirty-six squires dressed in Spanish fashion. After having saluted the sovereigns and the twenty-four ladies, they begin their games to the accompaniment of music. At a gallop they spear rings suspended in front of the imperial tribunal. They throw javelins at Turk's heads; they pick them off the ground at full gallop and throw them again. At full speed they cut an apple in two with a curved scimitar. They divide into two groups and face each other, charging in an attempt to unhorse their opponents. They perform maneuvers and jumps of all kinds that are just as graceful as they are swiftly executed. As a climax they perform an intricate dance in which their intelligent steeds keep time to the music.

Thunderous applause greets the prowess of the twenty-four paladins, their pages, and squires. The dinner hour is at hand. In the main room, the principal table, for the royal guests, is set up on one of the higher tiers and laid out in gold plate; at the left, another table for the princes, archdukes, heads of reigning dynasties, and ministers of the great powers; at the right, a third for the paladins and their ladies. All around the hall and in the adjoining rooms are a great many small tables at which those guests are seated who have no special distinction of rank. Never has there been seen in Vienna before nor was there ever likely to be seen again such a sparkling of silks and velvets, such a profusion of priceless lace and rare flowers, of tables groaning with the weight of gold they carried, a more dazzling and unlimited display of diamonds, rubies, and emeralds, so many minstrels in medieval costume strumming their harps and singing ancient lays to beauty and sirventes to valor; nor, underneath the materials, the laces, the wigs, the voluptuous charm woven by the minstrels, so much feminine beauty and human grandeur sitting at table and passing around golden baskets laden with fruit.

The festival ended in a huge ball, to which had been invited more than three thousand people. All night long there was dancing in the great hall, brilliantly illuminated by six thousand candles. The high spot of the evening was the great quadrille danced by the twenty-four ladies and their paladins, which was received with a tumultuous ovation.

Nunc est bibendum! They were celebrating the fall of the Revolution; while behind their backs the Old Regime was writhing in its death pangs. Though based on the dull and pompous model of the Old Regime, these parties were breaking through the stiff, correct, formal framework with which the Old Regime generally surrounded itself, even when at play. An orgiastic and leveling sensualism ran through them and set them on fire, transforming the Congress into a gigantic political carnival, at which scores of lovely women, enjoying a new freedom, pursued through the balls, receptions, and dinners, while pretending to be pursued themselves, the princes, kings, and emperors who were engaged in reconstructing Europe, and who no longer wished to follow the example set by the sovereigns of an early day and remain correctly bored while other people enjoyed themselves. They abandoned themselves to the intoxicating gaiety and the pleasures of a Vienna gone mad, losing all sense of proportion and caring nothing about their prestige. The young Alexander and the hardly older Metternich provided the chief scandals of the Congress. An official report states that the Emperor "apparently wishes to mingle in society as informally as possible; he sits down in mixed company at a table laid for twenty, and he has often danced with every woman at a small dance of forty people." [2] Talleyrand adds in a letter to Louis that "the time lost to business is consumed in parties. Emperor Alexander demands them, or even commands them, as if he were in his own palace." [3] The secret police reports are even more severe. A report dated November 4 says:

All sorts of stories are being told on Alexander, who is rarely at his office, spends all his mornings and afternoons watching the maneuvers and exercises of his troops, riding horseback or driving *en voiture,* hunting, and paying calls, and all his evenings dancing until after midnight.

·　·　·　·　·　·　·

Both Austrians and foreigners vie with each other in saying that Alexander, who had already made himself a laughingstock in Paris, where he had left a rather bad reputation, is making himself even more ridiculous, and even contemptible, in Vienna, where he will leave a terrible impression behind him.

And another report, dated November 16:

Some persons close to the Emperor of Russia who have had the opportunity of studying his character, insist that Alexander, too, is slightly deranged and will end like his father. The kind of life he has led in Paris, in France and Austria, in London and in Vienna, has ruined his reputation everywhere and the rumor of his notoriety has even reached Russia. These persons even go so far as to say that neither the ministers, nor the army, nor even the people, in other words no one, has confidence in Alexander, and that no one loves or respects him. He is reproached with Tilsit, the firing of Moscow, and all his stupidities in Paris with his Constitution, which he wishes to repeat in Warsaw. One hears them saying on every occasion: "The events of 1813 and 1814 prove that Alexander is neither a general, nor even a soldier, but simply a bungler, a man with no character who passes from one extreme to the other without transition or motive, a man

[2] *Correspondance inédite,* p. 146, no. 1.
[3] *Ibid.,* p. 172.

no one could fear as an enemy, and who deserves no personal consideration." They add that Russia constitutes a far greater danger than France to the peace and liberty of the Continent; that the King of Bavaria, the Grand Duke of Baden, the King of Württemberg, as well as the German princes and ministers here in Vienna, detest Alexander and have no more liking for Russia than for her Emperor.

Was he really bitten with *"dansomanie"* as the Viennese were saying? In any case, during November all the dissatisfied members of the Congress were putting their hopes on the approach of Advent, which would soon put a stop to the dancing. "The Emperor of Russia will have to stay home, so perhaps a little work will get done." The police kept careful record of the nocturnal visits— from ten at night till two o'clock in the morning—which he paid to Princess Bagration. They were frequent; but all this homage to the fair Princess did not prevent Alexander from rushing to the conquest of each and every pretty woman he met, and he had his own approach, which was somewhat original, to say the least, consisting of a complete disregard for any preliminary tactics and an immediate frontal attack made in all haste. A secret police report, dated November 21, says:

At the ball given by Count Francis Palffy, Alexander, who deeply admires the beauty of Countess Szechenyi-Guilford, said to her: "Your husband is absent. It would be very pleasant to take his place temporarily."

The Countess replied: "Does Your Majesty take me for a province?"

He seemed possessed by an erotic frenzy which made him a laughingstock. Metternich, his enemy, instead of taking advantage of this, apparently wished to discredit himself likewise in the same orgy of pleasure. "He spends most of his day at balls and parties," wrote Talleyrand to the King.[4] He even went so far as to confide to a lady,

4 *Ibid.,* p. 146.

probably in order to stir her imagination, that he was defending the interests of Murat with such tenacity because "he was passionately in love with the Queen, and had continual relations with her." [5] It would be hard to believe such an outrage if Talleyrand himself had not related it in a letter to the King. And one of his secretaries, M. de la Tour du Pin, wrote to the department: "What can be expected from one who, placed in the most solemn position a man could hold, does nothing but spend the greater part of his time in foolishness, who does not fear to have the *Bacha de Surêne* acted in his quarters, and who, since the opening of the Congress, has spent a great number of equally futile days?" If Alexander and Metternich were the outstanding male examples of scandal, the two titular mistresses of the Czar and the Chancellor occupied analogous positions in the female world. Here is an edifying police report on the reputation of the two most talked-about ladies of the Congress:

The Duchess of Sagan said to her worthy friend, the Countess Fuchs: "I am being ruined by my husbands (alluding to the income she gives to Louis de Rohan and Troubetzkoi). I shall have to give up that luxury, and I shall never have another husband."

At one of the last parties given by Princess Bagration, attended by one of the daughters of Prince Starhemberg with her parents, childish games were being played—forfeits, round games, and the like. While these were going on, the girl retired to the most distant room with a Russian, who locked the door. Prince Starhemberg noticed it and had the lock broken. Once again it was said that the Bagration house was a brothel, and that it was surprising to see a mother bring her daughter there.

"I am being ruined by my husbands!" In other words: "Divorce is too expensive; I shall have lovers in the future, these at least can be changed at will without expense." There is no doubt that both the public and the police

[5] *Ibid.*

were exaggerating. Alexander, for example, even though he was bitten with *"dansomanie"* and was suggesting to every lady who caught his fancy that she go to bed with him, was watching out for squalls. The police informer who had been told by one of the Czar's ministers and counselors that the question of Poland worried his master less than the difficulty of finding a fine hussar costume in Vienna has recorded a piece of nonsense.[6] In the midst of his joyous frolics, Alexander was busily carrying on intrigues and persecuting Metternich, keeping an eye on both his friends and his enemies, watching the salons and corridors, the alcoves and offices, still set on his plans in spite of appearances. He was struggling frantically to escape the fate which awaited him—his father's fate—if, after having saved Europe, he should return to Russia without a rich prize; and, at the same time, to escape the shame, the remorse, and the humiliation with which he would reproach himself, if he should return without having done something noble and great for humanity. Although Metternich was far from being the pitiful victim of circumstance and of temperament, neither had he abandoned himself completely to pleasure, as the scandal-mongers of Vienna were claiming; and, if the Congress was getting nowhere, it was not because its president "was enterprising only with women." But the exaggerations of public opinion and the police give some idea of the strange atmosphere which surrounded the Congress. Frivolity? Cynicism? Unconsciousness? No, there is something deeper in this sensuality: a dull pain, almost despair. Pleasure— a good dinner, an agreeable excursion, a party, any sort of erotic ecstasy—revives in a man who knows how to enjoy it with a little intelligence, his will to go on, after it has been weakened by the insoluble contradictions and ultimate uselessness of life. That is why man reaches out for it whenever he can. For a quarter of a century, an unhappy and fearful generation had been destroying the

6 Weil, *op. cit.*, no. 336, p. 266.

order of the world, in the belief that it was accomplishing
great deeds; now it was clear that all these great deeds
had been nothing but the ephemeral creations of the spirit
of adventure; in a few days everything had collapsed,
leaving only an immense abyss which was swallowing up
a part of mankind. It was imperative to resist the attraction
of this abyss, and to construct across the great void an
order wherein men might live again as men, without being
a constant prey to fear, as they had been for a quarter of a
century; a fixed point had to be found in a terrifying
and perpetually changing world. And the unfortunates
who were condemned to this forced labor of reconstruction
were all out of breath. But they had been so ill-prepared
for the task, by the twenty-five years of adventure they
had passed through! In order to be constructive they
needed courage; and all of them were seized again from
time to time by the old terror of France, revolutionary
and Napoleonic France!

On November 25, Talleyrand wrote to Louis XVIII that
two days before—probably at the great carrousel—he had
reproached Castlereagh with the way he had been manag-
ing things for the past two months. Castlereagh had answered: "I have always thought that when one was in a
league one should stick with it." Talleyrand added in
comment:

He considers himself in a league. This league is certainly
the result of treaties made previous to the peace. Now, how
can he be expected to agree with those whom he admits he is
leagued against? The other members of the league or coalition against France are in the same position. Russia and Prussia expect only opposition from us, Austria may desire our
support on the question of Poland and on that of Saxony;
but her minister desires it for those two matters less than he
fears our intervention in the others.

The four allied courts, having each some reason to fear the
influence which France might exert in the Congress, have
naturally united, and they fear to approach us when they

disagree among themselves, because any *rapprochement* would entail concessions they do not wish to make.

Vanity, of course, is also involved. Lord Castlereagh thought himself in a position to make the Emperor of Russia give in, and he has only embittered him.

Finally, a feeling of jealousy against France is added to all these motives. The allies thought that they had defeated her more severely; they did not expect her to have the best army and the best state of finances in Europe; now they realize it and admit it, and they have reached the point where they are regretting the Treaty of Paris, are blaming it on each other, and are unable to understand by what magic they were induced to make it, and are saying so, even in the conferences and to our faces.

The peace of 1814 was the greatest victory achieved by the monarchy. It was by that peace, and not by the Battle of Leipzig and the invasion of France, that it vanquished the Revolution for a century, until 1914. A Napoleonic peace would have preserved the Revolution in its most dangerous form. And yet already in November, 1814, the great monarchies of Europe, exasperated by the difficulties of reconstruction, were beginning to wonder if it would not have been better to have dismembered France; they were regretting the great triumph of the constructive mind over the spirit of adventure, of courage over fear, of good over evil, which had saved the world, and they wanted to re-establish their league against France. It was a tremendous piece of luck that the great powers had committed themselves on several essential matters in the Treaty of Paris. Many mistakes, which the confused state of affairs during November and December might have led them to make, had thereby become impossible.

Yet, though they were beginning once more to fear their former enemy, were they at least working in harmony to give peace and order to the world? Each of them understood that, in order to reconstruct Europe, he would have to make concessions. The question of Saxony, for instance.

In the conversation which had taken place between Talleyrand and Alexander in the middle of November, Talleyrand had received the impression that the Czar would
have been disposed to yield on this point, if he had not
considered himself bound by his promises to the Prussian
King.[7] About that time, after Bavaria had refused to enter
the Confederation if the Saxon Kingdom were suppressed,
Austria had determined to save the small state, and the
Court of Berlin was beginning to understand: the grapes
were sour. The Prussian chancellor had given the Bavarian
minister, Prince Wrede, to understand that the Saxon
King might be allowed to rule over a million subjects.[8]
Prussia was at that time coming up against more or less
sincere scruples on the part of Alexander. As Talleyrand
wrote Louis, the possibility of an amicable solution of
the Saxon problem was increasing. The Congress should
have been more hopeful at this point. On the contrary,
during November and December the Congress was under
the impression that things were going from bad to worse.
During these two months, alarming rumors multiplied,
following each other like breakers on a shore, each one
larger than the one before it. No agreement had been
reached. There was going to be war any minute. Fear of
what France might do fanned the flames of suspicion
among the four Allies. They all admitted that concessions
had to be made, but none of them made any move, for
fear that it would be the only one and that the others
would then have the advantage. Each one distrusted his
own wisdom and desire for peace, as though it were a
trap into which his own interests might fall. No one took
the initiative; and the most excellent schemes, even those
proposed by the purest constructive mind, were known
only to a few privileged persons.

Fear and suspicion were smothering the constructive
mind in the escape provided by the dangerous spirit of

[7] *Correspondance inédite,* pp. 127-128.
[8] *Ibid.,* p. 133.

adventure. The former was still confused and weakened by the interference of its disloyal competitor—the spurious constructive mind, which is so often preferred to the real by the variability and vanity of men. Toward the end of November, it seemed to be Castlereagh who was making use of the counterfeit. Just when Prussia was beginning to listen to reason, he had become infatuated with his idea of a large Prussia, strong enough, allied with Austria, to become a counterweight to an alliance between Russia and France. An absurd plan and a fantastic construction, of which Talleyrand complained to Louis in a letter dated November 30.

Besides, Your Majesty will see that Lord Castlereagh has been concerned only for Poland, determined that Saxony must be sacrificed, following the policy which considers only the groupings without paying any attention to the elements which compose them. A policy of schoolboys and allies.

A policy of allies and schoolboys! Of allies, because to combine in one state populations which are hostile to each other, with the intention of aligning military forces against a designated enemy, was to deal with peoples and states as with divisions or corps of a coalition army. Schoolboy policy because only a beginner in diplomacy and statecraft could dream of applying the same rules to the reconstruction of Europe as would be applied to a military coalition. To the aberrations of this spurious constructive mind were added the insufficiencies of the genuine. The constructive mind can only work along certain principles. But every principle capable of being conceived by the human mind is limited; not one is able to cover and dominate completely the reality to which it is applied. By one means or another, the reality always escapes, even from the broadest and most elastic principles which the mind of man can create. The most crucial illustration of this truth was furnished by Switzerland. On November 30, another attempt was made to solve the latter's problem.

On that occasion France was represented by Dalberg. It is not known why France was admitted to the discussion. Perhaps the Swiss had protested against her exclusion, as Talleyrand intimates. Or perhaps the failure of the committee on German affairs had made the Allies more cautious. Be that as it may, when the meeting was opened, the deputy from Berne, M. de Zerleder, presented an extremely able statement,[9] in which Argovie was claimed in the name of the law of nations and the confusion pointed out into which Switzerland had been thrown by the diversity and uncertainty of the principles of legitimacy. After having recalled that "every state of possession was formerly based on treaties; there was not one inch of land in Switzerland for which the right of transmission by the preceding ruler could not be produced," he ended with the following considerations:

Two principles exist in Switzerland. Four cantons recognize that of the former law; the others recognize that of popular sovereignty as the law. In several new cantons, popular sovereignty has been introduced without regard for what has gone before. In view of such conflicting elements, can one hope for a sincere union? Would it be honorable for those who, encouraged by the powers, have put forth claims based on everything which establishes them among men, to abandon completely those claims—an abandonment which would certainly be imputed to weakness?

A long discussion followed, and no decision was reached. The principle that occupying territory does not create sovereignty had helped the Congress to restore order in a large part of Europe. But it was a terrible obstacle in Switzerland, where it was about to provoke civil war.

Italy was no more acquiescent than Switzerland to the solutions thought up in Vienna. What was to be done with Murat? Metternich's fear continued to prevent any settlement of this problem. The powers must be patient, must proceed cautiously, must not precipitate anything.

9 D'Angeberg, *op. cit.*, pp. 468-472.

Naples was a mine which, if not handled delicately, might go off at any minute setting fire to Italy and all Europe. The Congress was impressed, and they dared do nothing against Murat. Every day the rumor came back that peace in Italy would be bought from Murat by offering him part of the Legations. Cardinal Consalvi was losing a great deal of sleep over this; he was doing everything he could to prevent it, buttonholing everyone at the Congress. But he was unable to obtain any definite promises. Everyone, especially Francis, avoided the subject. Francis told the Cardinal that he would not touch the Legations himself, but that he was not going to go to war in order to guarantee the Legations to the Holy See.

Now the Legations were far from being the only worry of the pontifical legate. There was also that terrible letter which had to be written and yet should not be written: a short letter to a lady; not even that, merely an address to be written and the envelope to be sealed. Ever since October, the Cardinal had been fearfully avoiding this address and envelope, had been in despair at not knowing what to do. Talleyrand had given him a letter from his wife, addressed to the Cardinal, full of friendly compliments. It was that letter which terrified the papal legate. He could not possibly address his answer to the Princess Talleyrand; by doing that he would recognize the marriage of a bishop. And neither could he address it to Mme. Grand, without insulting and outraging her as a concubine. In the days when Europe was dominated by the papacy, the Cardinal would not have hesitated one moment; he would have thrown the letter into the wastepaper basket and thought no more about it. For a month, he had been delaying his answer and torturing himself with what he should do. Not to answer would be an insult not only to the wife but also to the husband. And the Holy See was in dire need of France's friendship and that of her representative, in order to defend her interests in Vienna. Not knowing what to do, he had confided in

Cardinal Pacca; the Secretary of State had given him the excellent advice to reply with a courteous letter, headed simply "Madame"; to have another person address the envelope with all the prescribed titles and seal it with some other seal than his own; and to send the letter through the mail instead of giving it to Talleyrand.[10]

One should not be too hard on the merry cavortings of the Congress; it managed for a while to shake off the somber lassitude caused by its contradictions, fears, and mistakes, and to regain a measure of courage and confidence through the artificial stimulus provided by the celebrations. The carrousel on November 23 had been such a success that Francis had repeated it on December 1, with over ten thousand guests. Once again the Congress had shaken off its cares and danced all night. Only the aged philosopher of the Congress had occasionally cast a haughty and supercilious glance at this unprecedented revelry and at the strange company which reveled. Talleyrand wrote to Louis on November 6:

Everywhere one sees nothing but emperors, kings, empresses, queens, crown princes, reigning princes, etc., etc. All expenses are met by the Court; and each day's expense has been estimated at 220,000 florins in paper money. Certainly, at these events royalty loses a great deal of its dignity. It seems to me extremely improper to see three or four kings and more princes attending dances and teas given by ordinary commoners of Vienna. One has to go to France now to see the pomp and dignity which makes royalty both respected and loved by the people.

But it must be said that the amusements of the Congress were not all of a frivolous nature. On November 29, a huge Beethoven concert had been given, which gave rise to a great deal of talk. In the Congress, there were not only discussions about Poland and Saxony, but also about

---

[10] For a detailed account of this amazing story, see Rinieri, *op. cit.,* pp. 52-53.

music, past and future. Here is the police report on the Beethoven concert.

The English in Vienna attend religious services at the house of Lord Stewart. They are so strict in this respect that they refuse to attend concerts or musical seances on Sunday, and it was because of this that the Beethoven concert was postponed to a week day.

The concert, which was given yesterday [Tuesday, the twenty-fourth], did not help to increase the enthusiasm for the talent of this composer, who has his partisans and his enemies. Against the group of his admirers, at the head of whom are Razoumoffsky, Apponyi, Kraft, etc., who worship Beethoven, there is a vast majority of connoisseurs, who refuse absolutely henceforth to hear Beethoven's works.[11]

As for Neukomm, the police were now reassured. He had come to Vienna only as a musician. It seems that Talleyrand enjoyed hearing him play while he was writing his letters and observations.

[11] Weil, *op. cit.*, I, 619.

XIV

THE TRIPLE ALLIANCE

Alexander was an eternally discontented rebel, always in a state of opposition. He had not belied his nature in 1814. After having insured the triumph of the Old Regime, he had turned his back on it and begun to flirt with Napoleonism and Revolution. He was the anchor to which all the leftovers of the Napoleonic adventure tried to hitch themselves. Josephine, before her death, Eugène de Beauharnais, Élise Baciocchi, Marie Louise, the Emperor's brothers, had all become his friends and *protégés.* In Switzerland, he had become the most outspoken champion of the Revolution against the Old Regime. In December he went much further. The Austrian Emperor had decided to make another attempt to reach an agreement with Russia on Poland, through the intervention of Prussia. Hardenberg had agreed to confer with Alexander, as spokesman for the two German states. The Emperor and he met, probably on November 30. Alexander, who for some time had felt Prussia slipping away from him, was very friendly, listened to him kindly, and showed himself agreeable to reconciliation. But he did not come to the bottom of the matter. He declared that he would let Hardenberg know his intentions and objections in a short time.

In fact, on December 1 or 2, Prince Czartoryski and Baron Stein came to see the Prussian chancellor on behalf of the Czar and announced that Alexander was willing to concede Cracow and Thorn, which would become free cities "under the guarantee and protection of the allied powers," but on condition that Austria agree to the cession of the whole of Saxony to Prussia and that Mainz be declared a fortress of the Germanic Confederation. Toward the middle of November, Talleyrand had hoped that the Czar would agree to a compromise on Saxony; but nothing was ever definite with Alexander. There he was going back to his old idea of giving Saxony to Prussia, and this time—which was even more serious—justifying it not by the misdeeds of the King but by the interests and the wishes of the Saxon people. Alexander's thesis was as follows: the people of Saxony are against the partition of Saxony; they desire unity to the point of preferring to be completely under the sovereignty of Prussia; therefore one must respect their wishes. To the indefeasible right of kings, held up by the partisans of the Saxon King, with Talleyrand at their head, he was opposing the right of peoples to decide their fate. No less curious was the fact that Hardenberg had once enthusiastically endorsed this point of view, which was rather an advanced one for that age. When he reported the outcome of his negotiations with the Czar to Metternich, Hardenberg stated that "there are loud cries that to deprive the House of Saxony of its entire kingdom would be to adopt Napoleon's principles and act in a revolutionary manner"; but he was not afraid of this accusation, which he called "a figure of speech"; and he formally declared: "People persist stubbornly in an attempt to save part of his dominions for the Saxon King, which would be absolutely against the wishes of his people. . . . I may therefore boldly put the matter up to the Saxons themselves. If there were any possibility of counting the votes, they would almost unanimously be against dismemberment." [1]

In his greed, the Prussian chancellor did not hesitate to substitute the idea of plebiscites for the age-old principle that only cession by a sovereign creates sovereignty. For Hardenberg, this was only a political maneuver, albeit rather a daring one; for Alexander, a passing but sincere conviction, as were all the ideas of this restless individual. The proof of that lies in the fact that he made an attempt to win the Austrian Emperor's approval, which meant that he tried to convert the most complete living incarnation of the Old Regime. Talleyrand tells the story of this astonishing maneuver:

As M. de Metternich had emphasized the fact that his sovereign would never consent to the transfer of Saxony to Prussia, Emperor Alexander, wishing to verify this, accosted Emperor Francis that night, after the carrousel, and said to him:

"In these times, we other sovereigns are obliged to conform to the wishes of our peoples and carry them out. The Saxon people do not wish to be divided. They prefer to belong altogether to Prussia than to have Saxony partitioned piecemeal."

Emperor Francis replied: "I do not hold with that doctrine. This is mine: A ruler may if he wishes cede a part of his country and all of his people; if he abdicates, then his rights are passed on to his legitimate heirs. He cannot deprive them of these, and the whole of Europe does not have the right to do so."

"That is not conformable to the enlightened times," said Emperor Alexander.

"But it is my opinion," answered the Austrian Emperor; "it should be that of every sovereign and therefore yours. As for me, I shall never abandon it." [2]

The enlightened spirit of the times failed to dazzle so convinced a pupil of the Italian Counter Reformation.

[1] In connection with this matter, see the important "verbal memorandum" of December 2, reproduced in D'Angeberg, *op. cit.*, I, 485-491.
[2] *Correspondance inédite*, p. 167.

Francis, in polite phrases, was telling his imperial colleague that a sovereign should neither believe nor utter
such inanities, and with reason, the impartial historian
must admit. Even today the self-determination of peoples
is still a hoax; and it will be, as long as the will of the
people has not been more precisely defined and the instrument of its expression not been created. Think, then, what
it must have been at that time! The Congress already had
its hands full trying to find a solid base and to steer a sure
and clear path among the inconsistencies embodied in the
principles of legitimacy of the Old Regime; it would have
been confusion worse confounded to have added a revolutionary principle of legitimacy! Austria was by this time
convinced that, without an independent Saxony, there
would be no Germanic Confederation; and, as she had
understood what Alexander was aiming for with his revolutionary maneuver, she was willing to make concessions
in Poland so as to obtain a more conciliatory attitude from
Prussia and Russia with regard to Saxony. On December
10, Metternich sent Prussia a note which stated that Austria would yield to Russia on the Polish question, except
for certain points having military importance to Austria.
She would confine herself to asking guarantees from
Russia concerning the future constitution of Poland. But
Austria could not consent to the suppression of Saxony;
and she offered Prussia a part of it: lower Lusatia, half of
Upper Lusatia, and the Elba circle on both sides of the
Elba—altogether 432,000 people. With this and what she
would receive in Westphalia and on the Rhine, and what
Russia would restore to her in Poland, Prussia would be
reconstituted in the same proportions that she had before
the Treaty of Tilsit. But the Vienna government did not
only oppose the indefeasible right of kings to the revolutionary doctrine of Alexander and Hardenberg. A broader
justification was sought for the preservation of Saxony:
the general interests of Germany and of peace.

Both being German powers, Prussia and Austria enjoy simple and natural relations in their mutual influence on the Germanic Confederation, an influence which is generally desired because it offers a sure guarantee of peace. Everything points to harmony between the two courts; but this harmony must be made possible. The Congress must not degenerate into the sad spectacle of a fight between the two powers which are the most concerned with establishing peace in Europe. Germany must become a political entity; the boundaries between the great intermediate powers must not remain uncertain. The harmony between Austria and Prussia must, in short, be perfect, in order that the great task may be completed.

It is as a hindrance to that harmony, an insurmountable obstacle to the pact of federation, that we object to the total incorporation of Saxony in Prussia, and not at all from the viewpoint of the latter's aggrandizement. The incorporation of Saxony offers an obstacle to our concord because the Emperor's principles, the strongest of family ties, all our relations as neighbors are against it. There is also another obstacle, no less important to the settlement of German affairs, for the principal German states have expressed their unwillingness to sign a federative pact on so threatening a foundation to their safety as would be the incorporation of one of the principal German states by one of the powers called upon to defend the common nation. As France has also announced herself categorically against the total conquest of Saxony, an agreement between Austria and Prussia to uphold that conquest would only have the effect of restoring the protectorate of Germany to France. Therefore, what excuse could the Emperor find to give his consent to a matter which is so much against his principles, when it is directly bound up (as indeed it would be) on the one hand with a consent no less complete on the part of both our courts to the Russian plans for expansion, and on the other with a loss of the beneficial influence which the two powers are called upon to exert over Germany?

The Emperor is firmly convinced that by refusing to consent, under the circumstances, to the incorporation of Saxony, he is acting as the true and enlightened friend of Prussia, and not at all as a rival. But the question is to find the complement to the dimensions guaranteed to Prussia by treaty.

A rough estimate, based on a scale of values established by Your Highness, proves that those dimensions can be attained.

Francis I was no longer, in 1814, the young madcap he had been in 1797 and at Campo Formio; the hurricane of war which he had then unleashed on Europe with the destruction of Venice had taught him in some measure that force can only erect states when it is controlled. The Austrian note of December 10 was a masterpiece of constructive statesmanship. It should have settled the matter, since everyone wanted an accord. Instead, it brought about a storm. The Prussians were infuriated; after the conversation with Alexander, they had begun once more to hope that they would get the whole of Saxony; the offer of a fifth was an outrage. Hardenberg delivered a vehement note to Alexander on December 20, which the latter passed on to the Austrian Emperor.[3] Austria's offer was rejected, almost with disdain, and all of Saxony was claimed. Alexander, who was beginning to fear a rapprochement between France and Austria, sent Czartoryski to Talleyrand to say that he no longer desired the complete destruction of Saxony and would give his consent to a small nucleus being left independent. At the same time he asked Talleyrand if France had entered into any engagements with Austria. Talleyrand answered in the negative. Czartoryski thereupon asked whether, in case no agreement on Saxony should be reached, France would enter into any. "I would be sorry," was Talleyrand's answer.[4] Alexander also had a long interview with Metternich, in which he was "cold, sharp, and severe" with the unfortunate chancellor. He complained of not knowing what to believe of everything he was told by the Austrians and the Prussians, so contradictory were their statements. Was it then that an unusual incident took place, which was revealed after Metternich's death by the publication

[3] D'Angeberg, op. cit., I, 531-535.
[4] Correspondance inédite, pp. 180-181.

of his *Mémoires?* According to the story, the Czar had told the Austrian Emperor that Metternich had insulted him in his conversation with Hardenberg, and that he was going to challenge him to a duel.[5] All that unfortunate Europe needed was a duel, staged before the whole Congress, between the Emperor of Russia and the chancellor of Austria to settle the question of Saxony! Alexander was a little crazy. That story is sufficient proof of the fact. But, like Hamlet, he was only mad north-northwest; when his own interests were at stake, he knew a hawk from a handsaw.

Such a disagreement between the two great Allies could only give rise to a general discord. France, Bavaria, and the smaller German states stood by Austria. Alexander began to denounce Metternich to the whole Congress as the chief disturber of European peace. The Prussians began to think of nothing less than putting themselves at the head of the German revolution. They were taking to heart the revolutionary doctrines of the Czar. A police report dated December 16 reads:

Ever since the official note in which Austria must have offered Prussia lower Lusatia with Torgau and Wittemberg, an offer which the Prussian King formally refused, all the Prussians of my acquaintance, who are in the circle around the King and Prince William, have told me that, however little the King may be inclined to resort to war, they had no doubt but that it would take place. The Prussians flatter themselves that in such a war their alliance with Russia would be extremely close and based on mutual interests, whereas ours would not have that advantage; that the Russian army, strengthened by all the resources of Poland, would take the offensive and oblige us to oppose the greater part of our forces; and that on the Bohemian frontier the armies would be content to remain facing each other, while they could hold their grand army in readiness for France. They flatter themselves that they would have the majority of German

[5] Metternich, *Mémoires*, I, 326.

opinion on their side in such an event. Hanover would first be occupied. They are counting on Hesse, and even on the alliance with the King of Württemberg, whom they believe to be in sympathy with their interests. Besides, they hope that the other small states of Germany, seeing that the Congress of Vienna has accomplished nothing, being already hostile to the government of their princes, and feeling that actual war must decide whether Prussia or Austria will become the arbiter of Germany, will therefore turn more readily to that power whose Constitution is more liberal and more in tune with the spirit of the times. The Prussian government, which is working over this Constitution, is going to proclaim and introduce it the moment war starts.

As for the sentiment in Saxony, they admit that the army and nobility are against them, but they rely on the people and on the spread of the *Secte*.[6] They see in the coming war a struggle between democracy and aristocracy and believe that, by the nature of things, the former must be victorious. The moderates say, therefore, that this war will decide the fate of Germany between Prussia and Austria; the strict Sectarians, that possibly these events would give birth to causes, which could not be determined in advance, leading to the overthrow of everything; and they claim to have numerous partisans in Bavaria.

The Congress was neither a secret conclave of the great powers, as the victors had desired, nor a general European assembly of both great and small powers, as Talleyrand had proposed. Partly one and partly the other, the Congress was sinking deeper and deeper into misunderstanding and inconsistency, getting more and more lost as it sought frantically for some fixed point which it never found. The complete authentic contents of the Austrian note had only been known to a few people, all of whom were on the delegations of the eight signatory powers to the Treaty of Paris. The others had only heard about it at second-hand; but these others—that is, the delegations of the smaller powers and the Vienna salons—made up a

6 The Protestant faith.

circle around the eight powers which criticized them and
spurred them on, and which, only half-informed as to
what was going on in the conclave, was becoming more
and more impressionable, nervous, excited, one day pessimistic, the next optimistic, sometimes right and sometimes wrong. All this added still another complication, for
these currents of opinion, true and false, interfered with
the work of the Congress. Thus, toward the middle of
December, the opinion about the Congress was extremely
pessimistic: no agreement would be reached either on
Saxony or on Poland; on all sides the powers were arming;
war was about to begin! But Talleyrand, who was in a
position to judge, was far from sharing this opinion; and
on December 15 he wrote Louis that things were coming
along satisfactorily. At the beginning of the month, an
important change had occurred. Castlereagh had received
orders from London to join France and Austria in their
opposition to the annexation of Saxony. It appears that
Louis had persuaded Wellington in Paris, and that Wellington had persuaded his government in London, where
Castlereagh's policy had already been attacked in Parliament by the Opposition. Whatever the reason, England's
attitude had undergone a change; and Talleyrand intended to take advantage of it as well as of the effect produced by the Austrian note, to rupture decisively the
entente between the Allies and solve the chief question
before the Congress without resorting to war. He was certain that, when the day arrived on which England and
Austria would come to an understanding with France
and oppose a united front to the claims of Russia and
Prussia on Poland and Saxony, the latter would back
down. The day before he wrote his letter to Louis, December 14, he had taken the offensive by going to see Metternich, who had offered to show him the much-discussed
note. Talleyrand replied that he knew the contents but
wanted official confirmation. "My particular motive
for insisting on a formal disclosure lay in the fact that

this would mark the real date of the rupture of the Coalition," he wrote to the King on the fifteenth. Indeed, if Austria were officially to communicate the contents of the note to France because she knew that France was behind her, she would thus be seeking France's support against Russia and Prussia. After a slight hesitation, Metternich handed Talleyrand the note, accompanying it with a personal message, which concluded with this charming sentiment: "I am happy to find myself in agreement with your Cabinet on a point which is so nobly defensible."

At last the first split in the Coalition! Talleyrand did not delay to drive a wedge into this with a long letter which he wrote Metternich on the nineteenth and which is one of the greatest documents of history. After having thanked Prince Metternich on behalf of his King for communicating the contents of his note, he went on to reveal France's attitude with regard to Saxony. In his note, Metternich had envisaged the problem especially from the viewpoint of Germany and Austro-Prussian relations. With a few strokes of his pen Talleyrand raised it to the universal, philosophical plane of the European continent.

France [he wrote] has raised no claim, nor will she raise any. But she desires that the work of restitution be accomplished for all Europe, as for her, that everywhere and forever the spirit of revolt be quenched, that every legitimate right be made sacred, and that every ambition and unjust enterprise find both its condemnation and a perpetual obstacle in an explicit understanding and a formal guarantee of those same principles, the disregard for which was responsible for the long and deadly horror of the Revolution. That desire of France's should be the desire of every European state which does not blind itself to the facts. Without such an order of life, no one can be certain for one instant of his future.

Never has there been a nobler aim offered to the governments of Europe. Never has there been a greater need of fulfillment, and never has there been a more favorable opportunity to fulfill such an aim, at a time when all Christianity has for the first time been called upon to form a Congress. Perhaps this aim would have already been fulfilled if, as the King had hoped, the Congress had been immediately convened, and had, in defining the principles, established the aim and traced the only path which could have led to it. Doubtless, in that case, one would not have witnessed the spectacle of the powers thinking up pretexts to destroy that which the aim can only be to preserve. Certainly, when the treaty of May 30 expressed the will that the final aim of the Congress was to establish a real and permanent stability, it did not mean that all the territories and all the peoples were to be mingled in one indistinct mass, in order to divide them later according to certain proportions.

It was meant to preserve or re-establish every legitimate dynasty, to respect every legitimate right, and to govern the distribution of unclaimed territories, that is, territories without sovereigns, in conformity with principles of political stability, or, what amounts to the same thing, principles which preserve the rights of each one and the peace of all. It would moreover be a strange mistake to consider, as the only elements to be stabilized, those quantities enumerated by political arithmeticians.

Stability will be meaningless, if men persist in making an abstraction of the true moral force contained in virtue rather than of the ephemeral and deceitful force produced by the passions. Now, in the relations between peoples, the chief virtue is that of justice.

Actuated by these principles, the King has enjoined, as an unalterable law, upon his ambassadors to seek above all what is just, in no case to abandon justice and, whatever consideration may arise, not to subscribe to or acquiesce in anything which would be contrary to it, and, with regard to legitimate alliances, to join those which can the most efficaciously bring about the establishment and preservation of a true stability.

Of all the problems which are to be dealt with by the Congress, the King would have considered the greatest, most important, and most typically European one to be that of Poland, if it had been possible to hope ... that a people as worthy of everyone else's interest ... might be restored to their complete ancient independence.

The partition which eliminated it from the roster of free nations became the prelude to, perhaps in part the cause of, and up to a certain point an example for the calamities which have befallen Europe; but, when the force of circumstance, triumphing over the noblest and most generous instincts of the sovereigns to whom the former Polish provinces are subject, had reduced the question of Poland to a mere matter of partition and boundaries, which the three interested powers would discuss together, and in which their previous treaties had ignored France—no other course was left to the latter . . . than to desire that you might be satisfied and to be satisfied if you were. The question of Poland, therefore, did not have, either for France or for Europe itself, the importance that it would have had under the aforementioned circumstances; and the Saxon question became the most important because in no other question today are the two principles of legitimacy and balance so involved at one and the same time and to such a great extent as they are by the claims which have been put forth for the disposal of that kingdom.

To acknowledge the legitimacy of these claims would be to admit that kings may be judged; that they may be judged by whosoever wishes to seize their possessions; that they may be condemned without a hearing, without being able to defend themselves; that their condemnation necessarily involves their families and their peoples; that confiscation of property, which enlightened nations have made illegal, must in the nineteenth century be sanctioned by the law of nations, the confiscation of a kingdom being without doubt less objectionable than that of a simple cottage; that peoples have no rights distinct from those of their rulers, and may be treated like cattle on a farm; that sovereignty is lost and acquired by the sole fact of conquest; that European states are bound to each other by no other moral ties than those which bind them to the natives of the South Sea islands; that their mutual relations are governed solely by the law of nature; that what is called the European law of nations is nonexistent, inasmuch as, although civilized societies all over the world are wholly or partially governed by customs, which they observe as laws, those customs which have been established in international relations and which for three centuries have been universally, constantly, and mutually observed, have not thereby become laws; in other words, that might makes right. But Europe, which has suffered so terribly from such doctrines and paid for them with so much blood and so many tears, has well earned the right to loathe and detest them. They are equally detestable in Vienna, in St. Petersburg, in London, in Paris, in Madrid, and in Lisbon.

The disposition which has been intended for Saxony, bad enough as a precedent, would be worse in its influence on the general stability in Europe, a stability which consists in a balance between the forces of aggression and the forces of resistance to aggression; and it would upset that balance in two ways, both equally dangerous:

1. By creating an extremely strong force of aggression against Bohemia, and by thus threatening the security of Austria as a whole, for Bohemia's individual force of resistance would then have to be increased proportionately and could only be so increased by weakening the general force of resistance of the Austrian monarchy. Now, the security of Austria is of too much importance to Europe not to arouse the personal anxiety of the King.

2. By creating within the German nation, for one of its members, a force of aggression out of proportion to the force of resistance of all the other elements; which, by putting them into imminent peril and forcing them to look for support abroad, would render useless the force of resistance which, in the general system of balance in Europe, the nation as a whole should possess and which it can only possess through the closest unity between its elements.

France may say in all truth, with Austria, that she bears Prussia no feelings of jealousy or animosity; and that it is precisely because she has her best interests at heart that she cannot desire to see her obtain superficial advantages which, acquired through injustice and being dangerous to Europe, would sooner or later become extremely disadvantageous to her. Let Prussia acquire all that she can legitimately obtain, and not only will France make no objections but she will be the first to approve. Let there be no more question of how much of Saxony the Prussian King will restore to the Saxon

King, which is a contradiction to all ideas of justice and reason.
But, if it becomes a question of how much of Saxony the
Saxon King will cede to the Prussian King, and if such concession on the part of the Saxon King is necessary in order
to restore Prussia to a size equal to that which she enjoyed in
1805, then the King of France will be the first to pledge the
Saxon ruler to make such concessions as will not harm the
interests of Austria and of Germany, which at present signify
the general interests of Europe. Your Highness would seem
to have shown me what those concessions should be, in the
list which accompanied your note.

His Christian Majesty, being unalterably determined not
to sanction, even by his silence, the carrying out of the plans
against the King and Kingdom of Saxony, yet preferring to
believe that these plans are the result of error or self-decep-
tion and that a closer study will dispel them; full of confidence in the personal integrity and feelings of His Majesty,
the King of Prussia, who has also had his misfortunes; realizing how much can be accomplished by the influence of His
Majesty, the Emperor of Russia, and how much is to be expected from the noble qualities which he possesses; finally,
convinced that one must never despair in a just cause, has
never despaired in that of Saxony. He is even less in despair
upon learning that His Majesty, the Emperor of Austria, by
a resolution worthy of him, has come boldly to its defense,
and he declares that he will never abandon it.

Politics or philosophy? A mixture of both; therein lies
the incredible singularity of this document. Gentz called
the letter "an extremely remarkable piece of work, composed with as much fervor as strength and nobility, embracing great truths and astonishing judgment." Gentz is
right: great truths, in particular two great truths which
the nineteenth century was to disregard more and more.
The first is that a system of states such as Europe can only
remain peaceful if it is governed by principles which are
respected by the most powerful states, even though these
states are able to violate them and gain an immediate
advantage. The second is that those principles, though

limited and reversible, are sacred because they are rational crystallizations of a deep feeling of justice and humanity which alone is strong enough to check the most dangerous abuses of force. That is what Talleyrand meant when he referred to virtue. Woe to the age which takes advantage of their limitations and reversibility in order to falsify them and use them to justify force and its abuses! The sublime spirit of the eighteenth-century law of nations, which was not a legal document but a moral and almost religious law, was here apparent in all its splendor and profundity. Somewhat vague and uncertain in most of the preceding writers, it is revealed in perfect clearness by Talleyrand's great mind.

A few days later, Castlereagh paid a call on Talleyrand, who took advantage of the occasion to show him a copy of his letter to Metternich. "He read it very calmly," Talleyrand wrote Louis; "he read it completely, and returned it without a word, either of approval or condemnation."

Graecum est, non legitur. It had meant nothing to Castlereagh. But he had not come to talk political philosophy with his friend; he had come to suggest the formation of a new committee to verify the Austrian and Prussian estimates on the population of Saxony. Talleyrand gave his approval to the plan, but seized the opportunity to attack Castlereagh's latest policy of taking refuge behind complications and uncertainties. He wrote to the King on December 28 as follows:

I told him that I had no objections against that; but that, if we handled it in the same way that we have handled so many other matters up till now, by trusting to luck and following neither principles or rules, we should come to no decision; that we should therefore begin by laying down principles; that, before verifying estimates, we should acknowledge the rights of the Saxon King; that he, M. de Metternich, and I should make a private agreement regarding this matter.

"An agreement?" he exclaimed. "Are you proposing an alliance?"

"That agreement," I told him, "might be possible without an alliance; but it will be an alliance if you wish; I have no objection."

"But an alliance implies war, or else it may lead to it; and we should do everything to avoid war."

"I agree with you; we must do everything, except to sacrifice honor, justice, and the future of Europe."

He replied: "War would not be favorably looked upon in England."

"War would be popular in England if you were to give it a noble aim, an aim with significance to all Europe."

"What would that aim be?"

"The restoration of Poland."

He made no effort to repel this idea, and merely replied: "Not yet."

Besides, I had only guided the conversation into this channel in order to feel him out and discover what he would be likely to do if such an occasion arose.

"Whatever it be," I said, "whether by agreement or by notes or by a protocol signed by you, M. de Metternich, and myself, providing we acknowledge the rights of the King of Saxony, I am indifferent to the form; only the thing itself interests me."

"Austria," he answered, "has officially acknowledged the rights of the Saxon King; you have also *officially* acknowledged them; I have *openly* acknowledged them. Is the difference between us then so great that it requires such an action as you are asking?"

British resistance was weakening. But Alexander, who had foreseen Talleyrand's maneuver, launched a surprise counterattack at the end of December by making a supreme effort to restore harmony among the Allies. On his initiative, the allied representatives—Razoumoffsky, Metternich, Hardenberg, and Castlereagh—met on December 29 in order to arrive at a definitive solution, without the intervention of France and the Congress, of two insoluble problems—Saxony and Poland. At the first meeting, nothing was decided. Finally, on the thirtieth, Razoumoffsky decided to lay his cards on the table by revealing Alexander's exact plans. Russia wanted the whole of the Duchy of Warsaw excepting the former palatinates of Gnesen and Posen and the former provinces of western Prussia, in all amounting to 850,000 people, which Russia agreed to let Prussia have; and also a small piece of land on the right bank of the Vistula that included the salt mines of Wielicza, which she agreed to restore to Austria, together with the circle of Tarnopol—400,000 people—ceded by Austria in 1809. Cracow and Thorn were to be declared free and independent cities. With regard to Saxony, Alexander, who had recently begun to waver and show signs of being ready to compromise, now reverted to his original idea, which was the destruction of the kingdom and total incorporation with Prussia. Russia intended to indemnify the Saxon King with a state of 700,000 inhabitants on the left bank of the Rhine, including the Duchy of Luxembourg, parts of the archbishopric of Treves and Cologne, together with Bonn and the abbeys of Pruyn, Stavelot, and Malmédy.

The Prussians, who had been extremely annoyed with Austria's last proposal, were this time delighted. Both satisfied and dissatisfied, Austria approved the plan for Poland but again rejected the one for Saxony. But it was written that the four powers would never agree. This time it was Castlereagh who was angry, whether over Poland or Saxony no one knows. Had the Russian delegate been abrupt or haughty? Had Alexander's obstinacy finally exhausted his patience? We do not know for certain; but the next day Castlereagh went to Talleyrand and complained violently about Russia, protesting that Russia was behaving in a dictatorial manner and that England would not be told what to do by anyone. Talleyrand took advantage of his anger to bring up the subject once more of an alliance between England, France, and Austria. Castlereagh this time showed more enthusiasm, admitted that something should be done, and ended up by suggesting that he draw up a draft of the proposed alliance in black and white. In fact, he soon returned with the draft; Talleyrand leaped at the opportunity, read the draft, touched it up here and there, and suggested a few moderations. As soon as the actual text was agreed upon, he communicated it to Metternich. On January 3, 1815, the three powers signed the treaty in the utmost secrecy and pledged themselves:

... to act in concert, with the most complete impartiality and good faith, to see that, in the fulfillment of the Treaty of Paris, the measures which must execute its dispositions are carried out in such a manner as to conform as nearly as possible to the true spirit of the treaty.

It was thus a question of defending the Treaty of Paris against one of its authors, and by every means which might become necessary, including war. In a series of extremely detailed articles, the treaty considered the eventuality of a war carried out by the three powers in defense of the Treaty of Paris. This proved conclusively that the Treaty of Paris was the cornerstone of the new European order which the Congress was attempting to build. England and Austria had now acknowledged it. Europe could be saved only if it succeeded in completing the task in Vienna that had been started in Paris in May, 1814.

XV

EARLY SOLUTIONS:
POLAND AND SAXONY

Was it to be war then? On the contrary! The treaty had been signed on January 3; the same day, at the meeting of the four powers, Metternich declared that the Emperor of Austria was prepared to discuss the proposals of the Czar.[1] Nine days later, on January 12, Castlereagh asked for the insertion of a statement in the protocol, declaring that England abandoned her opposition to Alexander's Polish plans, since Berlin and Vienna had accepted them, but on condition that the three courts would commit themselves to giving their subjects "a system of administration whose form would be both conciliating and in harmony with the character of the people."[2]

England had capitulated; the condition imposed by England did not bother Alexander in the least, since he wished to give a representative constitution to the future Kingdom of Poland. He was no longer a hero, but the gambler had won his game.

No sooner had the Triple Alliance been concluded,

[1] D'Angeberg, *op. cit.*, p. 1874.
[2] *Ibid.*, p. 1796.

than, instead of resisting Russia's ambitions with more
energy, Austria and England proceeded to grant almost
everything that Alexander had been vainly demanding for
four months. Wherein lay the explanation for this paradox
to which the historians of the Congress have paid so little
heed? Was it necessary to make a Triple Alliance in order
to capitulate? Castlereagh and Metternich, that is, Francis
I, whose wishes Metternich was carrying out, both preferred a bad peace to war. Neither one had ever seriously
considered waging war over a few fragments of the Duchy
of Warsaw. As Talleyrand had said to Castlereagh, Europe
could only have taken up arms again in order to reconstitute ancient Poland; which meant nothing less than
thrusting Russia back into the almost Asiatic isolation
from which she had emerged twenty years before; ex-
pelling her from Europe just after her rather unexpected
and enigmatic intervention had made possible the re-
establishment of the European system destroyed by the
Revolution. Neither England nor Austria desired any
such adventure. But then why and against whom had the
treaty of January 3 been concluded? Against the ambitions of the Russia of the future, enlarged by the Duchy
of Warsaw. The English and the Austrians were very
much afraid of the future King of Poland turning into a
second Napoleon. On January 3, with the new alliance
signed, the Hofburg and the English Embassy felt more
at ease. Austria and England would no longer be alone if
Russia tried to take advantage of her strength; therefore
it was possible to satisfy her demands without too much
risk, and extricate the Congress from the Polish impasse.
For it was an impasse; it was obvious that Alexander was
ready to run any risk rather than give up the Duchy of
Warsaw.

But all these fears were imaginary; the history of the
nineteenth century has made it clear. History was to bear
out Pozzo di Borgo, who had considered the Kingdom of
Poland to be an illusion, since the same sovereign could

not possibly be an autocrat in Russia and a constitutional king in Poland. History was also to bear out the Prussian government, which had always thought that the annexation of the Duchy of Warsaw would weaken Russia rather than strengthen her. The Kingdom of Poland was only to survive its creator by a few years; and it was by attacking the Polish salient of the Duchy of Warsaw from both sides that Austria and Germany were to give the *coup de grâce* to the empire of the Czars during the World War. Not one of the catastrophes which Castlereagh predicted would come to pass as a consequence of the Polish annexation came true.

Europe had lost four months in Vienna because the English government and the Court of Vienna had suffered an hallucination, brought on by what was left of the great panic. It is not astonishing; life would be simple and easy if humanity had only to fight against real dangers. The great torment and the great trial of life are the imaginary fears, which surround, obsess, blind, and drag down to perdition simple mortals as well as kings and emperors. The Court of Vienna and the English government had been the victims of one of these imaginary perils.

Talleyrand believed the treaty marked the end of the exclusion which the four allied courts had imposed on France until then. "The Coalition is dissolved, and forever," he wrote to Louis XVIII on January 4.[3] Austria and England would no longer be able to act in the Congress without first having come to an accord with France. Indeed, on January 3, the very day on which the treaty had been signed, Metternich proposed at the meeting of the Allies that Talleyrand be admitted to the future meetings. But Talleyrand hoped for more; he already saw France at the head of a sort of coalition of big and little states, in the role of European champion of legitimacy and the law of nations against the revolutionary follies of Russia and Prussia. He did not even shrink from the idea

[3] *Correspondance inédite*, p. 209.

Switzerland; it had even plunged into the jungle—the matter of boundaries between the cantons. But the committee had not yet come to any definite conclusion on all this wealth of documentation, save for two important resolutions taken on December 10, during the fifth meeting. The first resolution adopted the Russian thesis contained in the note of November 16, and recognized the integrity of the nineteen cantons named in the act of mediation, as the basis on which Switzerland would be reconstructed. A question of principle, vital to Switzerland, was thus resolved; the parchment legitimacies presented by the aristocracy of Berne were buried in the archives, and the living legitimacies which were growing in the heart of new Switzerland were called upon to inherit the estate. At the same meeting, the Austrian plenipotentiary having declared that the Court was ready to restore Valtelline to Switzerland, the Swiss legation and the deputies from the cantons of Grisons and Valtelline were invited to appear before the committee, in order to make suggestions on a method to incorporate Valtelline in the Swiss Confederation.

Neither had the Congress come to any decision about Italy, whether to expel Murat, or to recognize him; to restore Parma to the Bourbons or to install Marie Louise there; to accept the former Grand Duke in Tuscany or to chase him out. The papal legate kept on buttonholing everyone, without obtaining anything from anyone. The same was true of all the other official and semi-official representatives of the small Italian states: Neri Corsini, who represented the Grand Duke of Tuscany; Count Ferdinando Marescalchi, former representative of the Italian kingdom in Paris, whom Marie Louise had charged with the care of her interests; Count Antonio Aldini, whom Élise Baciocchi had charged with saving the principality of Lucca at any price, even that of surrendering it entirely to the conquerors. The representative of Piedmont was meeting with no success in his efforts to obtain the territorial expansion desired by his sovereign, while Cardinal Consalvi was still complaining. The Congress was really causing him too much anguish! After all his trouble with the Legations, and with Princess Talleyrand, here to plague him anew was the committee on precedence, charged with the burial of the diplomatic etiquette of the Old Regime, which had died in the middle of the Revolution, and the establishment of a new etiquette in accordance with the spirit of the times. The committee had evolved a system much more simple and democratic than the system of the Old Regime. Sovereignties were made into a hierarchy of three classes. The first, the superior one, which had precedence over the other two, included emperors and kings, who were all made equal, regardless of the extent of their dominions. The second, which held precedence over the third, included princes, grand dukes, the Swiss and American republics. The third and last class included dukes. In each class, precedence would be ruled by seniority, each representative taking rank according to the date he had presented his credentials. It was a sort of arithmetical standardization of the whole infinitely complicated and contentious system of hierarchies in the Old Regime. It had the advantage of being simple, clear, and beyond dispute.

The committee had decided to enroll the Pope in the first class, in company with kings and emperors. The decision had filled the cardinal-legate with joy. But the committee had decided that papal legates should also come under the rule of seniority, whereas under the Old Regime they had always possessed the right of precedence. Wounded to the core by this decision, Cardinal Consalvi had been doing everything in his power to recover the former privilege for the Holy See. Talleyrand had hastened to his aid, and it had been easy to win over the Catholic powers: Spain, Portugal, and Austria. It had been more difficult to persuade Prussia and Russia, but all efforts to persuade Castlereagh had come to naught. The latter had declared that England, as a Protestant state, could not acknowledge in principle the precedence of the papal legate, although willing to acknowledge it in practice. At the beginning of January, the matter had broken down before this opposition, and Cardinal Consalvi was in despair.[7]

The tragedy lay in the fact that this was an authority whose prestige had outlived its power. If the Pope, besieged by revolutionary anarchy, had refused to consecrate Napoleon; if he had suffered persecution for having declared the French Empire an illegitimate authority—persecution which came to him later, anyway, when he denounced the despoilers of St. Peter's—he would have become the spiritual head of the Congress. But the Pope had instead made an attempt to legitimize force, although an unsuccessful one, and his legate meant no more to the Congress than the curator of an archeological museum in which the last vestiges of the medieval grandeur of the papacy had been collected. When the papacy had sunk to such a degree, what could the Italian states do or hope for? The consequences of Cherasco and Campo Formio were making themselves felt more and more. Italy had neither defended the Old Regime nor fought on the side of the Revolution. She had submitted and attempted to exploit the Revolution without accepting any of its principles or doctrines, and hating it while she submitted; and in the end she had allowed it to fall without raising a finger, either for or against it. As a neutral spectator, therefore, she had no voice in the Congress. Her ruling classes merely hoped that Austria would give them an ordered government, without despotism or violence.[8]

In short, the delegates continued to banquet, to dance, and to court beautiful women; and nothing was accom-

[7] Concerning this matter, see Letter XIII (pp. 155 *et seq.*) and Letter XX (pp. 192 *et seq.*) from Cardinal Consalvi to Cardinal Pacca. Rinieri, *op. cit.*

[8] On the popularity of Austria with the upper classes of Italy in 1814, cf. Bianchi, *op. cit.*, I, 76.

plished. Then, abruptly, all this gaiety and frivolity was interrupted by a funeral mass—and what a mass! Talleyrand had conceived the idea for January 21, the twenty-second anniversary of the execution of Louis XVI. At the invitation of the French Embassy, all the sovereigns and the nobility of Europe that were in Vienna assembled in the Church of Saint Stephen to pray for the soul of their unfortunate brother and render thanks unto God for not having shared his fate. Alexander, however, always on the other side, had denounced this idea of Talleyrand's as an antirevolutionary provocation. The others had flocked to the church, had wept over the moving sermon by the abbé de Zaignelins and the music by Neukomm; but had they also drawn from the ceremony the "great lesson" which Talleyrand had hoped they would?[9] That was more doubtful. Talleyrand himself had not yet been able to pierce the veil surrounding this tragedy of royal destiny; only today are we in a position to understand. Louis XVI had been the victim of the great panic which had taken hold of his people on the day that law, weakened by decay, had disappeared in France. His brothers, praying in Vienna for the repose of his soul, might still be kings, emperors, and princes if they succeeded in freeing the world from the great panic; but woe to them, and to all who succeeded them, and to their peoples, if the great panic should return again!

In the second half of January, a fortuitous circumstance brought the problem of Saxony out of the pit into which it had sunk. This was the recall of Castlereagh to London and his replacement by Wellington. There had been dissatisfaction in London with Castlereagh, even in the ranks of his own party and in the government to which he belonged. His policy was considered weak, irresolute, and uncertain. The opposition had been attacking him unmercifully. It seems that Louis XVIII had spoken to Wellington in Paris and that the latter had in turn advised his

[9] *Correspondance inédite*, p. 236.

government to recall Castlereagh. The recall was justified on the grounds that Parliament was sitting and that Castlereagh as minister should be present. But he did not want to leave Vienna without having accomplished something, and he made a last effort to settle the Saxon problem at least before going back to London. He worked day and night with Alexander, Frederick William, Metternich, Hardenberg, and Talleyrand. Finally on February 6, he reached an agreement with Hardenberg on a definitive settlement. Saxony was to be divided in half. The more populous half was to be left to the King, and included 1,200,000 subjects, with Dresden, Leipzig, Bautzen, and the entire territory bordering on Bohemia. The part which Prussia was to receive covered more ground but was not as wealthy or important; to console Prussia for not getting Leipzig, Alexander agreed to let her have Thorn with its zone. Only Cracow was to remain free. But this decision was not yet final; the consent of the Saxon King still had to be obtained. An act of force, even if it were accomplished by the whole of Europe, was not capable of creating sovereignty. To save the principle, Metternich, Wellington, and Talleyrand would go to Pressburg as representatives of Europe and lay before the Saxon King the earnest plea of the Congress that he would agree to make certain sacrifices for the general peace.

By the middle of February, the five great powers had at last reached an accord on the two problems of Poland and Saxony. The remainder—Germany, Italy, and Switzerland—were still up in the air. As the Congress had been palavering for five months, the results were meager. For that reason, must we, therefore, join in the nineteenth-century chorus of recriminations against the Congress? Obviously, Napoleon's treaties had been accomplished more rapidly. In three weeks, for instance, he had polished off the Treaty of Pressburg. Twenty weeks to acknowledge the territory which the Emperor of Russia already possessed, and to decide whether the little Saxon Kingdom should be entirely suppressed or divided in half—that seems like a rather long time. All right for Poland; the British government and the Court of Vienna had been the victims of an imaginary fear. But Saxony, a little state with 2,000,000 inhabitants! Was it conceivable that the five greatest powers in Europe threatened to go to war about this tiny state? Yes, we have seen them at it; what was at stake in Saxony was a principle of the eighteenth-century law of nations, the principle which had been the cornerstone of the European order before the Revolution and which was to be that of the new order—the principle that sovereignty cannot be acquired by conquest but only by cession. If the great powers of Europe, by taking advantage of their strength, had violated this principle in the person of a little sovereign like the King of Saxony, they would have destroyed the foundation of the building they were erecting, before they had put on a roof; they would have opened a breach in the new order, a small one but one that would have upset it completely. That was Talleyrand's thesis. But if this thesis was correct, how was it that the Congress, which had applied this principle without any trouble to more important territories—all those which had been restored without question to their former sovereigns, forcibly despoiled by the Revolution— came to grief on this last application of the principle, in itself quite unimportant?

Principle vs. expediency—always the same tragedy. The leaders of the Congress were men of the eighteenth century. They understood the law of nations in the spirit of the Old Regime, which had conceived it: as a body of rules of wisdom, to be followed by every enlightened statesman because, by applying those rules, he would serve the interests of his own country by harmonizing them with those of the others. The majority of them had been more or less influenced by the wave of rather mystical enthusiasm which, in the spring of 1814, had swept over Europe and made people see in the restoration of the law of nations the pledge of Europe's coming regeneration. But all of them had lived for the last twenty-five years in a chaotic world where abuses of force followed each other with increasing rapidity. They came to Vienna in order to reconstruct at one and the same time both Europe and their own states, which were parts of Europe—a dual task, concordant as a whole but easily inconsistent in its parts. They were constantly afraid that force might win another victory that would be their loss; that the principle of the law of nations might be used by others to harm their own interests; that they might be betrayed in the end by those with whom they wanted to build a new Europe and sacrificed on the pretext of saving the peace and stability of the world. Saxony—a tiny piece of land, a microscopic state of no importance—by bringing into conflict principle and expediency, both equally overexcited by suspicion and general uncertainty, could suffice to endanger the entire work of the Congress, the entire reconstruction of the European order. There was only one man in whom the vision of the universal problem, which conditioned the individual interests, was clear, precise, and unshakable. That man was Talleyrand. Therein lay the tremendous role he played. He was the loudspeaker for the secret conscience of the Congress, crying out in clear, concise words what the others vaguely and hesitantly thought. But he was all alone, for Alexander, who had helped him in Paris, had deserted him in Vienna. He was forced to find another collaborator.

But, while the Congress was dancing, Europe was cold and hungry, Europe was trembling under the menace of cholera, Europe was being gradually ruined by the military occupations. The intolerable present and uncertainty of the future multiplied and brought together rival dissatisfactions: the people who looked back regretfully on Napoleon and the revolutionary despotisms by which they had lived, those who hoped for the restoration of the Old Regime, and those who demanded constitutional monarchies. Europe, unable to distinguish between them, was equally scandalized by justifiable delays and inexcusable delays in the work of the Congress. A provisional state of affairs which is prolonged too far ends by exploding. The irresolution of the Congress could only, in the long run, end in a catastrophe. This was realized by nearly everyone, and nearly everyone protested to the Congress. Gentz's was the most persistent voice which emerged from this universal condemnation that was only partly justifiable.

The Congress should have made a strenuous effort to pull itself out of the lethargy into which it had sunk. But it seemed unable to find any support for such an effort. The settlement of the Saxon problem had eliminated the chief obstacle to the reorganization of Germany; but the committee for German affairs had not yet met again. As a creation of the most powerful German states, it did not represent Germany and lacked the authority to reconstitute Germany without the latter having any say in the matter. As for Naples, Talleyrand would have been satisfied if the Congress had declared Ferdinand IV to be the king and if all the powers had pledged themselves to respect his rights. After the Triple Alliance of January 3, the Vienna government found it increasingly difficult to support Murat against France and drifted gradually away from its Italian ally. In February, Austria had begun to collect an army of 100,000 men in the Po valley, which was obviously to be used in the event of a break with Murat. Moreover, Talleyrand had been working against Murat with redoubled energy ever since the Triple Alliance. But Austria was still fettered by her alliance with Naples of the year before and was still frightened of war. Metternich continued to avoid the issue, and nothing was settled. Castlereagh had left, and Wellington had taken his place. For a while Talleyrand hoped that Wellington would be more of a help to him in overcoming Austria's resistance than his predecessor had been.

But this was a false hope, for Wellington, while showing no sympathy for Murat, declared that England had ratified the treaty between Austria and the King of Naples and could not recant at this point. He made no bones about the fact that England did not view favorably the union of two crowns—those of Sicily and Naples—on one head. Talleyrand verified his former opinion that the English did not comprehend the principle of legitimacy, probably because they thought of Europe in terms of India. The only change in the status of Italian affairs at the Congress was that, at the eleventh meeting of the committee on Swiss affairs, the Austrian delegate requested that the question of Valtelline be reserved. The Austrian government had changed its mind and was thinking of annexing Valtelline to Lombardy.

The Congress became more and more sunk in lethargy. At the beginning of March, Talleyrand, Wellington, and Metternich set out for Pressburg on their mission to the King of Saxony. Vienna meanwhile continued to play. On March 5, the Court finished off the carnival with a splendid fête, at which the highest-ranking noblemen, clothed in the most elaborate Flemish costumes of the Middle Ages, acted out, in a series of living tableaus, the meeting of Maxmilian I and Marie de Bourgogne. Suddenly there was a flurry of excitement; groups began to gather, and the actors were forgotten. A courier from the King of Sardinia, who had crossed the Alps in three days by forced marches, had just arrived with the amazing news that Napoleon had landed at Cannes. Talleyrand had found the new collaborator he needed after Alexander's defection.

XVI

THE HUNDRED DAYS OF THE CONGRESS: SWITZERLAND AND ITALY

———————————————————— ⟶»»⟨⟨⟵ ————————————————————

The fête went on, but the same idea immediately occurred to everyone: that England had allowed Napoleon to escape. Later, this suspicion was extended to Austria and France. This, however, is an extremely doubtful point. What is certain is that Napoleon could only have been able to embark and take his departure with a following of 1,000 people because of the carelessness of the Anglo-French fleet, which was supposed to guard him. Could it be that England and France, if not Austria, having been forewarned of Napoleon's *coup de main,* had let him go ahead, expecting to stop him as soon as he landed in France, and send him to a remoter exile? If this is the correct hypothesis, the adventure baffled all these too astute calculations by an initial stroke of luck beyond all expectation. What is the explanation for this initial success? Why was Napoleon, one year after his abdication, again able to assume the throne of France for a few months without a single shot being fired? The leading role in this comic opera could only have been played by the army. But the army could not have reversed itself so completely in twenty days if it had not been supported or forced to do so by a strong current of general opinion. The Restoration and the treaty had apparently been received with almost unanimous enthusiasm in France; why did a part of France revolt a year later? Was it the "blunders" of the Bourbons, as many historians assert? But the so-called "blunders" of the Bourbons were merely the complications presented by the insoluble problem which the Restoration had to resolve. We have seen that Louis XVIII had possessed the courage to strike off the chains with which the Revolution had shackled France after having promised her liberty. This was the first move necessary to the re-establishment of the European system. But, once freed from the repression in which the Revolution had held them, all the fears, hates, and illusions, magnified by twenty-five years of adventure, had blown up in a series of terrific explosions of counter frenzies, which had inflamed the whole of France. The Hundred Days were only the greatest, the most violent, and the most inflammatory of these explosions. Talleyrand had said at Erfurt: "The Rhine, the Atlantic Ocean, the Pyrenees, the Mediterranean, and the Alps are the conquests of France; the rest is the conquest of the Emperor, and France cares nothing for it." This was true and profoundly human. Presumably not only the history of France but that of Germany and Europe would have been happier, if at the beginning of the nineteenth century France had been able to reconstitute the boundaries of ancient Gaul. But the left bank of the Rhine had been lost when the allied armies had crossed the river. By May, 1814, for France to have regained the Rhine, instead of making peace, it would have been necessary to resume the war of 1792 by making the Allies recross the Rhine. But how many Frenchmen besides Talleyrand and Louis XVIII understood the turn of events and its inexorable fatality so as to resign themselves to the inevitable?

There is no doubt but that after the signing of the

peace treaty the French people were in a painful state of worry, worry over the loss of a great aim, over a catastrophe involving the most serious consequences, for which someone was responsible. Someone—but who? Napoleon, who had not been able to halt the Allies at the Rhine; the Revolution which had mired itself in the quicksands of the Po in 1796, answer historians today. But public opinion, overwrought by so many calamities, did not see so far ahead in 1814; there was now a government in Paris which no longer exercised any censorship and which allowed itself to be criticized. Therefore, it must be responsible. It was inconceivable that Louis XVIII and Talleyrand had been unable to negotiate for the return of the left bank by the Allies, who held it by force of arms.

The incendiary explosion of the Hundred Days is understandable; but it was as dangerous for France as for Europe. It was a revolt carried out by the spirit of adventure against the constructive mind, which was painfully trying to re-establish the peace of the world in Vienna. Napoleon had re-entered France with an olive branch in each hand: a promise to France to constitutionalize the monarchy, a promise to Europe to respect the treaties and to become the great defender of peace. "Enough glory has accrued to each of the flags belonging to the various nations. . . . A door to fairer things is now open to sovereigns, and I am the first to pass through it. After having shown the world the art of great warfare, it will be sweeter to know in the future only the rivalry afforded by the advantages of peace." Fine words, but only words. Through Paris, Napoleon was marching against Vienna and the European system which they were struggling to reconstruct there, in order to make a shambles of everything— work and work room. At Vienna, in 1814 and 1815, Europe did not have to choose between the Declaration of the Rights of Man and the absolute monarchy of the Old Regime, but between revolutionary dictatorship and legitimate government, based on a principle of right, monarchic or republican, parliamentary or absolute. It was no use for Napoleon to promise France and Europe that he would govern with parliamentary institutions; in seizing France by means of a fantastic military coup, he had re-established the revolutionary dictatorship of force, which the Congress of Vienna wanted to eliminate from Europe entirely. What authority would Parliament be likely to have over the army which had mastered the country and the government by a surprise attack? Napoleon might swear a thousand times to respect the treaties; where would the wave of public discontent over the loss of the Rhine, which had swept him to the gates of Paris, ultimately leave him? If Napoleon should gain control of France, all that would be left for the Congress to do would be to close its doors and disperse. The war of 1792 would begin again, and into what new chaos would Europe fall? Napoleon might win further victories and conquer more territory, but would a revolutionary dictatorship be any more capable the second time of establishing an order and balance acceptable to all in Europe, than the first time?

The Congress showed itself to be, not a *thé dansant* as scandalmongers claimed, but a powerful instrument of the constructive mind, by not letting itself be overcome by the spectacular coup, but by accepting the challenge. It met again in a dual role: a Committee of War as well as a Peace Congress. It did not hesitate to answer Napoleon's peaceful overtures with cannon balls; but, while it prepared Europe for the new war, it put forth a tremendous effort to hasten the solutions which up till then had been stagnating in the devious convolutions of the "confidential approach." These were the hundred days of Congress, which paralleled the Hundred Days of Napoleon, the hundred days during which Napoleon prepared for the new conflict with Europe, and the Congress came to a close.

Talleyrand, having hastily returned from Pressburg,

requested the Congress to allow no doubts to linger but that Napoleon, if he should regain power, would declare war on Europe. On March 13, the committee of the eight signatories to the Treaty of Paris made public a declaration which, in the name of Europe, including France, placed Napoleon "beyond the pale of civil and social relations" as the "enemy and disturber of world peace." The declaration refused to believe that France would have any part in Napoleon's scheme.

And, although firmly convinced that the French nation, rallying around her legitimate sovereign, will immediately destroy this new attempt on the part of a criminal and impotent frenzy, all the sovereigns of Europe, inspired by the same feelings and guided by the same principles, declare that if, against all reckoning, this event should result in some real danger, they would be prepared to give the French King and the French nation, or any other government attacked, as soon as the demand should be made, the assistance required to restore the public peace, and to make common cause against those who undertake to compromise it.

That is an example on which European statesmen of today might well reflect, for it might be of use to them in the more or less distant future. The Allies might also have incriminated France for her share of the responsibility, which was evident. But what would they have gained besides aggravating her discontent and hate? And, since France, too, was to be included in the new European order, why antagonize her? At the same time, the Congress awoke from its lethargy, determined this time to finish its work.

Switzerland was the first to benefit by this new energy. On March 20, the delegates of the signatories to the Treaty of Paris, adopted, in a common declaration, the resolutions reached by the committee on Swiss affairs. The twenty-two cantons were acknowledged and the adherence of all the cantons to the federal pact was warmly recommended. Bienne and the bishopric of Bâle became an integral part of Berne, except for what had been ceded to Bâle in order to disenclose it. The boundary of the principality of Neuchâtel was rectified. Communications between Geneva and Switzerland were assured by way of Versoix. Compromises were suggested to determine the disposition of territory in litigation between cantons. Lastly, all these decisions were not arbitrarily forced on the Diet but suggested to it. The day before the committee meeting, it had been decided, at Talleyrand's suggestion, that the decisions would be "confidentially" and officially communicated to the Diet after it had accepted them. The declaration added that

...as soon as the Helvetic Diet will have given its formal acquiescence to the stipulations included in the present agreement, it will become an act bearing the recognition and guarantee, on the part of all the powers, of the permanent neutrality of Switzerland within her new boundaries, which act shall be a part of that which, in execution of Article XXXII of the aforesaid Treaty of Paris of May 30, must fulfill the dispositions of that Treaty.

The neutrality of Switzerland had ceased to be one of the variables in the policy of the Confederation; it had become an established principle of international law, a cornerstone of the new European order.[1] The affairs of Switzerland had been put in shape. The Congress, after the long makeshift protectorate of the mediation, restored to Switzerland the independence she had possessed in the eighteenth century, enriched with the liberty and equality of the nineteenth, which began to penetrate Switzerland with the 1815 regime. The Declaration of March 20, 1815, was the door through which Switzerland entered on the greatest period of her history—a century in which she was to establish the most human system of government that the world has ever seen.

But the thunderbolt which had just shaken Europe had

[1] D'Angeberg, *op. cit.*, pp. 932-939.

also brought to life in Vienna the question of Germany, dormant for three months. The committee on German affairs had not met since November 16. On March 22, the plenipotentiaries of the sovereign princes and free cities of Germany delivered a note to the chief plenipotentiaries of Austria and Prussia:

The undersigned, assembled plenipotentiaries of the princes and free cities of Germany, find in the events now taking place a powerful motive to declare unanimously that their constituents are prepared to co-operate with every effort and with levies that are proportionate to the populations of their dominions and to their forces, in the re-establishment of peace and order in Europe and in support of an independent Germany.

At the same time, because of the influence which it might have on the success of the common enterprise, they cannot neglect to reiterate their desire that Germany's future finally be made secure through a firm and lasting union. In this respect, they call attention to the contents of their notes of November 16, 1814, and February 2, 1815; and they suggest that immediate and general discussions be initiated, based on the fundamental principle of a federal pact guaranteeing rights to all members; that such a pact be signed in Vienna; and that in this pact, not only the relations between members of the union be determined and their independence and integrity guaranteed, but also that the citizens of Germany be assured a liberal constitution and accorded political rights.[2]

That was straight from the shoulder. "If you want us to help you conquer Napoleon, give Germany a liberal constitution." That was the literal meaning of the note. The next day, March 23, at the fifteenth meeting of the five-power committee, Wellington revealed that on March 14, the day after the manifesto drawn up by the eight powers against Napoleon, His Royal Highness, the Prince of Orange, sovereign prince of the United Provinces, had taken the title of King of the Netherlands. Wellington

[2] *Ibid.*, p. 951.

suggested that he be recognized as such. This, however, would be to anticipate the conclusion of the Vienna treaty; as long as this had not been signed, the Prince of Orange did not have the right to proclaim himself sovereign in Belgium. But the news had rapidly become worse; France was opening her doors wide to Napoleon; the Restoration was collapsing everywhere at the mere appearance of the former Emperor; by March 13, he had already reached Lyon without having struck a blow. The movement spread to Italy. On March 5, Murat had written the Vienna and London governments that he would remain faithful to the alliance, whatever Napoleon did.[3] But on March 15, he launched an invasion of the papal states, with 35,000 men, 5,000 cavalry troops, and 60 guns.

Under the circumstances, therefore, if a general war were to break out, it would be dangerous for the Allies to hold Belgium by nothing more than a military occupation. It was better to inform the Congress who Belgium's new sovereign would be. Wellington's suggestion was approved. But Napoleon was advancing rapidly. By March 17, he had reached Auxerre. On the nineteenth, Louis and his court fled Paris, and Napoleon entered the capital on the following day. On March 25, the four Allies concluded an alliance which renewed the Treaty of Chaumont, and invited France to join it. Two days later, Talleyrand accepted.

The new danger had brought Alexander to his senses. He had made up his quarrel with Metternich, turned his back on the Bonapartes, abandoned his revolutionary ideas, and quenched his mania for contradiction. For the first time since the Congress had opened, he was in agreement with everyone else. It was obvious that he had been mistaken when in April and May he had appointed himself guarantor of France's behavior and her reconciliation with the rest of Europe. Yet he was by no means an intractable egotist who became obstinate and annoyed

3 *Ibid.*, p. 1049.

when proved wrong; he had moods in which he was humble and almost happy to admit his mistakes and do everything possible to rectify them. Prussia, on the twenty-ninth, and Austria, on the thirty-first, both sent identical notes in reply to the one sent on the twenty-second by the sovereign princes and free cities of Germany. This time Hannibal was knocking at the gates; there could be no more delay, no more evasions. The Prussian note read as follows:

The undersigned, plenipotentiaries of His Majesty, the King of Prussia, to the Congress, did not delay in calling the attention of the King, their master, to the note of LL. EE. MM., the assembled plenipotentiaries of the sovereign princes and free cities, dated the twenty-second of this month.

His Majesty finds the declaration by the princes embodied in this note, stating that they are prepared to co-operate with every effort and with levies proportionate to the population of their dominions and to their forces, in the re-establishment of peace and order in Europe, and in the support of an independent Germany, as much in keeping with the patriotic feelings and thoughts of these rulers as with the significance of present circumstances. His Majesty has requested the undersigned to make known to the plenipotentiaries who delivered to them the said note, that he accepts their offer with pleasure, and that, together with the Imperial Court of Vienna, he invites the assembled princes and free cities of Germany to accede to the obligations contracted by Prussia and Austria in accordance with the enclosed copy of the Treaty of Alliance with Russia and Austria, for the re-establishment of peace and legitimacy in Europe, obligations in which the other governments will share. The powers believe that the most prompt method of attaining this end will be to use as a foundation, with regard to war, the covenants agreed upon at Frankfurt in 1813, with the modifications required by circumstances.

The royal Court of Prussia shares in the desire expressed in the declaration of the princes, namely: that Germany now receive the surety of its future peace by a firmly established constitution. Ever since the initiation of the Congress, the efforts of this Court have been turned toward the formation of a union which would guarantee both independence and legitimacy of government; and nothing proves better that its efforts have been fruitful than the declaration in the note of the princes, according to which they wish to combine their efforts for the re-establishment of peace with the setting up of the Confederation, making their efforts in accordance with this Confederation, and giving them, by means of the Confederation itself, a greater importance in the eyes of the German people.

Consequently, the undersigned take pleasure in declaring to the plenipotentiaries that, feeling the strong necessity of subscribing to the Germanic Confederation at once, and, in the case of its development being put off until quieter times, of at least determining its essential foundations, they are ready to enter into conference on the subject immediately.

As to the manner and form of settling, without delay, the two matters in question in the plenipotentiaries' note and in the present reply, the undersigned wish to confer beforehand with the plenipotentiaries; consequently they suggest that certain of the plenipotentiaries be chosen for the purpose of conferring with the courts concerned.[4]

The response was enthusiastic and binding, even if not specific. During the month of April, the princes and free cities of Germany held numerous meetings to determine whether they should accede to the treaty of alliance of March 25 against Napoleon. Negotiations toward the same end were actively carried on by Austria and Prussia with Bavaria, Württemberg, Baden, and all the other German states. Since the Confederation did not yet exist, the alliance had to be negotiated with each individual state. The urgent need for the Confederation was only felt the more strongly; indeed, Prussia and Austria made up their minds to prepare an extremely liberal plan for a federal pact. This recognized the equality of all members of the Confederation, great and small; it instituted an assembly to administer the affairs of the Confederation; it retained the existing constitutions; and decreed that constitutions

4 *Ibid.*, pp. 986-987.

would be introduced where there were none, "in such a way that the assemblies might possess the right to consent to taxes, deliberate on the laws of the land relative to freedom or property, complain of abuses in the administration, and defend the constitution and the rights deriving therefrom." Active negotiations were also begun between the German states, in order to come to an agreement on the exchanges of territory which were to establish the new balance within Germany, although the new war with Napoleon made definitive decisions on a number of questions difficult.

At the same time, matters in Italy were coming to a head. Murat had continued to advance peacefully toward the Po, without having met any resistance until March 30. On that day, he had reached the Legations, which were occupied by the Austrian army.... The Austrian outposts had put up a resistance before they retreated; on April 2, the Neapolitan army entered Bologna, which had been abandoned by the Austrian general. War between the Kingdom of Naples and Austria had begun without a declaration; the Pope and the Grand Duke of Tuscany had fled; uneasiness was spreading among the populations, who were beginning to wonder whether Italy was about to become once more a part of the French Empire. Murat did not wish an open break, in order to leave himself an out if Napoleon should fail. On April 8, his plenipotentiaries presented a note to Vienna, which, after complaining of the unfriendly attitude of the Court of Vienna, declared that the King remained faithful to the alliance, and that he intended, merely as a precautionary measure, to occupy the bank of the Po so as to guarantee order in central and southern Italy! [5] But the die of war had already been cast in Vienna. The day before the presentation of the note, Francis I had issued an imperial manifesto stating that "as a result of treaties concluded with the allied powers and also of our agreements with them

5 *Ibid.*, pp. 1047 *et seq.*

... he was annexing the Lombard and Venetian provinces in their full extent as far as Lake Maggiore, or Ticino, and the Po, with that part of Mantuan territory situated on the right bank of these rivers, as well as the province of Valtelline and the counties of Cleve and Bormio." To give the Lombards and Venetians "an unequivocal proof of the imperial good will," the manifesto offered a royal title to the annexed provinces—the Lombardo-Venetian Kingdom—and armorial bearings to the new Kingdom, which would be added to the Empire's coat of arms. The Emperor of Austria, like the Prince of Orange, was anticipating the end of the Congress, and for the same reason. Having decided to eliminate Murat, the Court of Vienna began by publicly notifying Italy of Austria's status as dominating power. Until then, Italy had only been able to guess, through a few vague proclamations by the Austrian generals, what Austria's intentions were—there had been nothing official and irrevocable. After the manifesto of April 7, Italy realized that Murat could no longer do anything except by agreement with Vienna and with her consent, at least as long as Napoleon did not re-enter Italy at the head of an army; and it did not take her long to become aware that Vienna had no more use for Murat. On April 10, Metternich replied to the plenipotentiaries of King Joachim with a declaration of war; [6] the Austrian army went into action by taking the offensive; on April 28, the Court of Vienna signed a treaty of alliance with Ferdinand IV, King of the Two Sicilies. Abandoned by Italy, vanquished at Tolentino and Mignano, Murat signed the Treaty of Casalanza on May 20, and relinquished the crown. Three days later, Austrian troops entered Naples.

Talleyrand and Louis XVIII had won out in Naples; the Kingdom of the Two Sicilies was reconstituted under the former dynasty. The solution was none too good for the unfortunate populations, but it precluded an even

6 *Ibid.*, p. 1061,

worse solution—a revolutionary dictatorship of force. Thanks to the return of Napoleon, it was Austria who imposed her solutions on the rest of Italy. France now had too much need of Austria to be able to make an effective resistance in Vienna on matters of relatively little importance. Happy at having had his way in Naples, Talleyrand yielded on the rest. Marie Louise obtained the duchies of Parma, Piacenza, and Guastalla for life, with the reservation that the five great courts of Europe would decree on the reversion of the duchies at her death. Archduke Ferdinand of Austria was re-established in Tuscany with his former title of Grand Duke and with a slightly increased territory. The Queen of Etruria received for herself and her descendants the principality of Lucca, erected into a duchy, and revertible to the Grand Duke of Tuscany. Archduke Francesco d'Este was acknowledged Duke of Modena, Reggio, and Mirandola.

The affairs of the Pope were the hardest to settle. On March 19, 1815, the Congress, in the "Ruling on the ranking of diplomatic envoys," had granted precedence to the papal nuncios, decreeing in Article IV: "The present regulation will not make any innovation relative to the representatives of the Pope." [7] Cardinal Consalvi might rejoice. But he had never ceased to clamor, not only for the Legations, but also for Avignon, maintaining that no cession on the part of the Pope had any validity, since the Pope was merely the administrator and not the proprietor of the patrimony of St. Peter; he threatened the Congress with a sort of papal appeal to the world if the rights of the Holy See were not respected; and he hinted at the use of spiritual thunderbolts—excommunication—against recalcitrant sovereigns. All of which had made even the Emperor of Austria frown. As they wished to satisfy him as far as possible, they had finally agreed to grant him the Legations, except for a small loss in Ferrara, which would be Austria's gain. In April, the Cardinal was reassured on

[7] *Ibid.*, p. 940.

that point at least: the Pope would have the Legations. But he was not content: he wanted to have it specified in the treaty that the Legations were not *given* but *restored*. This meant that the Congress would have to declare the Treaty of Tolentino worthless. The claim met with strong opposition, as much for principle, as for possible consequences. If the Legations had never ceased to belong to the Pope, it was impossible to negotiate their restitution. Now Austria and France wanted the Pope to give up Pontecorvo and Benevento, which formed two islands in the Kingdom of Naples, and not to object too violently about Avignon and Ferrara, since they had no desire to be denounced by Rome to the Catholics of Europe as the swindlers of Jesus Christ. They wished to obtain a promise from the legate that the Holy See would not make too much of a fuss in exchange for the Legations; in other words, strike a bargain on the vehemence of the pontifical rage.

Cardinal Consalvi was an intelligent man, but he was also violent, outspoken, obstinate, and sometimes irascible. He stuck to his guns with such a stubborn persistence and a passionate zeal that the Congress became thoroughly annoyed. He himself admitted in one of his letters that by May he had become the object of general hostility. Every day he was subjected to having his ideas on papal rights refuted by persons of the highest rank. His critics were saying that it was incorrect to believe that an administrator could not transfer property; indeed, under certain circumstances, he was obliged to do so. His duty was not to return the property exactly as he had received it, but to watch over it carefully, disposing of part, if necessary, in order to save or ameliorate the rest. Pius VII had only to follow the example set by Pius VI, who had ceded part of his states by formal treaty in order to save the rest.[8] While the Cardinal was being lectured, the Congress delegates were trying to isolate him and

[8] Rinieri, *op. cit.*, pp. 571-572.

frighten him. During the spring of 1815, he kept writing Cardinal Pacca that it was becoming more and more difficult for him to see the Congress leaders, especially *"il signor principe"* Metternich, who was deaf to all his pleas.[9] And from time to time, the Cardinal was told that the Congress would finish its work and ratify the treaties without resolving the problems dealing with the Church states, which would be postponed indefinitely—a prospect which made him boil over with rage.[10] In the end, however, an agreement was reached. The peace treaty would not "give" but would "restore" to the Pope, the Legations, Pontecorvo, and Benevento. The Holy See was to hold out for Avignon, for the dismembered particle of Ferrara, and for the right to garrison Ferrara and Comacchio, but with moderation and without setting a torch to Christianity.

Poor Italy! She came out of the Congress stripped of almost everything, including her very soul. The Old Regime had apparently returned in force. Rome was restored to the Pope, Turin and Naples to their kings, Modena to its duke, and Florence to its grand duke. But Venice, shining light of all that was best in the Old Regime, had disappeared, together with Genoa, its ancient rival. Of the satins, taffeta, damask, brocade, velvet, tapestries, sculpture, paintings, ivory, diamonds, pearls, rubies, gold, silver—of all the splendid regalia of the Old Regime, there were left only the fragments in Italy— monuments and buildings too heavy to be carried away. Monasteries, churches, palaces had all been stripped. The gold and silver which had still covered the magnificent monuments to a medieval theocracy, had been melted into money and scattered throughout Europe. The wealthiest industries, having lost their private clientele—church, aristocracy, and courts—as well as their general customers, had been ruined. Italy had reverted to a country pro-

9 *Ibid.*, pp. 562, 631.
10 *Ibid.*, pp. 529, 530-531.

ducing raw materials: silk, hemp, skins, metals. With the splendors of the eighteenth century had flown its soul. In general, Italy was still a believing Catholic nation in 1815, but no longer in the same sense as in the Old Regime. During the quarter of a century between 1789 and 1815, the papacy had ceased to be what it had been, although even then weakening, during the eighteenth century—an impressive and inseparable union of spiritual and temporal power. The Revolution had permanently weakened both powers by separating them. In the temporal field, the Pope in 1815 was no more than a very poor sovereign of a small and tattered state; in the spiritual field, a great theological leader, but one who was criticized and open to criticism by skeptics even in Italy, formerly his most submissive fief. The Revolution, although it had not given Italy her freedom, had secularized her culture, her social life, her laws, her economy, her education, and her political institutions. If on the one hand the Church, stripped and mutilated though it was, hoped with the Restoration to recover a privileged position in Italian society, on the other hand a section of the upper classes had already conceived the notion of and desire for a completely secularized state and society, in which the influence of the Church would be confined to theology and morality.

In 1815, Italy came out of the Revolution terrified by the new ideas—liberty, equality, unity—which the Revolution had tried to give her. Since 1796 these new ideas had only served to justify the abuses of force which had victimized her, beginning with the distorted democracy. Italy had been the testing ground for the latter. The Congress of Vienna, which wanted to purge Europe of revolutionary dictatorships, had been right to restore the former dynasties in Italy. They were the only powers who still retained a certain amount of prestige and whose sovereign rights were still acknowledged by a considerable portion of the people. Could this Italian, product of the Counter Reformation, who concealed from no one his intention of reconstructing in Italy the paradise in which he had been born and had grown up—Francis I—be the liberator who would break the chains with which the revolutionary dictatorship had bound Italy? In 1815 there were a great many Italians and foreigners who hoped so, Castlereagh among them. In a conversation which took place in Paris in May, 1814, between Castlereagh and a delegation from Lombardy which had come to request that an independent state with a constitution be created in northern Italy, Castlereagh had stated that Europe had gone to war in order to free Italy from the yoke of revolutionary tyranny. But, he said, Austria had a steady government which was paternal, respectful of laws, and did not abuse its force; there was nothing to fear from it; the Lombards would be happy under its rule.[11]

But this was to prove a false hope. After 1815, Italy was to fester more and more from the humiliation and devastation which she had suffered during the Revolution, become more and more desperate over her poverty, her weakness, and the insignificant status to which she was reduced, left with nothing but memories of the time when she had been the center of the Holy Roman Empire and of the Christian world. In 1815, Italy, although she still respected the governments of the Old Regime, no longer believed in them as she had before the Revolution. She had seen them flee, these governments once venerated as perfect, before the little armies of France, abandoning their faithful subjects to the horrors of invasion, humbling themselves before the Revolution. They had come back, it was true, but at the cost of what struggles on the part of others, what bargaining, what compromise! And besides, people were beginning to look upon them as petty, weak, worthless! Parma, Modena, Florence! Trampled upon, outraged, dismembered and put together again at the whim of the revolutionary powers which had invaded her in 1796, Italy had also begun to feel capable of found-

[11] Bianchi, *op. cit.*, I, 341.

ing a powerful state modeled after the other great states of Europe. A spirit of nationalism had been born. It was to develop; and it was finally to convince part of Italy—but only a part—that the little states of the Old Regime and the ornate paradise created by the Austrian Emperor were at the root of all Italy's misfortunes, her poverty, her weakness, her obscurity. An irreconcilable dualism was to rend Italy more and more: which was the enemy, the danger, the source of the evil? The Old Regime or the Revolution?

The surviving dynasties of the Old Regime in Italy were legitimacies, but they were dying legitimacies. For that reason, the solution of the Italian problem by the Congress of Vienna must be considered ineffective and uncertain, although the Congress cannot be blamed. It was the only possible solution, and can only be judged in the light of what the Congress had to and could do. Nineteenth century historians have seen fit to blame the Congress for not having created a strong state in the north of Italy, either by enlarging the dominions ruled by the House of Savoy or by establishing a new dynasty. But such a plan was impossible. Austria had already made sure of obtaining Lombardy and Venetia at the Treaty of Paris; the fate of northern Italy had already been sealed when the Congress assembled. Austria's seizure of Lombardy and Venetia was the result of Campo Formio, Italy's penance for not having resisted the French invasion of 1796; the Congress had nothing to do with it. Moreover, if northern Italy had been given to the House of Savoy, the new sovereign would have found himself in the same position in Milan and Venice as Murat had been in Naples: a government imposed from outside, its authority, like that of a revolutionary dictatorship, supported by force. Sooner or later this government would have been dragged into adventures that were incompatible with the "tranquillity of Europe," as the European order to be constructed was called in Vienna. For a century, Italian historians have been too much given to thinking in terms of Italy alone; they have forgotten that in Vienna the Italian problem, like all the others, was solved in relation to the general European order which had to be created. Therein lay the unappreciated greatness of the Congress.

Once again, poor Italy! She was entering upon the new century humiliated, bruised, impoverished, and torn apart by the dualism between the Old Regime and the Revolution! Even more unfortunate, because she would seek to escape from being torn apart by rejecting both the Old Regime and the Revolution! Italy had acquired a horror of both aspects of the Revolution, the new orientation and the subversion of laws. By rights, she should have become the champion of the Old Regime in Europe. But she no longer had the strength to resist the encroachments of nineteenth-century ideas, as became the oldest representative of the qualitative societies in bygone times. What changes were to take place in her soul? The hatred for the new orientation was rapidly to pass into indifference. After 1815, Italy became the country least receptive to the great ideas of the Revolution. The right of opposition was never sincerely accepted by any school, party, or institution, particularly by those who should have been the instruments of the new right—the press and parliament, for instance. Liberty was only a weapon used insincerely by various parties and groups in their struggle for power. But, though the great ideas of the Revolution met with indifference, the spirit of adventure, that gigantic subversion of laws which the Revolution had accomplished, began more and more to fascinate Italy. What if the real Revolution were not the Declaration of the Rights of Man, but instead an attack on the law and its fabrications, a conquest and amplification of power by unrestrained, unscrupulous, and self-assured force? True, Napoleon had failed in the end, but he had succeeded for a while; another might succeed for a longer time, perhaps permanently. These were subversive thoughts, the negation of everything great and fundamental in the Old Regime. But Italy will never succeed in ridding herself of them, in spite of the efforts she has made since 1815. On the contrary, from generation to generation they will grow stronger without ever coming into the open. They will exert a secret influence on philosophy, on art, on literature, on politics; they will combine with souvenirs of ancient grandeur, and finally they will explode. One man, a great man; one war, a great war; one conquest, a great conquest —and Italy will be able in a few years to reconquer and magnify her former grandeur by the subversion of all rules and laws invented by mediocrity, by throwing herself, like Napoleon, into a great adventure.

We have seen how Italy in the eighteenth century was an "ornate paradise" which "concealed in its heart an inferno." [12] The Revolution shattered that paradise and sent flames leaping through the cracks. Little by little they spread over all Europe. How can it be doubted that the order of the eighteenth century was nothing but a great disorder which was inverted?

[12] See the chapter on Italy in *The Gamble*.

XVII

THE HUNDRED DAYS OF THE CONGRESS: GERMANY

<hr>

Only Germany remained, the most difficult problem before the Congress. Already, in April, Prussia and Austria had drawn up a draft of the federal constitution. A committee had been formed to examine it. This committee was much more inclusive than the one before. Besides the five plenipotentiaries of the larger states, it was composed of representatives from Saxony, Baden, and Hesse-Darmstadt; five deputies chosen by the sovereign princes and free cities; the plenipotentiaries of the King of Denmark as Duke of Holstein; and the plenipotentiary of the King of the Netherlands as Grand Duke of Luxembourg. The times were grave; it was impossible to deny Germany, whose help was needed for the new war against Napoleon, the right to be consulted about her future. But during April and the first half of May the federal Constitution was laid aside, in spite of the earnest entreaties of the smaller states. Before taking up the all-important matter of the Constitution, Vienna and Berlin wanted all the German states to come to an accord on the territorial questions which divided them, so that each state might enter the Confederation with its boundaries firmly established, being sound in limb as well as mind. There had been much negotiating in April on these matters, and it was continued into May; but the negotiations were tedious, as each state sought to get as much as possible out of all the exchanges taking place. The differences between Bavaria and Austria were particularly knotty. Bavaria, at the time of her alliance with Napoleon, had taken important territories, like the Tyrol and Salzbourg, from Austria; she was disposed to return them, but wanted equal indemnities. It was on account of this that the committee to examine the Austro-Prussian Constitution did not meet for the first time until May 23. All the territorial questions between the German states were far from being settled; but time was short. On the twenty-third, Metternich presented the plan to the committee and set the opening of the discussion for the twenty-sixth. But on the twenty-fifth the sovereign princes and free cities of Germany met and declared that five representatives were no longer sufficient; each one wanted to be personally represented on the committee. The whole of Germany was putting the committee in an uproar. The same day, Alexander proclaimed the creation of the Kingdom of Poland in a long proclamation.

The war, carried into our country for the purpose of subjugating the world, reunited Russia to the whole of Europe, who together repulsed that war to the very walls of Paris. Ever since that day we have had the hope of restoring the independence of nations, and of giving as foundation for this, justice, moderation, and liberal ideas, which have too long been subjugated to the military despotism of the code of civil and political rights of the people.

The Congress of Vienna has been formed to gain the benefits of a lasting peace for Europe, crushed by the misfortunes of war; but in order to attain this much desired goal, it was indispensable for everyone, putting aside personal advantage for the general interest, to make concessions and

sacrifices demanded by the circumstances. It is on this principle that the fate of Poland was decided. It was essential to
include her among those nations who, by mutual sharing of
their well-being and the advantages of civilization, ameliorate
each other's condition.

However, while striving to re-establish this new link in the
chain of European interests, one could not only consider the
interests of Poland. The well-being of each individual state
and the necessity for guaranteeing the security of all, did not
permit of detailed arrangements especially appropriate to the
local interests of Poland, but which might not have been in
harmony with the common interests which assure the general
balance of Europe.

A healthy policy, past experience, and that same religion
which commands us to consider the long suffering of this
estimable nation, have imposed on us the duty to spare no
sacrifice in order to preserve Europe from new misfortunes,
and to assure the peace of the world.

People of Poland, new ties are going to unite you to a
generous people, who, because of former connections, courage
worthy of your own, and the common title of Slav nationality,
is disposed to receive you in a brotherhood, which will be dear
and useful to both peoples. A wise constitution and an un-
changeable union will bind you to the destiny of a great
monarchy, too widespread to have need of expansion, and
whose government will never have any other rules of policy
than an impartial justice and generous ideas. Henceforward
your patriotism, lighted by experience and moved by gratitude,
will find in national institutions a motive power and a goal
capable of occupying all its faculties.

A constitution suitable to the needs of the locality and to
your character, the use of your language preserved in the
public acts, offices and employments available only to Poles,
freedom of commerce and of the seas, the facility of com-
munication with those parts of former Poland which remain
subject to another power, your national army, every means
guaranteed for the perfecting of your laws, the free circula-
tion of knowledge in your country—these are the advantages
you will enjoy under our domination and that of our suc-

vague definition which the Austrian government was later to feel the need of defining more clearly. On April 6, 1818, it was officially to declare that the territories of the Empire participating in the Confederation would be: the Archduchy of Austria, the duchies of Styria, Carinthia, Carniola, Austrian Friuli, that is the district of Gorizia, the city of Trieste and its territory, the county of Tyrol with Trent and Brixen, the Duchy of Salzburg, the Kingdom of Bohemia, the margraviate of Moravia, and Austrian Silesia. In other words the greater majority of the German population of Europe, with some Slav and Italian minorities, while remaining subject to different states, was united in a Confederation, which became one of the great powers of Europe. But under what conditions? How was it organized?

The Germanic Confederation of 1815 was not a complete and total confederation like Switzerland and the United States today. It had not absorbed the armies of the individual states into one confederate army. The Confederation did not possess any army proper; its military force consisted in the aggregate of the individual armies, each of which depended upon its own government, and which under certain circumstances could have acted in combination with the others; the Austrian, Prussian, Bavarian, and Saxon armies carried on as before. Unarmed, the Germanic Confederation of 1815 did not have the powerful and absorbing sovereign character of the Swiss or American confederations. Its affairs were in the hands of a Federal Diet, situated at Frankfurt, in which seventeen votes formed a decisive majority; eleven belonging to the more important states, each of which was represented by a permanent plenipotentiary; six to the myriad small states—principalities and free cities—divided into six groups. Austria had the presidency of the Diet. When it was necessary to vote, or to modify the fundamental laws of the Constitution, or to create organic institutions, or to take measures which concerned the whole Confederation, the

Diet would meet in General Assembly. All the states which formed the Confederation—there were thirty-eight—had to be represented at the Assembly by a plenipotentiary; but with a different number of votes depending on the importance of the state. Austria, Prussia, Saxony, Bavaria, Württemberg, Hanover each had four votes; Baden, electoral Hesse, the Grand Duchy of Hesse, Holstein, Luxembourg, three votes; Brunswick, Mecklenburg-Schwerin, Nassau, two votes; the others, one vote—in all, sixty-nine votes.

An impersonal Constitution and a headless Confederation! The Emperor, the former head of the Holy Roman Empire, had been replaced by a small assembly of seventeen plenipotentiaries, led by Austria, and in which Austria and Prussia shared the predominating authority; a diarchy, which depended on the collective and mobile authority of the Diet. The party which had wanted to give the Confederation only one head, the Emperor of Austria, and to make him a real power, not Austrian but German, as the symbol and instrument of United Germany, had met with failure. Francis I had been stronger than the party, which had many followers in all of Germany, and particularly in Prussia; he had refused to become the first Emperor of Germany in accordance with the idea of this party, which seemed to him too revolutionary; he had managed to remain in the intermediary position of Emperor of Austria, as he conceived it, better adapted to the preservative role he expected to play. The relations between the states, their respective duties and rights, were defined by a considerable number of articles. The most important were those which determined reciprocal duties and rights in case of aggression. Any state of the Confederation, threatened or attacked on its territory, or in that part of its territory forming a part of the Confederation, had the right to invoke the *casus foederis*.

But the main article, the keystone of the Confederation, was the thirteenth, which concerned the political institu-

half a century. Germany was transformed from a haphazard conglomeration of mutually distrustful states into a constitutionally organized federation capable of placing a restraint on the spirit of adventure and all revolutionary forces, a federation which, as Metternich had said, became an important force in the peace and stability of Europe. The Congress of Vienna had forged the chain of liberty that Germany and Europe needed; it had resolved for the next half century the great contradiction created by the Revolution; it had shattered the heavy shackles with which force had enslaved Europe after 1805, by making force a prisoner in a new and more peaceful order which would restrain it from warlike adventures until 1863.

Was this a triumph of the constructive mind? Only in part. Partly through certain structural faults, but more especially because of the spirit in which it was applied, the federal Constitution of 1815 ended up by becoming more the achievement and the instrument of the conservative mind than of the constructive mind, of which the former is a distortion.

Nevertheless, Germany got more out of the Congress than Italy. She was completely secularized, and she was unified. In Germany, all the ecclesiastical principalities had disappeared, while in Italy there still remained the most important and the most difficult either to overthrow or to reform—the Church states. The Confederation was already a kind of unification which made Germany a political entity, whereas Italy was still only a geographical expression. Germany had at least acquired the semblance of a liberal Constitution, in which the promise of a more definite one was incorporated, although in rather sibylline terms; Italy had merely received the gracious concession to include her armorial bearings on the Hapsburg coat of arms. But destiny was taking its course. The good and the evil which the Revolution—including the Congress of Vienna—accomplished in each country were proportional to the resistance offered to the violence of the Revolution and to the intelligence and courage with which its great ideas—liberty, equality, fraternity—were accepted and put into practice. Switzerland had taken to arms when the Revolution had tried to impose its decrees by force; but she had accepted and put into practice its ideas, and during the nineteenth century she followed them to a greater extent and more successfully than any other country in Europe. Switzerland became the country which gained the most and lost the least from the Revolution, the country which most benefited from the European order established at Vienna. Germany had resisted the revolutionary invasions and accepted the doctrines of the Revolution to a far less extent that Switzerland, but at least she had offered some resistance and assimilated some of the doctrines. The Revolution accomplished less good and more evil there than in Switzerland, but at any rate it did accomplish some good. And Germany did obtain important concessions from the Congress. Italy had offered no resistance whatsoever to the armies of the Revolution, while she had shut her heart and her mind to the great doctrines, and kept them shut until 1922; she became the country in which the Revolution accomplished the greatest evil and the least good, the Cinderella of the Vienna Congress.

Finally, it must not be forgotten that, thanks to the Congress of Vienna, Italy and Germany lived until 1848 under peaceful, economical, and conservative governments which did not burden them with the costs of a cumbersome administration or a too adventurous policy. Ruled by governments which recognized their duty to help their peoples work and increase their wealth, Italy and Germany, between 1815 and 1848, were able to build up their wealth, sadly depreciated by the devastations of the revolutionary adventure. And that in itself is important; in order to become a great power, a people must first be assured of their daily bread.

XVIII

ASSETS AND LIABILITIES OF
THE REVOLUTION

───────────────── ▰▸▸▸◂◂◂▰ ─────────────────

The work of the Congress was ended. On June 8, the sovereign princes and free cities of Germany, the Emperor of Austria, the Kings of Prussia, Denmark, the Netherlands, Bavaria, Württemberg, and Saxony affixed their signatures to the federal Constitution of Germany. The next day, at 10 P.M. after the great court gala, seven of the eight powers who had ratified the Treaty of Paris signed, "in the name of the very holy and indivisible Trinity," the great treaty which became the cornerstone of the nineteenth century. The Spanish plenipotentiary refused to sign as a protest against the attribution of Parma, Piacenza, and Guastalla to Marie Louise. The King of Spain was not to ratify it until May 7, 1817.

Nine days later, on June 18, the Revolution's last adventure came to grief at Waterloo. The great panic was over. Its causes had been extremely simple, but its results had been enormously complex. In 1789, the French monarchy had been tottering. Louis XVI had remained on the throne until August 10, 1792; but his reign had really ended with the capture of the Bastille on July 14, 1789. From that day on, he had been a king who had neither an army, police force, judiciary, nor treasury. Endless dissertations have been made on the reasons for this sudden toppling of the monarchic legality. But the fundamental reason was the era, the decay of a secular legitimacy which failed to revivify itself in time and which abused its power at the beginning of the seventeenth century by compelling France to submit to absolutism. The fall of the French monarchy was like the fall of a very old tree which seems to be an immovable giant until the very end but which suddenly topples over, because it has lost its roots. Eaten through by insects and rotted by damp, it may topple to the ground at a gust of wind or the mere weight of its branches. That was how the French monarchy crashed, just as France was making a valiant attempt to give a new orientation to Western civilization, a broader, more liberal, more humane orientation. According to tradition, France would have had to overthrow her monarchy in order to have brought about the triumph of the new orientation, but quite the contrary occurred. The fall of the monarchy, by causing a wave of terror to sweep through all classes, prevented France from following out the new orientation which she had chosen. In order to set up a government which would have recognized the right of opposition and in order seriously to put into practice the Declaration of the Rights of Man, France would have needed a vigorous legitimacy, capable of guaranteeing liberty and equality. It was thus that the monarchy, by its fall in 1789, dragged down to ruin with it the Revolution as well as the new orientation of the human mind. France lost itself in the vicious circle of fear which provoked abuses of force and abuses of force which aggravated fear, leading to terrorism, *coups d'états*, revolutionary dictatorships inside France, and invasions, endless wars without rules, absurd and impossible peace treaties outside France. All Europe was dragged into the vicious circle, and the great panic began. At the heart of a Europe which had been a balanced arrangement of great and little states, an Empire rapidly grew to immense size, an Empire which was the first to become frightened by its own unsteady grandeur. The Empire and Europe were constantly at war because they mutually feared each other. The Empire was afraid that Europe would form a coalition to overthrow it; Europe feared that the Empire would reduce her to slavery. Each war increased the fear on both sides, peace became impossible, and the war seemed endless.

Once before, at the beginning of the third century of our era, the central pillar of law and order—the authority of the Roman Emperor and Senate—had crashed in ruins. An immense fear had taken hold of mankind, and this fear had unleashed force, which in turn aggravated the fear. The Roman world had not been able to break that circle; war had raged for centuries, and in the end all civilization had perished. Why was it, then, that in the nineteenth century, after a generation marked by panic and the abuse of force when mankind was beginning to despair of any end to war, during the brief space of three years Europe was able to break the same circle, set up a new and stable order, and take up the march toward progress with an enthusiasm that had never before been witnessed?

Three men accomplished that miracle, three extraordinary, enigmatic men, who seemed to have been placed by fate in widely varying positions, but who, at the critical moment, met on common ground, drawn by we know not what incomprehensible and metaphysical law of safety or by a no less inexplicable and almost transcendental accident of fate.

It was Alexander, the youngest, who in 1812 took the initiative. No sooner had Russian territory been freed of Napoleon's invading armies than the one thought of the nobility and the bureaucracy had been that the war was over for Russia; let Europe extricate herself as best she may. The generals had been of that opinion. The commander-in-chief, Koutouzoff, had begged the Czar to have pity on the army, which had been bled white by so many battles! What would have happened if Alexander had listened to his people? Germany was an ally of Napoleon, and England by herself was not strong enough to reconstruct the European order, no more so than Napoleon was to replace it. The latter's Empire was being maintained by such a ruthless pressure on so large a section of Europe that it was impossible to understand why it was accepted, even through resignation and despair, by so many varied peoples. Left to its own devices, it is difficult to see what other perspective would have confronted Europe than to have suffered the fate of the Roman Empire, with the same endless series of wars and fruitless revolutions. But, in that decisive hour, a youthful Emperor understood that his victory in Russia would be of no value, would only be the start of an interminable war leading eventually to universal chaos, if the reconstruction of Europe were not accomplished. It was with the intention of accomplishing that reconstruction with the help of Russia's might that he threw himself into a war whose objectives were tremendous and farsighted.

Never before had a sovereign taken a more absurdly grandiose decision. Alexander I, the leader of a crusade to re-establish the European order! But he was a revolutionary Czar, with a restless, inconsistent, rebellious nature, continually being forced by an unhealthy instinct to violate and overthrow the very laws which he should have respected and made others respect. Surely, never before had there been so astonishing a paradox! And yet the fact is that this crusade for the European order against the revolutionary spirit of adventure was in itself one of the most foolhardy adventures ever dreamed of by the ruler of an empire. By the end of 1812, Alexander stood alone in Russia, supported only by a few personal friends.

His own country was unwilling to continue the war; two thirds of Europe was under Napoleon's heel; and Germany, the ally of the French Empire, was about to make war on her future liberator. Alexander could only count on the meager support of an exhausted England and the impoverished Spaniards, who were still waging a desperate struggle with flintlocks against the artillery of the imperial armies. But Alexander is one of history's enigmas. The son of a lunatic, an eccentric himself, he was at times transformed, by some mysterious power, some secret illumination, into a genius and a champion of lost causes, who went beyond the bounds of rational state policy and challenged the future.

Thus, in 1812, Alexander had invaded Germany in order to carry out his plan to save Europe, dragging with him a Russia that was exhausted and hostile. He had succeeded in separating Austria and Prussia from their alliance with France, in driving Napoleon back across the Rhine and following him into France. But then the real tragedy began. The farther the Coalition advanced the more impossible it became to attain its objective. In order to re-establish the European order it was necessary for its negation, the Empire of Napoleon, to disappear. But would the Empire assent to its own destruction? And if peace could not be made with Napoleon, with whom should it be made? After twenty-five years of terror, the Revolution was heading toward the most unexpected and terrible catastrophe of all—a great war which everyone wanted to end but which no one knew how to end because there was no one with whom to make peace. In despair, so as not to neglect any chance and because it saw no other alternative, the Coalition had made treaties at Frankfurt and Châtillon. But there was no confidence in those treaties, and they met with no success; the Empire and a European order were an impossible contradiction. Since the Battle of Leipzig, Alexander had been desperately seeking the man, the government, the combination, with which he could make peace. He could find nothing and was becoming more and more frightened and thinking up more and more fantastic plans. By March, 1814, he was gradually losing himself in the immense void through which he was leading his army, not knowing where to find peace.

When, all of a sudden, a mysterious little sign—one man's hand—was raised in this immense void, pointing out to him the scarcely visible path which led to peace. The second of the three men destined to save the world had come into the picture. This was the degraded nobleman, the apostate and married bishop, the nonconformist who had always served the Revolution and the spirit of adventure. But he was also a great constructive genius who, in the midst of all his aberrations and in spite of serving the Revolution, had discovered, without leaving his house in the rue Saint-Florentin, what Alexander had been seeking everywhere. He had discovered the man who could make peace and why he alone had that power. This was Louis XVIII; and he was able to make peace because, if not the whole of France, at least the greater part still acknowledged his authority and power, even though he was in exile. The European order could be re-established on the day that Europe regained her respect for the most fundamental of all the laws pertaining to civilized society—that which recognized the principle of legitimate government. By communicating his discovery to Alexander on March 31, Talleyrand, in twenty-four hours, managed to put an end to a war which had lasted twenty-two years and which might have gone on intermittently for fifty or a hundred years, becoming ever more destructive, more senseless, and more difficult to end. It was in that conversation of March 31 that Alexander finally understood what he had been wanting to do since 1812, when he had hurled himself single-handed into the great adventure of reconstructing Europe; whence also the courage which led him to the proclamation of April 1. But, if Talleyrand had been able

to show him the path to safety because he was a constructive genius, a creator of laws, he had also been able to
meet Alexander in Paris because for forty years he had
been a nonconformist. If his life had been that of a nobleman of the eighteenth century, who knows where he would
have been on March 31, 1814?

But it was not alone sufficient to have found in Louis
XVIII the government which could lead France back into
the European order. Louis's personal qualities had to be
adequate for his position. Fortunately, he turned out to
be a capable ruler. Like the other two, he was a tragic
individual. A man of superior ability, he had been condemned to prove his superiority by remaining quiet and
doing nothing for a quarter of a century while suffering
the most most cruel blows. He had kept quiet, he had
done nothing, he had waited all that time, never giving
way to despair and secretly nursing a great idea: that he
should resolve, by means of his authority as legitimate
king, the problem which the Revolution had been unable
to resolve, by granting the right of opposition to France.
A noble idea, but one which alone was not sufficient; the
courage to put it into practice was needed. And Louis had
that courage; he had it because he was a king of the Old
Regime!

Quantae molis erat. In order to put an end to the wars
and revolutions loosed on Europe by the fall of the French
monarchy in 1789, it had taken a revolutionary Czar who
was a little crazy, brilliant, and courageous by turns, as
much in love with the theory of order as he was incapable
of making it or observing it. It had taken a great legislator
who had spent his life at variance with laws. And it had
taken a king of the Old Regime to dare and know how to
accomplish the task of the Revolution. Words fail us in
the face of so many contradictions. What riddles, then, are
order and chaos, between which a wretched mankind is
continually being torn! And not only had those three
men been forced to prepare themselves for their great

achievement by going through the most extraordinary, the most fantastic, the most repugnant, and the most inexplicably unhappy trials; at the crucial moment all three of them had had to risk their lives. But at least they managed to rescue nineteenth-century Europe from the fate of the Roman Empire in the third century; and to prevent the new orientation of the human mind—liberty, equality, fraternity—from being completely submerged by the frenzied subversion of laws, which had begun with the great panic of 1789. Alexander, Talleyrand, and Louis XVIII became the glorious conquerors of the great panic. But to what extent and with what results? In order to understand their work, and the whole history of the nineteenth century which resulted from it, this question must be answered. They thrust back and imprisoned the great panic, that is indisputable; but did they destroy it utterly and uproot it? No, they did not destroy it utterly and uproot it, because they were not able to suppress all the institutions, the ideas, the follies, the illusions which the great panic had created. The Revolution left both *assets* and *liabilities:* assets, which derived from the new orientation, and liabilities, which derived from the great panic. In order to arrive at a true estimate of the Congress of Vienna and to appreciate its ultimate achievement, we must ascertain both of these. The task is made possible because over a century and a half we have acquired a proper perspective.

Let us begin with the assets which were accomplished by the new orientation. The Revolution fundamentally secularized and simplified society and the state in the whole Western world. The Catholic Church had finally become an immense crystallization of secular-economic, political, spiritual, and social interests; the monarchic and aristocratic system which governed Europe had crumbled and crystallized into a great number of courts and tiny, little, medium, and great dynasties, which, mummified by an ancient ceremonial, had become centers of degeneracy and corruption. The Revolution made a thorough clean-up of these institutions, and the Congress of Vienna established the most important alterations in the new European system. The Catholic Church lost a great part of its wealth and political power; but it became a more serious and sincere religious force. Alongside of religious culture, a laic culture developed and flourished. Having shaken off the guardianship of the Church, the states became freer in their movements and more active. The monarchic system also became simpler, more serious, more effective, through the assimilation of a great many small dynasties by a smaller number of medium and large monarchies.

The Revolution spread the ideas of liberty and equality widely throughout Europe and America. This was the second phase of its assets. It spread the idea of liberty in two forms: intellectual liberty, as a result of the secularization of society; and political liberty, whose most important manifestation was the right of opposition. The Revolution also disseminated far and wide the idea of political and social equality, which had a greater significance for Europe than for America. In the eighteenth century, Europe had become an ultra-aristocratic organization, which was not only contrary to the principles of Christianity, but which had become an obstacle to the development of new creative forces.

In short, the Revolution accomplished a fundamental humanization of Western customs, government, and law, particularly the penal code. Although the eighteenth century had attained a high degree of refinement in many angles of social life, its penal code had remained positively barbaric. It was the Revolution which humanized the penal code everywhere. In this humanization of customs, government, and law, one must include freedom of worship, the emancipation of the Jews, the elimination of all the restraints surviving from the religious wars—the Inquisition, for instance.

By means of all these transformations, the French Revolution freed latent energies of thought and action, which had been accumulating in Western civilization since the Renaissance, and which were violently released during the century from 1814 to 1914—the real nineteenth century, rather than that of the calendar. No other century has displayed such inventive and active energy; and it was the Revolution which set it in motion.

And now for its liabilities, which resulted from the great panic.

Above all, the abolition of the law of nations, which had been the best and the greatest of eighteenth-century creations; the initiation of conscription and total war, as a result of which Europe is today threatened with destruction. The fifth of September, 1798, the day on which the Directory approved the law establishing conscription, is a decisive date in the history of the Revolution and of Europe.

The political confusion of a certain number of countries in Europe must also be laid to the door of the Revolution. The revolutionary invasions spread the great panic everywhere; the great panic weakened the Old Regime everywhere, at the same time that it instilled hatred for the principles of the Revolution. The result has been that, since 1814, certain countries of Europe have been unable to govern themselves either by the principles of the Old Regime or by those of the Revolution. For more than a century, they have sought everywhere for a political principle which is neither of the Old Regime nor of the Revolution; they cannot find it because it does not exist, and, frightened by their failure to resolve an impossible problem, they become in their turn a terror to other countries.

In short, it was the Revolution which created dictatorship as a stable form of government. Europe, if she wishes to find her way out of the chaos which is threatening to be her doom, will have to make up her mind to re-evaluate, in the light of the present, the true significance of the 18 Brumaire and of Napoleon, who was, in spite of himself, through the force of unforeseen and unforeseeable circumstances, the creator of the government we now call totalitarian.

The effects of the Revolution have been contradictory, because the Revolution itself was a dual force, containing elements in conflict with each other: a new orientation and the subversion of laws; principles of liberty, equality, and fraternity, and the great panic. But it is this dualism which allows us to establish today the respective positions in history of the Congress of Vienna and the Revolution. Were the Congress of Vienna and its prologue, the treaty of 1814, the negation of the Revolution, as historians have reiterated again and again during the last century? By no means. Powerless to stamp out the great panic, the treaties of Paris and Vienna, by checking its progress and limiting it, considerably increased for the next century the value of what the Revolution had accomplished, and minimized the effect of its evils. They enabled the constructive mind, which seeks happiness for mankind in the creation of laws that are more humane, wiser, and more just, to resist the spirit of adventure, which seeks it in the subversion of all laws. The Congress of Vienna was not, as has been claimed, the ecumenical council of European absolutism. It was by means of the two treaties of Paris and Vienna that France and the Kingdom of Poland—the part given to Russia—obtained representative institutions and the right of opposition. The same treaties enabled Switzerland to free herself from the protectorate of the mediation government, become independent, and begin making her institutions democratic. Again, it was these treaties which accomplished the unification of Germany and guaranteed her from the fear of her upper classes by Article 13 of the federal Constitution, which forced all the confederate states to grant representative institutions. It was in Vienna, whence a reconstructed Europe was emerging, that the principles of the Revolution saw the light again after the long darkness of Napoleonic dictatorship. It is true that Article 13 of the German Constitution was to remain a dead letter—a great misfortune which was to plunge Germany into panic again until 1848. But the Congress was not responsible for this misfortune. It had made German liberty a pillar of European international law; what more could it do?

Italy alone reaped no benefit from the efforts of the Congress of Vienna to carry out the doctrines of the Revolution, but that was because she was not willing. Italy—that part of society which counted—remained, until 1922, the country in Europe most inimical to the doctrines and principles of the Revolution. The Congress of Vienna was merely conforming to Italy's wishes when it replaced the revolutionary despotisms of the Napoleonic regime with the absolutism of the Old Regime. In other words, Vienna strove to satisfy Europe as far as possible. Although Europe—both large and small states—was not officially recognized in Vienna as an authority capable of legislation, she was able, with the assistance of France, to make her voice heard in the Congress, and her wishes harkened to by the four great allied powers. Despite inevitable mistakes, she managed on the whole to have the vacant territories allotted in such a way as to take into account the possibilities of adaptation and development, which was more important than the so-called will of the people, nonexistent at that time and very vague even a century later. The one exception was Poland.

Poland was the real victim of the Congress of Vienna. There was a general conviction in the Congress that a sincere reconstruction of Europe required the revival of an independent Poland. Like the papal states in Italy, like the Holy Roman Empire, Poland had been dismembered in the darkness of the revolutionary chaos, if not by the Revolution, then with its complicity; like Italy and Germany, she should have recovered and been put together again at Vienna. It did not turn out that way; the Congress was forced to carry out a new partition, the fourth and the most cruel of all, for it lasted a century. Why? Austria and Prussia could have given their consent to the resurrection of Poland, because they could easily have found the necessary indemnities in Germany, and they would have had the advantage of pushing the Russian Empire back toward Asia. Russia, however, could not. Alexander I, by taking the initiative in reconstructing the European system, had made Russia a great European power, the equal of Austria, of France, of England, not to speak of Prussia, which was not at that time a really great power. In 1815, Russia had to advance into Europe, that is into Poland, as far as she could, even at the risk of perishing as a result of it a century later; in 1815, Europe could not force her back into Asia, because without the annexation of the Duchy of Warsaw, Alexander could not have made Russia accept the treaties of Paris and Vienna. And if Russia had not become a European power the construction at Vienna would have collapsed. That is why the fate of Poland was irrevocably decided at Vienna, for as long as the system of Vienna lasted. The desperate revolts of Poland were to be in vain.

It was not to be the same for the other peoples when they became dissatisfied with what the Congress had accomplished: Belgium, Italy, and Germany. During the nineteenth century, three great crises were to be provoked in Europe by the combination of the Revolution's spirit of adventure with its new doctrines, and by the ferments and explosions which resulted from that combination: in 1830, the fall of the legitimate monarchy in France and the revolt of Belgium; in 1848, the European Revolution; and from 1860 to 1870, the creation of the Kingdom of Italy, the destruction of the Germanic Confederation, and the formation of the German Empire. These events were profoundly to alter the system set up by the Congress, while satisfying the desires of Belgium, Italy, and Germany, but they were not to destroy it. The system remained strong enough to restrain and canalize the spirit of adventure and the fears which those upheavals spread throughout Europe; strong enough to multiply and distribute the benefits of the Revolution all over the world, and finally to accomplish yet another, even more important task, the greatest one of all. The existence of a strong European system has never implied and never will imply perpetual peace; wars may be necessary for the maintenance and the further development of the system. But every worth-while system, if it wishes to exist, must be capable of localizing and limiting the wars which may occur in it. The system created by the Congress of Vienna succeeded in doing that with the wars caused by the Revolution of 1848 and those which followed it: the Crimean War in 1856, the Italian War of Independence in 1859, the Austro-Prussian War in 1866, the Franco-Prussian War in 1870, and the Russo-Turkish War in 1877-1878. It did not fall until 1914, with the start of the World War, and it fell then because it was no longer strong enough to localize and limit the war. And then, in a flood of misfortunes, all the evils of the Revolution swept down on the world: the overthrow of the law of nations, the militarization of peoples, *coups d'états,* unrestrained wars, totalitarian governments, distorted democracies, the subversion of laws in every country, universal fear. The second great panic in modern history had begun.

The Revolution as a creative or a destructive force? A new orientation of mankind, liberty, equality, fraternity? Or permanent revolution, subversion of all laws, universal chaos, panic, and brutality? A century and a quarter later, mankind once again, like the Congress of Vienna, is facing this dilemma. Why? Wherein lies the fundamental significance of the antithesis between the good and the bad of the Revolution, which we are unable to eliminate? In order to answer this important question, let us take another look into the mysteries of order, after having determined, by a specific and definitive formula, why we must acknowledge that the Congress of Vienna was a great success. All the solutions which it gave to the immense problems caused by the Revolution were not good. Some of them were mediocre; and they created new problems—Germany and Italy, for instance—over which men have not stopped worrying and will not stop for a long time. But the Congress freed Europe from the great panic; therein lies its brilliant and immortal success. During the century between 1815 and 1914, Europe suffered less than in any other period of its history from the fears which cause mankind to tremble and become frantic, and had more confidence than ever before in the present and the future, which is essential to every real civilization. That is the difference between 1815 and 1919. The Congress of Vienna marked the end, the Congress of Paris the beginning, of one of the greatest panics in all history.

XIX

RECONSTRUCTION

———————————————— ·>>> <<<· ————————————————

In the city which Fate, in a happy moment, chose as a refuge for the last years of my life, I am an occasional witness of a spectacle which has always impressed me deeply. The city is governed by a two-party democracy, each of which has its own processions, parades, and outdoor meetings to declare its program. Sometimes both parties may be seen holding their parades at the same time, filing through different streets with banners and music. Between these two processions there is a wide difference in everything—insignias and individuals, prejudices and doctrines. What one procession believes in, the other condemns, and vice versa. In the two processions are symbolized the ideological contrasts and rivalries for power which have made so many pages of history run with blood, the contrasts and rivalries about which all Europe fought between 1789 and 1814. These processions are not made up of angels singing hymns in honor of an idea; they are composed of passionate men contending for power. Yet they march peacefully in perfect order, watched over only by a few stolid policemen, unarmed and friendly. Why?

They have an understanding between them that they will settle their differences through discussion and ballot; that the majority will determine the right to rule; that a majority of one will be the deciding factor in favor of the truth of the ideas under discussion.

The most tenuous of all conventions! It is obvious that a majority proves nothing: neither the ability of a government, nor the truth of an idea, nor the justice of a decision. How then can a convention which it is so easy to prove absurd be sufficient to canalize such violent passions as rivalry of ambitions and ideological discord? I have always looked upon the two human torrents as passing between two almost invisible silken threads capable of being broken by a small child. And yet the two threads hold them in and direct them as though they were steep banks. Why? Illusion, timidity, a belief in false principles invented a few centuries ago? No, the two processions are right. If they broke the threads, they would fall on each other, law would no longer exist, and fear would invade the minds of men. And then the silk threads would have to be replaced by iron fetters.

Silk threads or iron fetters—there is the dilemma. Let us return to the problem which we touched upon at the beginning: what is order? We have seen the answer: it is the aggregate of laws which man must respect so as not to live in permanent terror of his fellows, of the innate folly of man, and of his unpredictable outbursts, which philosophers call liberty. Man is a sublime brute, an angelic monster, a bundle of contradictions in perpetual motion. The greatest of these contradictions is that he is afraid and wants to be brave, because fear is the diabolical force which lets out all the evil in his nature. The most valuable function of order is to help man to be brave, by eliminating the most dangerous cause of his fear. But the laws which allow us to foresee the individual and collective conduct of men are of two kinds—silk threads and iron fetters. The more afraid men become of each other, the more they resort to iron fetters, which are the coercive laws of an ever-increasing brutality. It is in dark periods of history that law maintains order by legalizing terror. But order imposed by terror is a false order, and a contradiction in terms, for it can only be maintained by increasing man's fear, whereas the aim of order is to free him of that fear. For that reason, mankind has tended toward reducing the innumerable constructions of law, so as to entrust more and more the maintenance of order to moral, ritual, and religious laws, laws of prudence and wisdom, which individuals and groups impose upon themselves without physical coercion, by means of a reciprocal moral pressure. In other words, silk threads rather than iron fetters. Self-discipline is the highest form of the constructive mind. A great civilization is merely a system in which the process of self-discipline has become more and more complex and refined.

But, if that is true, then order should be the supreme good of mankind. On the contrary, it is the greatest tragedy. Why? Because self-discipline is the greatest necessity but the most contradictory and most difficult to which man has been condemned. The constructive mind, like the human mind, of which it is an instrument, is limited and variable. Being limited, it always creates laws which are applicable only to certain cases, and which, from being wise and just, become unwise and unjust when new interests and needs arise which they are unable to satisfy. Being variable, it can only create variable laws. But, as laws are created to stabilize the variability of human nature, they are only efficacious to the extent that they are fixed, permanent, and stable. That is another contradiction. In order to escape it, man clings to God; he tries to fasten human laws to that fixed point, projected into eternity. But the human mind, when it conceives God, no matter how hard it strives to tear itself away from the perpetual motion which is the condition of its existence and to attain the eternal, never succeeds in escaping completely. In conceiving Him, it communicates something of its variability even to God and to the laws which it wants to establish in God.

All the laws which the constructive mind is capable of creating are limited and variable. The result is that no law can be justified completely and definitely. The fear of disorder, which the law should eliminate, is always an argument of prime importance in its favor. But that fear diminishes in proportion as the law is applied successfully. Men become accustomed to a social order, which is always an artificial state, as if it were an unalterable part of the cosmic order. The silk threads become invisible. If the world changes, if new desires and needs are born, a generation may end up believing, if it respects laws of fundamental value, that it is allowing itself to be bound by stupid prejudices and that it need only ignore them. The spirit of adventure is thereby awakened; the subversion of law begins; and all of a sudden the great panic returns. And so the iron fetters reappear.

That is why world order, in all its forms, from peace between states to legal documents which justify legitimate governments, is a labor of Sisyphus which man must always begin anew, a structure continually undergoing repair because it begins to disintegrate at the very moment that it is being built. One of the gravest mistakes committed by human indolence is the belief that order is best preserved by keeping it as it stands. It can only be preserved by continually reconstructing it. The only real guardians are those who reconstruct it. Unfortunately nothing is so necessary and yet so fruitless, so useful and yet so arduous, as the construction and reconstruction of world order; nothing is so rare as a great constructive mind. The Congress of Vienna was merely a grandiose example of this eternal drama of history, the labor of Sisyphus to which man is condemned—the subversion and reconstruction of laws. Maddened by a paroxysm of terror, Europe had everywhere multiplied the fearfully heavy iron fetters: military dictatorships, general conscription and militarism, a permanent state of siege. Finally, three men understood that universal chaos and slavery would be the result; and, risking their lives and reputations, they attempted to break the fetters and replace them with silk threads: legitimate governments instead of dictatorships in every country; the re-establishment of a European system governed by the law of nations and guaranteed by treaties, instead of forcible annexations, protectorates maintained by strength, and an interminable struggle for an impossible hegemony. But a fixed point had to be found to which the new silk threads could be fastened. Taking advantage of the general enthusiasm at the end of the war, the three men succeeded in getting the Paris treaty of May 30, 1814, signed. That was the first fixed point, for it set forth certain principles on which a new Europe was to be constructed. In order to put those principles into practice, Talleyrand had thought to find another fixed point in the Congress, the Congress as the mouthpiece of Europe, Europe conceived as a superior and almost mystical authority. That time he was unsuccessful; in Vienna the order that had been established in Paris seemed about to fall; there was a clash of wills which threatened to tear up the delicate fabric of silk that was being woven. There was ugly talk of another war. Was Europe once more to be bound with the same iron fetters that had just been removed? The return of Napoleon and the Hundred Days caused a reversion of feeling which saved the Congress. Understanding took the place of bickering, and a strong desire for unity reappeared. The great treaty was signed on June 9. A fixed point had been found to which were fastened for a century all the silk threads of international law which were to guarantee the individual boundaries within the new system; and also some—but not the strongest—silk threads of the new constitutional law, which should have insured, inside the states, the right of opposition and guarantees by the representative regime.

Europe gained an immediate peace, a less precarious

peace than the truces to which she had been condemned for a quarter of a century; and in peacetime she quickly recovered from the great panic. She was forced to wait for a while before tasting freedom. But no sooner were the iron fetters broken, and the European system re-established, than the constructive mind which had created the latter disappeared.

A strange fate awaited the three men who had wrought this great and good work together! They separated and each one went alone to an inexplicable destiny. Alexander went back to Russia, broken-hearted, and with his mind unsettled. He had made his great youthful dream come true, he had saved Western civilization by reconstructing the European system. A rebel and a revolutionary by temperament, he had accomplished this great reconstruction chiefly by a challenge to his era, and to the frenzied subversion of all law and order which had been its dominating madness; but he was only a constructive genius intermittently, and he ended up by not believing in the reconstruction of which he had been the architect. The Hundred Days, which had saved the Congress, had seemed to him the disastrous warning of a new war and the destruction of his labor. After Waterloo, he was obsessed with the despair of an imaginary failure, which threw him into the mystical vagaries of Mme. de Krüdener, and gave him the strange idea of the Holy Alliance. In his famous manifesto, he beseeched God and asked his crowned confreres to give to the world the peace which he had already given without realizing that he had done so. Never has a man of power more naïvely humiliated himself before God and man, in order to accomplish a task which he had already done without knowing it.

Talleyrand was, of the three, the great constructive genius, the one who knew best the reasons and the deep significance of his labor. By the breadth, the depth and humanity of his ideas, by the courage with which he applied them at the most critical moments, by the sort of

haughty disinterest which ennobles the most important
part of his work, Talleyrand seems to have the right of
precedence over all the statesmen who have appeared in
the Western world since the Revolution. During the
eighteen months when at long last he was able to guide
world affairs himself, after having been for so many years
the executive of leaders who should have been his secretaries, he overcame the greatest panic ever to devastate
history, created a world which was to outlive him for
a century, helped Alexander to save Western civilization,
and left a work which had no faults. I believe he is the
only statesman in history for whom this honor can be
claimed. But he was to remain in power only a year and
a half. A few months after signing the treaty, Louis XVIII
took advantage of the complications and difficulties provoked by the Hundred Days and the second Treaty of
Paris, to dismiss him. He was a married bishop and an
outcast noble in spite of his princely title; he had served
the Revolution, and pleaded the indefensible cause of the
duc d'Enghien before Europe. In short, the order which
he had reconstructed immediately drove out its creator,
whose existence had been one long discord after another.
His strange and implacable fate never let him go: the
great dissenter was dismissed by the very laws which he
had established. He did not complain then, any more than
he had ever complained. Only once was he to remind
the world of the abominable violence which had victimized him in youth and which explains all his misfortunes as well as excuses many of his mistakes. This was
in his letter to the Pope which he signed on the last day
of his life, less than twenty-four hours before dying. "The
respect I owe to those who gave me birth does not prevent
me from saying that all my youth was devoted to a pro-
fession to which I was not born." But a century weakened
by romanticism was not to understand this silence any
better than his actions and his principles.

Louis XVIII was a monarch of the Old Regime who believed in the divine right of kings, who had never compromised with the Revolution, who had known how to bide his time, and who had wished and known how to resolve the major problem before which the Revolution, after creating it, had succumbed. He, also, had a contradictory nature, but it was not as complex a contradiction as with the others. Perhaps for this reason he at least was to have the reward of dying on the throne of his ancestors.

But he, too, like Alexander and Talleyrand, was to be submerged in the success of their common labor. From 1815 on, the Western world, free of fear, acquired such an *élan,* such confidence in itself, that, for the first time, it was able to enjoy all its benefits: wealth and power, liberty and order, knowledge and security. Everywhere, silken threads replaced iron fetters. For a moment, a part of mankind, the wealthiest, the most powerful, the most intelligent part, believed in unlimited progress. But it was only an illusion. Men fell once more into the snare of their eternal contradictions; as they became so well accustomed to the order created in Vienna, they began to confuse it with the cosmic order, and its invariable everlastingness; they lost sight of its fragility, of the contradictions which secretly sapped it, of the sacrifices and the struggles of self-discipline which had made it possible. Deceived by this mirage, successive generations have less and less understood the Revolution, the great panic which devastated Europe, the mighty, courageous effort which saved it, the Congress of Vienna, and the famous men of that day—the truly great and the falsely great. More and more, they have allowed themselves to become dazzled by the accomplishments of the spirit of adventure in that great tragedy; they have come to attribute the happiness they enjoyed, not to the constructive mind, which overcame the great panic, but to the men and events which had created it; and they have ended up by believing in the romantic legend of the Revolution. A heady wine on which the nineteenth century became more and more intoxicated.

One must return to the original observation. Revolution is a word with a double meaning: sometimes it means a new orientation of the human mind, and sometimes the subversion of law and order. More and more, during the great peace of the nineteenth century, the Western mind came to confuse the two meanings of the word, and ended up by convincing itself that every subversion of law and order, every destruction of an existing legitimacy is, and must of necessity be, the beginning of a new and better orientation for humanity. The fallacy of this confusion is now apparent; if, by a lucky chance, the subversion of a long-established legitimacy be accompanied by a new and better orientation, nonetheless it is always, by its very nature, followed by universal panic. But the nineteenth century, made smug by its security, had forgotten even the notion of a general fear. As long as the order created by the Congress in 1815 lasted, that delusion cropped up in literature, in history, in philosophy, in the theoretical parts of political platforms, and was confined to a few attempts at fanciful revolts. When that order collapsed in the World War, the delusion swept through Europe. Young and old, rich and poor, wise and ignorant, conservatives and radicals, were all eager for revolution, were all seeking happiness in the total destruction of rules and laws in every phase of human activity. The most essential laws—the ones on which the legitimacy of government depended and therefore universal security—were almost everywhere violated and overthrown with astonishing ease, and illegitimate governments were hailed, even by the elite, as splendid innovations. The religious and secular authorities—the papacy, the universities, the courts and academies, the banks and tribunals—offered weaker and weaker resistance to the universal folly and allowed the total destruction of the world to be accomplished; sometimes they even helped to destroy it.

Then, after the destruction of the Roman Empire and the French Revolution, began the third great crisis of

Western civilization. The fundamental reason was the same for all three: in the case of Rome, the downfall of the imperial government; in that of the Revolution, the downfall of the French monarchy; and today, the downfall of the monarchic system in Europe during 1918 and 1919. The war which began on September 1, 1939, was not born of a conflict of political interests between the great powers, as was the first World War; it was born, like all the wars of the French Revolution, of the intellectual, moral, and political disorder which Europe after 1919 was subjected to by the collapse of the monarchic system, by the universal cult of revolution, and by the frenetic subversion of all the laws. What is at the bottom of this disorder? A frightful clanking of iron fetters, forged and shaken by fear. The great panic, the symbol and result of universal disorder, has once more taken possession of mankind, the same panic in which Europe almost perished between 1789 and 1814. For a whole century it had disappeared, as the Rhone loses itself in the rocks at Bellegarde, because it was hidden beneath the splendors and happiness of the nineteenth century. Then it reappeared, for the same reason, the one Talleyrand had discovered in his solitary meditations during the winter of 1813-1814: the overthrow, in the midst of wholesale destruction, of those laws which safeguard the legitimacy of government; the spread of illegitimate governments, distorted democracies, counterfeit republics and counterfeit monarchies.

Once again the Revolution frightened those who began it more than those who were forced to submit to it. Along with the distorted democracies, Europe was being crowded with illegitimate governments, which live in permanent fear of their peoples and of other states; fear of their peoples because they tyrannize over them with regimes of mystification and terror; fear of other states, either because the conflicts inherent in all relations between sovereign states always loom as terrible dangers to their instability and weakness or because, having destroyed all principles and rules, their actions and attitudes can neither be explained nor foreseen. Every one of them, therefore, becomes a menace to other states, and every one becomes frightened of the fear it causes. It is this psychological game of crisscrossing fears, partly real and partly imaginary—almost incomprehensible to peoples still fortunate enough to be governed by legitimate governments—which caused the second World War, a war desired by no one, even less by those who were continually threatening the rest of the world in order to dispel the maddening fear felt by an illegitimate government, than by those who frankly confessed to fearing war as the ultimate evil. The tragedy of 1789-1814 is being repeated. What will be the result of this awful relapse into an old evil? A great reconstruction which will save us all, as in 1814? An endless succession of useless wars and revolutions, endless because no means will be found to end them, as in the Roman Empire after the third century? Wars resulting from the spiritual disorder of an epoch are far more dangerous than wars caused by a conflict of political interests. But there can be no doubt about the answer. Europe will be saved again if it finds, as in 1814, the courage to vanquish the great panic, and if, in order to vanquish this, it starts again, as in 1814, at the beginning—by recognizing the right of opposition to be the safeguard of Western civilization, the prerequisite for every legitimate government, the fundamental principle of peace and order, the keystone of every permanent structure.

That is the noble lesson which Louis XVIII left to his century, a sublime example of foresightedness and courage, because of which he deserved the title of great. Among all the fears which had beset the illegitimate governments created by the Revolution, the most dangerous, the one which led the Revolution to commit the worst abuses of force, was the fear of the right of opposition, the great innovation which the Revolution had promised France. All other fears, the aggregate of which made up the great panic, had stemmed from that one. Louis XVIII dispelled the great panic by attacking it at its source, because he had the courage to give an example of a government which was not afraid of opposition. A century and a quarter later the problem to be resolved is the same and the task to accomplish identical, if not in the method to follow, in the direction to take. The new great panic, cause of the second World War, also proceeded from the fear of the right of opposition which took hold of all the illegitimate governments, too many of which had resulted from the universal subversion of laws which threw Europe into confusion after 1919. Once more the great panic must be eliminated by tearing out its deepest roots, A new balance must be set up in Europe by a confederation of legitimate states, each of which will be free to govern itself as it wishes—republic or monarchy, aristocracy or democracy, corporatism or sovietism—but on condition that it respect two fundamental principles which alone can legitimize it—the right of opposition and the right to vote, the second of which is only partially separate from the first. Once they have again become legitimate, all the governments can rid themselves of their constant terror of the wretched subjects whom they tyrannize, and of the perpetual dread of an ever-imminent attack, which is wearing them out and weakening them today.

It seems unlikely today that a king, even a great king, would suffice to carry out, with courage, this saving task. Louis XVIII should reappear in the shape of a whole people or at least an elite, that would have the strength to win the war and the courage not to be afraid of its victory. Does that people, that elite, exist somewhere today? At the moment, there is only perplexity, hesitation, and uncertainty. But also in 1811 or 1812 everyone in Europe was afraid and desperate, no one imagined that in the fateful hour Europe would be saved by the courage of a radical czar, a married bishop, and an exiled king, whose cause seemed lost. And today the event or events which

will save mankind might be taking shape in latent greatness somewhere, no one knows where. The author of this
book would be happy—he has undertaken it with that
aim—if his work should help this latent greatness to become aware of itself and make ready for the fateful hour.
For, if it fails then, the people of the twenty-first or twenty-
second centuries will remember Europe as the seat of a
once-great civilization.